# MY FIRST TRIP TO CHINA

Scholars, Diplomats and
Journalists Reflect on their
First Encounters with China
**Kin-ming Liu, Editor**

# MY FIRST TRIP
# TO CHINA

**www.musemag.hk**

Published by 出版
East Slope Publishing Limited 東坡出版有限公司

Book Design 書籍設計
Ringo Hui (BW Design Consultants)
info@bwdc.com.hk

Cover Illustration 封面插圖
Mak Wah Cheong

Printer 印刷
Green Production (Overseas) Group

Edition 版次
1st edition, November 2012
2012年11月初版

ISBN 書號
978-988-16046-2-0

Retail Price 定價港幣
HK$180

Muse is a registered trademark of East Slope Publishing Limited
Post Office Box 33744, Sheung Wan, Hong Kong
Tel: +852 9170 5484  |  Fax: +852 2541 1527
Website: www.musemag.hk  |  Email: muse@musemag.hk

**My First Trip to China**

CONTENTS

First and foremost, I wish to express my gratitude to all the authors who have contributed to this series and have kindly let us reprint their stories, including those whose stories we did not have space to run in this collection (in the order of their appearance in the series): Michael Yahuda, Simon Long, Willy Lam, Anita Chan, Winston Lord, James D. Seymour, June Teufel Dreyer, Jan Wong, David Schlesinger, J. Bruce Jacobs, Ross Terrill, Chas W. Freeman, Jonathan Steele, Richard Baum, Gregory Clark, Wei Peh Ti, Philip Cunningham, Karen Smith, and Scott McDonald.

Two authors whose stories are not included in this volume—Szeto Wah and Robert A. Scalapino—are no longer with us. Mr. Szeto passed away in early 2011 and a chapter from his memoirs, published posthumously, was excerpted. Professor Scalapino accepted the invitation to join the series shortly before his death in late 2011. A story from his memoirs, published in 2008, was adapted.

The series first appeared on the website of the *Hong Kong Economic Journal*.

I am immensely indebted to Frank Proctor, the publisher of *Muse*, for having the interest and courage to publish this volume.

I am very thankful to Orville Schell for writing the Foreword. I am particularly grateful to Susan Jakes, a fellow at the Asia Society's Center on US-China Relations of which Mr. Schell is the director, for offering me the opportunity to continue the series, now expanded to cover the first encounters with America by the Chinese as well, on *ChinaFile*, an online magazine published by the Center.

With love, I dedicate this book to the center of my tiny universe: my wife Souhon and our two daughters Lila and Isabel.

*Kin-ming Liu*
*Hong Kong, September 2012*

## A China Frontier: Once the Border of Borders — Orville Schell

In 1961, when I first arrived in Hong Kong as an aspiring young China scholar, there was something deeply seductive about the way this small British enclave clung like a barnacle to the enormity of China's revolutionary. Because it shared a border with Hong Kong, China seemed at once far away and very near. Its proximity to this British outpost gave the latter an exciting air of immediacy that it would otherwise not have enjoyed. But the boundary that demarcated the New Territories from the People's Republic of China was actually one of the starkest dividing lines in the world. Most of those who crossed it were desperate Chinese refugees willing to risk death to escape their famine-plagued homeland for the uncertainty of life in the colony. And, because few did business in China there, and it hardly welcomed casual tourists, few expats had reason to cross the border. Indeed, many colonials referred to the Hong Kong-China boundary as the "frontier," a wonderfully redolent term that suggested their presumption that the known world ended there, while something else almost ineffable began on the other side. So, in the 1960s, the idea of a "frontier" was able to grip the imagination with the idea that the world was still divided into starkly differentiated areas with no-man's-lands in between which, if crossed, held the promise of ushering one into a completely different and fascinating parallel universe.

While so much of the rest of the world had been blurring its boundaries during the early stages of 20th century globalization, here was China, defiantly maintaining its revolutionary identity and isolation, becoming not only a *terra incognita* for much of the world, but also conferring on it an air of mesmerizing impenetrability and unpossessability. Its haughty detachment, fierce dedication to self-reliance and abject refusal to surrender to the outside world's pressure paradoxically also made it a strangely alluring place… at least, for some of us! This book chronicles the accounts of such people remembering their first passage to China after Mao Zedong came to power in 1949.

In many ways the yearning of such Westerners to be able to take leave of the known for the unknown world was a residual, if mutated, form of an older yearning that prevailed during the 19th and early 20th centuries. Then, the daring adventures of Western explorers like Richard Byrd, Henry Morton Stanley, Sven Hedin, Sir Francis Burton and Joseph Rock enthralled the "civilized world." Since they transported people vicariously from humdrum, post-industrial lives to exotic, unknown lands, we voraciously devoured the exploits of these intrepid men recounted in the pages of magazines like *National Geographic* as they risked life-and-limb to the elements, pestilence, disease, and hostile native peoples (even cannibals!), trekking the world filling in the last so-called "blank places" on the map in Africa, Tibet, the Amazon and the North and South Poles. But, by the middle of the 20th century, there were virtually no more such blank places left to slake the diminished longing of Westerners for "the faraway," "the other," and "the mysterious."

These days, the word "frontier" has fallen into disuse, precisely because our world has since become so homogenized that there are fewer real dividing lines between geographic places. As we approach international borders now, instead of having the sense of leaving one powerful gravitational field of culture and place for another, we hardly have a sense of going anywhere very different at all. Once strangely exciting, because it unsettled, travel has now been relieved of so much of its uncertainty that it is approaching the banal. We are assured that: English will almost always serve as a linguistic solvent wherever we land; familiar brand-name restaurants will be awaiting us; hotels with reassuringly recognizable names will welcome us; and CNN or the BBC will be available in our rooms.

Just as the last geographically unexplored pockets of our planet were vanishing and leaving us without our accustomed fix of exotica and romance, the second half of the 20th century arrived to produce a surprising new surrogate form of the forbidden. Out of the Second World War came the Cold War, re-dividing the planet into "the free" and "the communist" worlds, slamming shut the portals into socialist bloc countries with all the finality of the gates of Lhasa closing before the advance of Sir Francis Younghusband or Mecca for Westerners before Sir Richard Burton succeeded in penetrating its mysteries. And, as soon as we Westerners found ourselves denied ready access, we began to transfer much of our old fascination with the geographically remote that had so animated the previous hundred years of exploration to the new "hermit kingdoms" of Communism. Because there was also a new sense of threat aroused in us by the fact that these newly closeted lands were now irrevocably locked behind the "iron" and "bamboo" curtains of our new Cold War enemies, our fascination was only enhanced. Feeling that democracy was in a race against Communism for the hearts and minds of the world, we were fired with a new competitive sense to learn how effective Communism actually was. Did they have new powers of organization that might make them invincible? Might socialist revolution actually work better than democracy, allowing these "bloc countries" to ultimately "bury us?" Since it was so difficult to gain access and see their inner workings, we were left with an uneasy sense of confronting a phantom adversary that made it tempting for us to project unwarranted abilities and powers onto them.

Of all the new "Communist countries," there was none better able to foment such uncertainties within us and to goad us into generating such projections than Mao's new People's Republic of China. His distinctive brand of messianic, peasant revolution, his fierce determination to make New China resistant to any kind of dependence on the capitalist West, and his stubborn determination to make China "self-reliant," all helped create something of a legend of defiance, inaccessibility, and even invincibility.

So, we young American China followers who found ourselves marooned in places like Hong Kong and Taiwan studying Chinese were left to feel something like Jews exiled from the Holy Land. So inexorably isolated from the object of our study (and desire) were we, that we could only envy those few French, Canadian, and British nationals of our acquaintance who had managed—per force of their country's early diplomatic recognition of Mao's government—to penetrate the Chinese veil. (Even if they had only been allowed a short and superficial visit.)

Indeed, while in Taipei in the early 1960s, I had a classmate from Canada who had actually managed to visit "Peking" for a day or so while traveling on a ship to Hong Kong that just happened to stop in Tianjin. We Americans, who felt so terminally shut out of this beckoning land, treated him as if he were a pilgrim who had kissed the sacred hem of the pontiff's. Because he had sojourned—however briefly—in this red celestial kingdom, we enthroned him as a minor god.

As a substitute for actually being able to go there, our small band of overseas students would sometimes take weekend trips to a lovely little fishing village south of Keelung facing the Taiwan Straits. There we would sleep on the white sand beach under the dazzling stars and surreptitiously tune into the bombastic radio news programs that crackled in from Beijing over our small battery-powered transistor radios. We would fall asleep feeling connected for the moment to that exciting but elusive revolution that was aflame just a hundred miles across the water.

There was also, of course, something about the fact that the Chinese Communist Revolution was so well-personified—we would now probably say "well-branded"—by Mao Zedong's larger than life quality that made China all the more mesmerizing. Mao had seemed to have accomplished a historical impossibility: to have awakened the Chinese people from a century of deep torpor and then to have animated them with an uncharacteristic elan, mass-fervor and energy. Where all of the turmoil would take China was another question. But, as we contemplated his revolutionary drama from afar, it was not difficult to be drawn vicariously into it.

But our fascination was not born so much of sympathy for Mao's whole madcap experiment as curiosity. What I think drew us powerfully was China's apparent disinterest in us, indeed, in any kind of Western intrusion, even visitation. Like aspiring young swains who discover that the object of their desire is utterly disinterested in their attentions, we were, in a sense, a group of forlorn Swanns in love. And, like Marcel Proust's anti-hero's unrequited passion for Odette, our infatuation with China was only made more ardent by the hopelessness of any possibility of attention, much less consummation.

As my plane looped in over Hong Kong Harbor that day in 1961 and then descended over the rooftops of Kowloon to land at the old Kai Tak Airport, I remember the excitement I felt at actually being able to glimpse the faraway South China coastline. But, once in Hong Kong, with its plummy, colonial British expat culture, China had a curious way of receding from consciousness, only to burst back into consciousness as some explosive event happened across the border. Later during the Cultural Revolution when China was aflame with class warfare and Wuhan was in a state of civil war, I recall standing in the Kowloon train station near the Star Ferry dock one day looking down the glistening railroad tracks that headed north to the "frontier," and trying to imagine China. Of course, as Americans, we were forbidden from traveling there. Indeed, our US passports were stamped with an explicit prohibition forbidding such travel. But, for me, those tracks were like a magic highway to not only the unknown, but the unknowable.

It was not until almost ten years later that in 1975 I finally boarded a train at that same station. Filled with a certain delicious apprehension and excitement (the kind that makes the whole experience of "travel" more than just commuting), I set off, at last, for the "frontier" myself. And, as so many other China specialists in this volume so well describe, more rapidly than imagined, our train halted at an unprepossessing railway bridge near Shenzhen. Now a massive city and Special Economic Zone, it was then a rural fishing village. Here, because there were not yet any thru-trains to Canton, we were required to disembark. Following a simple black and white sign that said, TO CHINA, we wrestled our own baggage across a bridge under the watchful eyes of armed PLA soldiers stationed along the tracks. Their presence gave an added sense that we were, in fact, crossing from one universe to another. For, on the other side of that bridge was New China where Chairman Mao still lived in Zhongnanhai, the Cultural Revolution still continued, and where there were no advertisements, private cars, fashion magazines, or private property.

China was a society as seemingly different from the West as one could get and still be on planet earth. Indeed, when we landed at Beijing's Capital Airport a few days later, there was not a single other aircraft moving on its runways. And, when our plane's engines finally shut down and we stepped out onto the tarmac, except for the sighing of a soft spring breeze that blew and a few dim lights in the distance, it was as silent and dark as a tomb.

This book contains a series of narratives by some of those early Western pilgrims who made odysseys to China when it was still a world apart. Their trips, and their accounts now, stand as benchmarks for just how far China, and the world, has come since.

This volume is the brainchild of Kin-ming Liu, a Hong Kong journalist and editor who astutely recognized that for so many of us non-Chinese who have been drawn to China, these moments of first contact were among the most important in our ongoing professional lives. What made these moments of crossing so important for us was that with our entry into China, we imagined that we would finally pass over from the world of exclusion to the world of inclusion, that having crossed that once seemingly impassable frontier, we would, at last, become privy to China's secrets. But, as it turned out, the boundary that divided "us" from "them" was a lot more impenetrable than we had ever dared imagine from the outside. We may have managed to get physically inside China, but as "foreign guests," we were in so many ways irrevocably still on the outside.

And so began another quest, this one dedicated to divining exactly what really animated this provocative country whose geographic periphery we had at last managed to breach, but whose essence continued to remain so frustratingly opaque. But, perhaps it is this unfathomable, unpossessable aspect of China that has made it all the more beguiling to those of us who, decades after our first superficial encounters, still find ourselves today trying to make sense out of its curious progress into the modern world.

*Orville Schell*, *Arthur Ross Director of the Center on US-China Relations at the Asia Society, is a long-time China observer, author, journalist, and former Dean at the University of California, Berkeley's Graduate School of Journalism. He is the author of fourteen books, nine of them about China. He graduated Magna Cum Laude from Harvard University in Far Eastern History, was an exchange student at National Taiwan University in the 1960s, and earned a PhD(ABD) at the University of California, Berkeley in Chinese History.*

# Kin-ming Liu

I was startled by Richard Bernstein to start this series.

In his farewell column titled "A Bridge to a Love for Democracy," published in the *International Herald Tribune* right before the end of 2010, the US veteran journalist recounted his first trip to China through Hong Kong in 1972: "There was a short trestle bridge at Lo Wu. I've often wondered if it's still there. The Union Jack flew at one side, the red flag of the People's Republic of China at the other. The border town on the other side was a little fishing and farming village called Shenzhen, now a modern city of skyscrapers and shopping malls, an emblem of China's amazing economic development."

A graduate student in Chinese history and a stringer for *The Washington Post* at that time, Bernstein, who later became *Time* magazine's first Beijing bureau chief, "was favorably disposed toward China" when he strode across the bridge. "But it took only about 24 hours on that first journey to China for me utterly to change my mind and, indeed, to become a lifelong anti-Communist and devotee of liberal democracy, to find great wisdom in Winston Churchill's dictum about its being the worst of all systems except for all the others," he wrote. "The noxious cult of personality around Mao was the first thing that effected my political transformation. But deeper than that was the pervasive odor of orthodoxy, the uniformity of it all, the mandatory pious declarations, which, if they were believed, were ridiculous, and, if they were forced, illustrated the terror of it all."

Bernstein claimed that "nearly 40 years in the journalism game haven't shaken me from the essential belief that I formed during that first, memorable visit to China" and he continues to believe that "we're better than they are."

As an amateur watcher of China-watchers in the West, not only am I always curious about these foreigners' views on China, but I have also been fascinated by their personal experiences in China. Simon Leys' *Chinese Shadows* and Edgar Snow's *Red Star Over China*, to name just two very different works from different generations, remain as vivid as ever whenever I re-read them. Totally captivated by Richard Bernstein's account, I was stunned to learn subsequently from my friend Jonathan Mirsky that he was also a fellow traveler on the very same trip with Bernstein. Immediately, I invited Jonathan to write his story for me. He kindly agreed, disclosing more colorful details of the trip. My thirst for similar episodes refused to be quenched, though. I wanted more. "Why don't I ask other people to write their stories too?" I said to myself. Thus began the series "My First Trip to China." Throughout the year of 2011, I found myself inviting many journalists, scholars, businessmen, diplomats, and other individuals to recount their first encounters with China. A few shared the same first trip with Bernstein. Some made their initial visits in the earlier years of the People's Republic of China. Most went after US President Richard Nixon's trip to China in 1972, or later when China opened up in the late 1970s. A total of fifty-one stories appeared weekly on the website of the *Hong Kong Economic Journal*, my then employer, and thirty of them are reprinted in this collection.

Long-term strategic planning was a luxury I could not afford when managing the news website. Running the series involved knocking on the doors of many authors, thanking those who were willing to contribute, eagerly waiting for them to file, and uploading whichever story came in handy to beat the weekly deadline. It came as a nice surprise, therefore, to find that I could arrange the thirty selected stories into six groups under two categories. Please let me explain.

The first category of stories, divided into three groups, is defined by the background of the authors themselves.

- **Fellow Travelers**: The authors, all with academic credentials, debated the issue of deception and disillusion raised by Richard Bernstein in his column. Two of them (Jonathan Mirsky and Mark Selden) made the trip together with Bernstein.

- **Motherland**: The authors—despite their nationalities—are all of Chinese descent. One of them (C.P. Ho) recorded the earliest visit to China among all the contributors, in 1942.

- **Business**: The authors made their maiden trips either as businessmen or in association with a business organization.

The second category of stories, also divided into three groups, is defined by the timing of the trips being made.

- **Bamboo Curtain**: The authors visited the People's Republic of China in its earlier years when Mao was alive and well. One of them (Sidney Rittenberg) even landed in China at the end of the Second World War.

- **After Nixon**: This group of authors, more or less, rode the coattails of the US President's ground-breaking trip to China in 1972.
- **Opening Up**: Deng Xiaoping opened China's door further in the late 1970s and attracted another wave of visitors. One author in this group (Morton Abramowitz) facilitated the normalization of relations between America and China.

These personal stories contribute to a mosaic of a different and distant China, before it set off on a fast-lane journey to become the world's second largest economy.

*Kin-ming Liu is a ChinaFile Fellow at the Asia Society's Center on US-China Relations. A former chairman of the Hong Kong Journalists Association, he has worked for Apple Daily, the Hong Kong Economic Journal, and is currently with the South China Morning Post.*

# Fellow
# Travelers

## Fellow Travelers

### Jonathan Mirsky
*From Mao Fan to Counter-Revolutionary in 48 Hours (1972)*

I went to China in 1972 on the same trip as Richard Bernstein, and my painful memories of that journey remain the same as his.

The details are slightly different: I wasn't a graduate student. I was teaching Chinese and Chinese History at Dartmouth, an Ivy League college, and at forty, I was older than most of the group. Beijing had issued an invitation to the Committee of Concerned Asian Scholars, a radical coalition devoted to stopping the war in Vietnam and persuading Washington to recognize Beijing. The Chinese would pay for our six weeks in China.

All of us had studied Chinese and related subjects, and while some, like me, had studied in Taiwan, none of us had ever set foot in China. We were excited at the prospect of going there during the Cultural Revolution, now in its sixth year. As we reached the middle of the Lo Wu Bridge and crossed the dividing line into China we hugged each other and were greeted by our hosts, or minders, as they turned out to be, for our entire trip.

That night in Canton we had the first of many welcome banquets and were asked if the next day we would like to meet "a typical Chinese worker family." Absolutely! We were driven the next morning to a high-rise block of flats and ushered into the brightly painted three rooms plus kitchen, bathroom and toilet where the family enthusiastically welcomed us. They were father, mother, granny, and two children, one of them an infant. They had a radio, television, colorful satin covers on their quilts, and several shiny bicycles. We knew already to have notebooks and ballpoint pens handy and the father briefed us on his factory work: the number of workers, their pay, and how many owned wristwatches and bicycles.

We were encouraged to ask questions so we enquired why, if there was no crime in China, as our hosts had assured us, the windows were barred? We were told that the flats had been built in 1949, before Liberation, when there was crime, and the same explanation was given for why the bicycles had built-in locks: they were pre-Liberation models from when there was bike-stealing, and the model hadn't been changed. We loved this family, their warm welcome, and we loved that they seemed so prosperous.

The next morning I woke up very early, happy to be in China, and eager to go outside and join the throngs I saw walking to work. By an amazing coincidence I soon found myself outside the same block of flats we had visited the day before and in front of the door stood our typical Chinese industrial worker feeding his baby from a bottle. He gestured to me to come in and have some "white tea"—boiling water. But it was a different flat, shabby, poorly painted, only two rooms, no private kitchen or bathroom; such amenities were shared with the neighbors. There was no television, the quilts were gray and well worn, and the man owned only one well-used bicycle, which was locked.

I have thought for years that I had been in the presence of the bravest man in China, never equaled by anyone—and I met many brave Chinese—

I was to meet over the years until my expulsion in 1991. He told me we had been in the show flat, arranged by *shangmian*, the authorities, for "foreign friends," and that while the building looked old it had been built only ten years before, in 1962, and the reason there were bars on the windows— and locks on all bicycles—was that there were plenty of thieves about. He disclosed all this to me matter-of-factly, rather as he had briefed us the day before, and didn't ask me not to tell anyone what he had said.

I returned to the hotel, stunned by what I had seen and heard. In the foyer I met two of our minders who asked me where I had been. I said I had been for a walk. They pressed me hard, wanting to know exactly where and expressing alarm that I might have fallen down ill in the street. I observed that I could speak Chinese and could have dealt with any emergency. When I declined to tell them precisely where I had been they picked me up under the arms, carried me into the lift and to my room, which they locked from the outside telling me I would be let out when I apologized.

After some time my fellow trippers liberated me from my detention but I told them nothing about what had happened until lunch, when the minders were away. Several of my friends wondered if the man was a Taiwan spy who had somehow inveigled himself into a position of trust in China in order to betray it. Others insisted that there was nothing too bad about the day before; after all wasn't it just a case of a host putting his best foot forward to make a good impression on a guest? Only Richard Bernstein shared my distress and alarm.

For the rest of the trip, surrounded by Maoist enthusiasm from the Chinese around us and from our companions, Richard Bernstein and I were treated, as he says, like political deviants. Both of us were now suspicious of every venue, every briefing, and every account of how everything should be understood. Every school, every hospital visit, every commune, every discussion with intellectuals seemed suspect to Bernstein and me and I confess we seemed to our companions at best a pair of sourpusses, at worst turncoats.

After three weeks I announced my intention to return to the US and immediately was subjected to what might be called a *douzheng*, struggle session, by several of my companions who were all to become well-known academics. Their central point was that if I returned it would give comfort to reactionary people like Lucian Pye, a distinguished professor of Chinese politics at MIT, a well-known disparager of positive claims about Mao and the Cultural Revolution in particular and the People's Republic in general. I am ashamed to admit they convinced me to stay.

When we arrived in Beijing we wanted to visit the embassy of the Democratic Republic of Vietnam and were told, for the first time in our trip, that a wish could not be granted. We went anyway and were told, discreetly but plainly, by the Hanoi ambassador that the US and China seemed to be making a deal to end the war. This turned out to be true.

When we saw Premier Zhou Enlai as a special treat at the end of our trip—as usual with him, after midnight—he departed briefly from his celebrated courtesy and banged on the table, demanding we tell him what the

North Vietnamese had said. We were too frightened or discreet to tell him and he dropped the subject.

Several years later, after Mao's death in 1976 and the end of the Cultural Revolution, I chanced on one of our minders in the street in Shanghai. Over a cup of tea he disclosed to me in detail how our trip had been managed. Almost his last words were "we wanted to put rings in your noses, and you helped us put them there."

*Jonathan Mirsky was East Asia editor of The Times (London) based in Hong Kong, from 1993 to 1998. In 1989, he was named British newspapers' International Reporter of the Year for his coverage of the Tiananmen uprising. He has accompanied Prime Ministers and Foreign Secretaries to Beijing, has interviewed the Dalai Lama, Zhou Enlai, Deng Xiaoping and Lee Teng-hui, and during his long residence and travel in Asia has visited Tibet six times.*

# Edward Friedman
## Finding the Truth About Rural China (1978)

In May 1978, at age forty, accompanied by three colleagues who had already been to China, I made my first trip to the People's Republic of China. I was a critical and independent member of Amnesty International, Human Rights Watch, and the American Civil Liberties Union. I knew about Leninist dictatorships from reading reports of democratic exiles from the USSR and Eastern Europe. I knew Mao's Chinese Communist Party (CCP) had copied the institutions of Stalin's Soviet Union. I was confident that Chinese minders were not going to fool me.

There also was no way our team was going to be taken in by a Potemkin village. Before getting to China, our group asked to go to a village that was in a region studied by social scientists before 1949. We indeed ended up in the southeast of the much-studied Dingxian. We were not going to be taken in by fictions about the "bad old days."

We asked, in addition, not to go to a heroic mountain base region of the Red Army or to suburban villages enriched by a nearby metropole. We would see the real rural China. Indeed, we ended up in a very poor region of the North China Plain.

We read every village study we could find. We asked China's famous social anthropologist Fei Xiaotong about methodology. He told us we had to learn to see the invisible. That is, he could see in 1956 that Mao's forced collectivization had produced an economic disaster only because he had been in the village twenty years earlier and could see, after collectivization in Kaixiangong, that all the petty commerce had been destroyed by the collective. People were therefore poorer and more dependent.

We therefore had to learn local history in depth. We would interview the elderly, talk with local historians and go to libraries to locate accounts of the region from earlier times.

In May 1978, the four of us set to work for two months to study village China. We all tried to put in separate sixteen hour days, sharing our insights and concerns each evening after dinner in order to have a better learning agenda the next day. We would ferret out the truth, digging deeper and deeper. We took no time off from work.

We began by living in three different village homes. We sought out so-called black elements, villagers dubbed enemies of the ruling Leninist party. We visited neighboring villages for comparisons. We went to regional model villages. We went to the market. We created a context for evaluating the stories we were being told in our one village. We, however, did not know the villagers had been warned before our arrival to say nothing negative about the Great Leap famine or Cultural Revolution vigilantism.

We tried to see all parts of life. We ate in people's homes, got haircuts and chatted with the barber, interviewed school teachers, worked in the fields, went to weddings. We, however, could not see what the barber saw, that the customer who followed me into the barbershop was from the security apparatus.

All of our new knowledge would be put in the context of the best scholarship on rural China which we had already mastered long before going to do on-the-spot research in rural China. We were scholars building on the best scholarship.

We knew that the village was a node in a power structure. Therefore, we interviewed a wide spectrum of people who knew about the village—from the national center, where we spent four hours with China's most famous villager, Chen Yonggui, down through the province, prefecture, county and commune. We, however, had no way to know that this was the village's patronage network.

In short, in order to figure out how the CCP political system shaped life opportunities for villagers, we went at the topic from numerous approaches. We collected statistics and did a thorough household survey that revealed a mini-famine following collectivization. By the end of our initial two months, we felt ready to write a book that would tell the truth about the experience of Chinese villagers in a "socialist" state. Surely we had learned something substantial.

In addition, villagers introduced us to some issues we never had thought of. They could measure good and bad times by whether white rice was available or whether there was pork to eat on a significant occasion. Cultural signifiers—how one married or how one mourned the loss of a parent or celebrated the New Year with family or could build a home for married children—were vital. We had to understand how villagers evaluated life based on their values and not just impose our standards.

After leaving China, we went to the archives of the Union Research Institute in the British colony of Hong Kong and photocopied their file of clippings on the county (Raoyang) of the village (Wugong) we had been studying. We then learned that our "typical" village had actually been a socialist model since the 1940s. We learned that the village had reconstructed its narrative every time the Party line had changed. A critical reading of the URI files was more revealing than the prior two months in China.

We now knew we did not have enough material for a book. Some ninety-five percent or so of what we thought we had so cleverly unearthed by our shrewd interviewing was little more than the story the village leaders and their patrons had put together by 1967 so that the village could be presented to higher levels as a successful embodiment of Mao's Cultural Revolution line. That's how one won rewards from the state.

There was no way a one-time visit could seriously illuminate reality. We were fools, even though we learned a few things. We had learned that privileged access to monopolized resources came from satisfying the privileged and the powerful. This reality alienated hardworking neighbors who understood that copying models could not win what mattered, the access to state-controlled resources.

But we returned later that year. We now had real questions based on the URI files. Increasingly, villagers who did not want us fooled and who now thought we knew more than we really knew sought us out to tell us their truths. Whatever the value of the books we produced on village China after almost three dozen more visits over the next quarter century, *Chinese Village, Socialist State* and *Revolution, Resistance and Reform in Village China*, most of the credit should go to those brave, long-suffering and good villagers. Hopefully, some day they will be able to write their truths freely.

*Edward Friedman, coauthor of Chinese Village, Socialist State, has been a professor of Political Science at the University of Wisconsin, Madison since 1967. He received his PhD from Harvard in Political Science in 1968. His most recent coedited book is Political Transitions in Dominant Party Systems. He edited a condensed translation of Yang Jisheng's two volume study of the Leap famine, Tombstone: The Great Chinese Famine, 1958-1962, published in 2012.*

# Richard Kagan
## *Multiple Chinas, Multiple Americas (1975)*

I made my first trip to China in January, 1975. My itinerary included Hong Kong, Canton, Shanghai, Peking, Yanan, Xian, Lungmen, and Changsha. I was a co-leader with Professor Lu Chung-tai. We had twelve students on the three-week trip.

My attitudes toward China were quite different from the usual groups that traveled there.

In the late 1950s and early 1960s I had been deeply involved in the civil rights movement in Berkeley and in the South. In the early 1960s I also became involved in the teach-ins on the Vietnam War. From 1965-67 I studied in Taiwan, and did research in Hong Kong and Japan. In Taiwan, I became deeply involved in anti-war activities. Information was gathered and published on the movements of the US Army and demonstrations were prepared against America's policies in Taiwan, Hong Kong, and Japan.

These two commitments, to civil rights and against American imperialism, led naturally to a sympathy for the Taiwanese—especially those in southern Taiwan—who had been abused by the Kuomintang troops and secret police. America's support of Chiang Kai-shek's martial law in Taiwan, and the use of the Republic of China as an ally in Vietnam fueled my protests against Chiang and the War.

During my studies in Taiwan, a group of scholars and I formed an organization which called upon the Association of Asian Studies to allow for some political dissent and more academic freedom. We organized around two issues: anti-Chiang and anti-Vietnam War. After I returned to the US, this group became the nucleus for the Committee of Concerned Asian Scholars.

Recognition of China was a major policy of the Committee. For them, the issue was one of American imperialism. Some did idealize China. For them, China was creating "the new man," and a new pattern for foreign policy. A few did feel betrayed by the false promises of the Chinese revolution.

In order to understand these reactions and the consequent reflections on China, the political context of the 1970s must be taken into account. The anti-communism and pro-America campaigns were still aggressively applied to students and intellectuals alike. The key fuel to the protests of this period was the Vietnam War. China seemed to be the only major Asian power that stood up to American imperialism.

In addition, there was a great deal of powerful testimony describing China's positive revolutionary success. For me, Jack Belden's *China Shakes the World*, and his writings on the Second World War in Asia and Europe were a fascinating counterview to the popular American views on the War in the Pacific and in general. And of course there were the foreigners like William Hinton and Rewi Alley, among many others. None of us really knew what the social, economic, and political situation was in China. We were fêted with great meals, happy people, kind tour guides. It was a well-designed theater of deception.

While I was deeply committed to teaching about China, and supported America's recognition of China, I was not without severe doubts. I was put off both by those groups who continued to condemn it and those who looked to it as a model of a better world.

To compound my own reservations, I had to suffer with my co-leader, a Professor of Economics at Hamline University. I only learned later that he was invited to travel to China because Beijing was trying to win him back to the motherland. He and his wife came from two large and powerful warlord/landlord families in Manchuria. He was related to Chang Tso-lin, the warlord in Manchuria. Wherever we went, he was treated like royalty. He acted super patriotic to our hosts. He would tell them in advance to be careful talking around me because I knew Chinese. The students felt abandoned by his behavior and his insistence that nobody criticize the hosts or ask embarrassing questions; many felt very threatened and frightened. One consequence of this was that I wanted to distance myself from him as much as possible. This led to many adventures and many disagreements.

We visited a May 7th Cadre School, I believe, in Changsha. We sat in the typical conference room—a large table, tea cups, and book shelves against the wall. The lecture covered the usual topics: the role of Mao, the mass line, the need to work like the farmers, and the role of the cadres. They boasted of their library, and stated that at night they read and had study groups.

At this meeting, I developed a ruse that I have used in various modes at many times in China, and during the martial law period in Taiwan. I asked to go to the bathroom. I was taken there—at which time, I made it clear that it would take a while and I could return on my own. Then, without much ado, I hurried through the rooms. In the case of the May 7th Cadre School, I made my way to the library (like chicken feed for the academic in me). I took books off the shelves. They were published in the old-fashioned way—the pages still needed to be cut. And they were not. Furthermore, these cadres who had been working in the fields, with the pigs, and the wells, had not left any dirt on the pages. The books were squeaky clean—in both the brightness of the pages and the sound of opening them. This was a Potemkin library.

I returned just in time for questions. I pointed to the book case in the room and asked which books they had read. They said they had read them, but I could not get them to comment on which ones. I did not offer to take them off the shelves.

We were in Yanan in mid-January. It was cold. There was ice and snow. Luckily I was dressed like a Siberian Minnesotan. This is where I broke down any friendly views about China's leaders.

I bought some cans of fruit and made my way into the night up into the hills. I came to a cave with a quilt-like covering over the entrance. Inside there was an old, very poor family. The grandmother had no teeth—but a great smile. I only understood a few of her words, but her body language was warm and inviting. We sat and ate and talked. They warned me not to tell my guides that I had visited them. When I returned to the hotel, I was interrogated. Where did I go? What did I do? They threatened to send me back to Beijing.

There was a famous hilltop pagoda in Yanan. I was able to leave my group and climb the hill and then enter the pagoda. At the top I took a picture of the area. On the inner walls, there were inscriptions. Tourists would write their names and their units. My favorite was an intriguing message in French, which read, "*Je etait un mauvais etudiant*" (I was a poor student). I often have thought of him or her, and why this would be written. When I returned from the pagoda, I asked our guides if we could go there and climb up. They told me that it was closed. And people could not go inside.

I had many other similar episodes. There was one that inadvertently exposed my pro-Taiwan attitudes. My guides asked what countries I had visited. I told them: Israel, France, Japan, and Taiwan. The next morning they descended on me with anger. How could I call Taiwan a "country?" They ranted for quite a while.

I left China for a day or two in Hong Kong. I gave a report to some pro-China people in Hong Kong. I was not well-received. Upon returning to St. Paul, Minnesota, I gave talks to the US-China Friendship Committees. My criticism of China drew hisses from the audience. I soon gave up talking to these groups.

In my teaching career, I have tried to balance the many views of China: from human rights abuse to economic success; from being a Party state to promoting educational achievement. I find the problems in teaching about China similar to the problems of teaching American history. How does one balance the very negative with the positive? How does one prioritize the different levels of experience?

The first trip to China was a trip that has deeply affected many lives. The trip was a reaction to American values. For some, it made them further alienated and critical. Some were blacklisted and left the country for careers and lives abroad. For others, it made them feel betrayed by the realities they saw. They became bitter and hostile to China.

Some became super patriots for America. From my trip I learned that there were different Americas and different Chinas. Paraphrasing Judy Collins: I have seen China and America from both sides now—from the Ku Klux Klan to Martin Luther King Jr., from the Communist Party to the Chinese people who have stood for human rights and who have created artworks that reveal the human spirit. Our war in Vietnam was not superior in purpose or in practice to Beijing's actions in Tibet. Our treatment of the Native Americans is not a standard to apply to the world. And neither is China's threat to Taiwan's freedom.

As teachers, we daily face the problem of inappropriate comparisons, stereotyped descriptions, hyperbolic fears, and selective sculpting of facts and generalizations. The paradigm of the "discovery" of China in the 1970s still controls our perceptions. The division is between those who still see China as a positive personal experience, in terms of visiting it and helping it develop, and those who see it as a threat. As teachers and citizens, it is necessary to pull back from the extremes of blind loathing or admiration.

*Richard Kagan* *is Professor Emeritus of History at Hamline University. He was a founder, chairman, and editorial board member of the Committee of Concerned Asian Scholars. He has written books on North Korea and Taiwan and numerous articles on the Vietnam War and East Asia. He was the Taiwan history consultant for the movie, Formosa Betrayed.*

# Mark Selden
## *Understanding China and Ourselves (1972)*

I was a fellow traveler in the 1972 Committee of Concerned Asian Scholars (CCAS) trip to China with Richard Bernstein and Jonathan Mirsky… and in other ways with Richard Kagan and Edward Friedman who followed in 1975 and 1978 (Friedman and I visited rural Hebei in 1978 and then spent the next quarter century trying to fathom and write collaboratively about China's rural transformations). All five of us were or had been active members of CCAS, two of whose primary goals were ending the US War in Indochina and opening diplomatic relations with the People's Republic of China.

My experience on this first China visit was framed by my recent experience with CCAS and the anti-war movement; my understanding of America's Asian wars, military base structures and the US-China relationship; as well as my research on the Chinese Revolution.

Reading these accounts more than thirty years later, I am struck by the powerful influence that first experience in China had on all of our thinking and, indeed, our subsequent lives. For Bernstein and Mirsky, within days of their arrival in China, any illusions that they might have cherished about China and the Chinese Revolution were shredded. (Could those illusions have been larger than life given the sense of betrayal that resonates in their accounts decades later?) What replaced them were images of a manipulative totalitarianism that would drive their subsequent careers as leading China journalists. A theme that unites all four reports is the determination not to be duped by Chinese Potemkin villages or official lies.

That first visit left an indelible stamp on each of us in the course of lives substantially devoted to writing about China. Indelible... but in multiple and diverse ways, including not only our perceptions of China, but also of America. Richard Bernstein spells this out most clearly: for him, it was not only that "China was so backward," but, "we're better than they are." This was doubtless in part a response to the over-enthusiasm of some of our fellow travelers. Still, I wonder, can this provide a clue to the American passion for world travel: it allows us to return home with renewed conviction that we're number one?

What strikes me in three of these accounts is the absence of another theme that was central to the intellectual movements of the 1960s, including the currents that gave rise to CCAS and to my own thinking then and since: that is the imperative to understand other countries in light not only of their own history and culture, but also of the workings of global power, particularly American power.

Mirsky, Bernstein and Kagan were among the coauthors of *The Indochina Story*, the work primarily of Harvard Asian Studies graduate students, and perhaps the finest achievement of CCAS in providing a comprehensive, informed and accessible critique of the US Indochina Wars, one that reached a significant readership as a 1970 Bantam paperback. Not only that, Mirsky and Kagan had also contributed critical chapters about American blinders on China, and on US war-making in Laos, respectively, for a volume that Friedman and I edited. That was *America's Asia: Dissenting Essays on Asian-American Relations*, which appeared in Vintage the following year. Both were among early works that sought to rethink the reigning parameters of Asian Studies, above all in light of America's global role and the history of empire.

Reading these accounts, which rightly remind us of the need to exercise independent judgment when visiting another country, I discern little of the kind of critical thinking that animated some of our work at that time about the American exercise of global power that impinged on China and others, and that led to ways of thinking not only about China but equally about ourselves—that is, about the US-China relationship.

Mirsky and Bernstein appear to have been astonished to discover that China was a poor country, and Mirsky was outraged that the Chinese would go to great lengths to conceal that poverty and put forward the best possible face for one of the earliest groups to visit China, at a time when the US and China were groping toward establishment of diplomatic and economic relations.

I was a student of Chinese history and the Chinese Revolution, and had earlier spent a year studying in Taiwan and another in Japan. I was reflecting at that time on China's decline from its position as a major world power as recently as the eighteenth century, as a result of the disintegration of the Qing dynasty, the invasive imperialism that set off a century of war, and above all the decimation of the country and the loss of ten to thirty million Chinese in the China-Japan War of 1937-45 and many more in subsequent revolutions.

Moreover, I was recalling both a US-China World War II alliance and the quarter century that followed during which the US and China were perpetually at war, including US intervention in the 1947 civil war followed by the US-Korean and US-Indochina Wars, as well as American attempts to isolate the PRC internationally in geopolitical and economic terms.

During that trip, I certainly anticipated neither the speed nor the character of China's subsequent hyper-growth and social transformation. But viewing this poor, proud and determined country, it seemed to me that its poverty was hardly either unusual or surprising in light of conditions in much of the post-colonial world at the time, and in light of China's modern history of war and revolution. Indeed, there was much that struck me positively about China's achievements at the time.

I felt hopeful that the re-establishment of diplomatic, trade and cultural relations that seemed imminent could support positive trends in both our countries, the Asia region and the world. This was a sense reinforced by the nocturnal discussion magisterially presided over by Zhou Enlai in the presence of other Chinese leaders. Knowing of my interest in Japan and my recent book, *Open Secret: The Kissinger-Nixon Doctrine in Asia*, our hosts arranged several opportunities to speak with Chinese specialists on Japan and on US-China-Japan relations, at a time when these relations all seemed to be in flux. Chinese international relations specialists were deeply concerned about the revival of Japanese militarism at the time—even more, apparently, than they were about American militarism.

My own thinking centered rather on Japan's postwar subordination to US power under the US-Japan security framework (AMPO), and the uses and abuses of US base expansion and multiple Asian wars. But we shared a sense that Japan then (as now) had yet to fully come to terms with the crimes committed during the invasion and occupation of China and much of Asia. The discussions helped me to understand the deep legacy of the China-Japan War in framing China's international perspective and to think in fresh ways about the prospects for US-China relations.

On the other hand, I shared with Mirsky and others in our group the disappointment that our Chinese hosts blocked our attempts to arrange a visit to the North Vietnamese Embassy to discuss the ongoing US-Indochina War. This underscored what we knew prior to the trip: that relations between China and the Democratic Republic of Vietnam were deeply troubled, the conflict rooted not only in the *longue durée* of China-Vietnam relations but also in the China-Soviet rift.

It is a bit difficult to recall nowadays, at a time when China is among the nations most plugged into the international economy (far more than the US, Japan or Europe when measured by the extent of foreign trade or foreign investment as a share of GDP, or in terms of its grip on the US economy with the purchase of approximately $1 trillion in US treasuries) just how isolated China was in 1972 from world trade and contacts with the West. And how proudly it wore its self-reliance. That self-reliance I understood to be the product in large part of protracted guerrilla warfare, and above all, the fifteen-year resistance to Japanese invasion that became part of the national mythos.

But it was also, of course, the response to the US ability to isolate China from world markets... a pattern that was just beginning to reverse as the US opened the way for China's entry into world markets and world councils (above all the United Nations) as part of a strategy of isolating the Soviet Union and encouraging the opening of China's economy, with US trade and investment to the fore.

What could we learn about China during an officially sponsored and organized trip? Not surprisingly, we learned a good deal about the issues that preoccupied the Chinese party-state, our hosts, both directly and indirectly. Meaning, also, of course, that there was much that we did not learn about: it was difficult for us to discern the nature of ongoing tensions in society in the late years of the Cultural Revolution, when the party had regained power without resolving underlying tensions; we learned nothing about the way in which the *hukou* system divided society, about the devastating toll of the Great Leap Forward or about the structural foundations of Chinese poverty; and little about the early stages of reform that were just getting underway without fanfare, particularly in the countryside. And much more.

We were perhaps better able, by reading between the lines, to gain a rudimentary sense of the ravaging of the universities during the Cultural Revolution; universities were just beginning to resume teaching, with worker-peasant-soldier students chosen primarily for their activism rather than through the previous examination system.

For me, most memorable was our three-day rural visit to the Red Flag Canal in Henan province, inevitably a national model of self-reliance which proudly featured an "Iron Girls Brigade" comprised of young women who had distinguished themselves in physical labor and the embodiment of Mao Zedong thought. Living in villagers' homes for a few days gave us our first limited opportunity to talk with farmers and gain a first glimpse of rural life.

But what were we seeing? Was it perhaps a caricature of rural reality, precisely because we had been taken inevitably to a model village and because the families who hosted us were party loyalists? Most of us recognized, I believe, that we were seeing the state's display of its model agricultural community and its self-reliance policy. Indeed, I would later realize that the presentation of the model to us shared much in common with the Party's use of models to define its policies for the Chinese people.

That experience in Dacaiyuan village set off the desire to seriously investigate Chinese rural society, which I had been studying at a distance in the US. Over the next six years, a series of applications to conduct research in rural China languished until 1978 when the United States and China were preparing to establish diplomatic relations and, as Edward Friedman has described, we began (with Paul Pickowicz) the research in rural North China which would continue over a quarter century and produce two volumes on the theme of village and state in the epochs of war and revolution and of reformist transformation.

Aware as I am today of just how difficult it is to fathom the social dynamics of a village, let alone Chinese (or any other) rural society, what stands out is the value of that first visit in whetting my appetite to learn more, and the value of that experience as a first step in thinking about the issues, including the limits of "viewing flowers from horseback." Perhaps above all the visit deepened my awareness that our understanding of China and other countries is closely bound up with our place in, and grasp of, the global role of the United States.

*Mark Selden is a Senior Research Associate in the East Asia Program at Cornell University and was a founding member of the Committee of Concerned Asian Scholars in the 1960s. For more than thirty years he edited The Bulletin of Concerned Asian Scholars (later Critical Asian Studies). His books include The Yenan Way in Revolutionary China and Chinese Village, Socialist State (with Edward Friedman and Paul G. Pickowicz).*

# Perry Link
*Dawn in China (1973)*

My father was a radical leftist professor. He led study tours to the Soviet Union in the 1930s and later admired Mao Zedong. For me, that influence, in addition to the passion in the late 1960s and early 1970s within the American student movement against our country's war in Vietnam—a movement in which I was not only a participant but an activist—led me to look at socialist China with very high hopes.

The first time I tried to go to China was in 1967, the year after I graduated from college. I was living in Hong Kong and wrote a letter to Beijing. A few months later I received a charming reply: two sheets of paper that it appeared as if a Red Guard with little English and a faulty typewriter had spent days laboring over, a letter in which it was explained that the Chinese people had nothing against me, but that I was from a predatory imperialist country and could not visit the People's Republic. Before I left Hong Kong I bought four volumes of the *Selected Works of Mao Zedong* and, rather grandiloquently, ripped the covers off of them so that I might carry them safely back to the imperialist US.

Meanwhile, I found a corner of Hong Kong that was still legally part of China, and I settled for going there. The Walled City of Kowloon, formerly an outpost of the Qing empire, had been abandoned for decades by both Nationalists and Communists, and had been disowned by the British as well.

It had become a fetid labyrinth of alleys and tunnels, the lawless bailiwick, I was told, of drug dealers, prostitutes, and gangsters. A group of Baptists ran a primary school there—and yes, there were children. I volunteered to teach English at the school. I knew this wasn't socialist China, but it was "China."

The first time I set foot in socialist China was May of 1973. A year earlier, in April 1972, the Chinese ping-pong team had visited the US to break the diplomatic ice of twenty-three years, and I had served as an interpreter traveling with the Chinese and American teams. Chinese officials on that tour got a good political impression of me, in part because I led four of the six American interpreters in a boycott of the teams' meeting with President Richard Nixon at the White House. (Nixon had ordered a bombing of Haiphong just the day before; to me, small talk in the Rose Garden just didn't seem right that day.)

Anyway, a year later we US interpreters asked if we could visit China, and the answer was yes. During four weeks we visited Guangzhou, Shanghai, Suzhou, Xian, Yanan, Beijing, and Tangshan. The bill for the trip—room, board, airfare, rail, sightseeing, everything—was US$550. It was a friendship rate.

But it was during that trip that cracks began to form in my ideal image of the People's Republic. I carried a small camera and took walks on my own, in search of "real life." I had learned in graduate school that there were no flies in China after the Anti-Four Pests Campaign of 1958. When I saw a fly on a white stone table in Suzhou, I photographed it. I thought I had something.

In Yanan, when four of us foreign guests boarded a crowded bus the driver shouted *waibin!* Immediately four seated passengers stood up, offering us their seats. The old man who stood up next to me did not, in my impression, seem to want to. I said, "Please, you sit," but he said nothing and remained standing. Embarrassed, I remained standing, too, and for the rest of the ride the people on the bus endured the ludicrous spectacle of an empty seat on a crowded bus.

We foreigners always rode "soft sleeper" class on the railroad, while most people on the same trains were riding "hard seat" class. I asked our guide about it.

"Why is there a soft-sleeper class?" I said, my socialist principles in mind. "Who rides in it, besides us?"

"The leaders," the guide replied.

"Why?" I asked, unaware that it was a stupid question.

"They are busy. They have many burdens. They need soft-sleeper."

My image of a classless society had suffered a blow, and it suffered a few more blows before the tour was over. The example that sticks most in my mind happened in Tangshan, where we visited the huge Tangshan coal mine. We descended in an elevator far below the earth's surface. (This was three years before a Richter 7.8 earthquake buried countless workers in that same mine.) Riding small railroad cars through a maze of tunnels deep underground, I noticed various signs: "slow!", "sound horn!", etc. The signs were in traditional Chinese characters, not simplified ones, and I also couldn't help noticing that there were no political slogans among them. All the signs were strictly business. This contrasted sharply with the surface of the earth, where slogans and quotations from Chairman Mao, on splendid red-and-white banners, or giant red billboards with gold writing and trim, were everywhere.

After emerging, I asked our guide: "Why are there no quotations from Chairman Mao down there with the miners?"

Her immediate reply: "Oh, it's too dirty!" She seemed a bit irritated at me for suggesting such an inappropriate location for the Chairman's thoughts. To me, though, it was a hard fact to swallow: the dirt of the mines was OK for the working class but not for the thoughts of its leader.

The inner insecurity of the guides became apparent to me in something that happened in Shanghai, when I bought a souvenir of my trip for my mother. My mother was born on a farm in Nebraska and was a salt-of-the-earth type. Her name was Beulah, she ate wheat germ, and brown was her favorite color. In a small shop I found hand-brooms that I knew she would like. They were crafted of sorghum stalks, light brown with dark flecks. Lovely. And symbols of the dignity of labor—which I knew she also would like. I imagined that she might hang it on a wall in her home, so I bought one.

Afterwards one of our guides, very nervous, accosted me. He seemed torn between handling an emergency and trying to maintain politeness.

"Why did you buy this?!" he asked.

I explained about my mother.

"Let me get you a better one!" He took the broom back to the shop and returned with another—not much better or worse, to my eye, but in his view more nearly perfect. Then, sitting next to me on the mini-bus ride back to the hotel, he began a deeper interrogation.

"Doesn't your mother like silk?… China has silk. China has jade carvings, China has cloisonné. Why do you buy a farmer's broom to represent China to your mother?" I began to realize that the guide saw what I had done as "unfriendly." My mother and I were looking down on China.

And this started me wondering: did this guide, deep inside, respect China's working people, the wielders of brooms—and want my mother to have the impression that "China is silk" only because he guessed that she, from a bourgeois society, would respect silk but not brooms? Or was it maybe worse than that? Was he participating in a societal hypocrisy that pretended to value brooms over silk but in reality did not?

From time to time during the trip I tried to strike up conversations with ordinary citizens, people with whom meetings had not been arranged. This was not easy. People constantly formed crowds to look at us, but kept their distance and stayed quiet. I have a vivid memory of one man—I would guess he was about thirty—who was part of a crowd but made eye contact with me. When I tried to address him personally—"What's your name?", "How are you?", etc.—his lips and eyebrows contorted wildly, from what seemed to me like severe pain, so I stopped.

Children were a bit less inhibited, and plainly curious about us. Any walk of ten minutes or more on a city street attracted a long train of them, as if we were pied pipers. I was amused to note, one day as we were walking past the gates of the Beijing Zoo, that some children who already held tickets to go see hippos and giraffes chose instead to come out of the zoo and follow us.

During one meeting with children—this was in Xian—a number of them gathered around us and seemed willing to talk. I asked a boy what he wanted to be when he grew up.

"I want to go to the toughest place and serve the people!" He pronounced the words in a sharp, confident, high-pitched voice.

"And you?" I asked another.

"I want to go to the toughest place and serve the people!" A sharp, confident, high-pitched voice—and exactly the same words.

I asked three or four more, of slightly different ages and of both sexes. All the answers were identical. I do not believe our handlers had prepared this scene for us; it had come about in too casual a manner. And I don't know how much of the conformity resulted from training in how to answer this question and how much may have come just from others seeing that the first boy had produced a good answer and wanting to play things safe by doing the same. In any case, it left me with a deep impression.

In the years since 1973 I have learned much, much more about how wrong I was in the late 1960s to take Mao Zedong's "socialism" at face value. I could not have been more mistaken. I am a bit puzzled that others among my leftist-student friends from the 1960s sometimes seem reluctant to face this obvious fact. Is it embarrassing? Why should it be? We were naïve, yes. We believed lies. But we were not the ones who spun the lies. Aren't the lie-spinners the ones who should be embarrassed? Besides, I feel no need to explain any reversal in my underlying values, because I don't find one.

In the late 1960s, I admired Mao because I felt strongly about things like peace, freedom, justice, truth, and a fair chance for the little guy. Today I detest Mao and his legacy. Why? Because I am drawn to things like peace, freedom, justice, truth, and a fair chance for the little guy.

*Perry Link is Professor Emeritus of East Asian Studies at Princeton University and Chancellorial Chair for Teaching Across Disciplines at the University of California, Riverside. He wrote Evening Chats in Beijing, coedited The Tiananmen Papers and recently coedited No Enemies, No Hatred: Selected Essays and Poems by Liu Xiaobo, winner of the 2010 Nobel Peace Prize.*

# Bamboo Curtain

## Bamboo Curtain

## SIDNEY RITTENBERG
### *Looking Back from Age Ninety (1945)*

May 1944: Based on a language aptitude test, I was taken out of the infantry, training in the Oregon snows, and shipped down to sunny Stanford, to be trained in Japanese. I opted for Chinese instead, thinking this would bring me home earlier. And then…

And then I totally fell in love with the Chinese language, the culture, my Chinese teachers. And it was two generations and three worlds later before I finally came home.

But that's another story. This is about my first trip to China.

In 1945, after forty-five days crossing the Pacific on an Army transport, we finally arrived—not quite in China, but in Calcutta, India. Then, four months later on September 16, as the Japanese were surrendering, I flew over the Himalayan Hump to China.

I didn't realize it at the time, but that flight, in a sense, previewed what awaited me in China. Our unit climbed on board and sat in a long row, backs against the wall, wearing our steel helmets, carrying full pack and gas mask, holding our rifles. Each of us was ordered to pay a one dollar deposit and was issued a parachute for the dangerous flight, by a First Sergeant who assured us that if the chute failed to open our deposit would be refunded.

But we were finally going to China!

As the plane rose steeply from the airport at Barrackpore, Bengal, one of the engines shut down and the propeller stopped turning. At the same time, a steaming hot liquid seeped back out of the flight deck and started down the aisle past where I was sitting. One of the flight crew came down the aisle, headed for the "head" (bathroom, to you civilians). I said, "Look that engine's stopped, and what's this hot stuff?" He glanced through the porthole at the motionless propeller and said, "Humph." He pointed at the hot liquid as he went on down the aisle and called back over his shoulder, "Battery."

But we were finally going to China!

They got the engine restarted and we crossed the Himalayas without further incident. And as the dawn gently broke over the Western Hills of Kunming, we saw the airport below us.

China! A softly-tinted red basin with tree-lined canals snaking through the fields, the fields themselves in bits and snatches, looking like somebody's crazy quilt. As we swooped down to land, we could see endless lines of carts pulled by great black water buffaloes or by the little Yunnan ponies.

China! This was where we could "use our language"—"ours," because we had put a full year into the Army's immersion study program at Stanford. Then, since the Army urgently needed Chinese language personnel, we were shipped out the day after graduation—to Camp Crowder, Missouri, where we were told to "forget about your Chinese" and were trained for one year to climb telephone poles, run field switchboards, and repair telephone lines. (You've heard about Army efficiency?)

We raged for a year about "not being able to use our language," we complained to the Inspector General in Washington—and now, finally, we were in China, where we could use "our language" to make a difference.

When we landed, we were taken to our barracks at "Hostel #8," and introduced to our logistical hosts, the Nationalist WASC (War Area Service Corps). Our hosts proved skilled at showing GIs around, quietly relieving them of many prized possessions, procuring village girls for one dollar a night, and scrutinizing their activities.

But I would have none of that—I went out, as soon as my duffle bag was stowed in the barracks, to see what friends I could make with "my language."

Of course, I found that "their language" was quite another story. They spoke a Yunnan dialect, which I learned to understand only after some time. But they could understand my amateurish Beijing dialect.

On the first afternoon, I went with two of my buddies to visit the Nationalist Army company command post, across the road from us. This was part of Chiang Kai-shek's elite Fifth Army, commanded by Generals Du Yuming and Qiu Qingquan—both of whom ended up as POWs in the later Civil War days.

The square in front of the command post was an amazing sight. It looked like the set for some Cecil B. DeMille movie: medieval instruments of torture lined the square—stocks, a crooked bench for bending the spine, rings for hanging victims up by their thumbs… I asked one of the guards on duty— a chubby, baby-faced Hunanese farm boy—"What are these for?"

"For us, when we're naughty. And for bad *lao bai xing* (civilians)."

Everything we had learned at Stanford about the Old Regime in China suddenly became very real.

On the way back to the barracks, I ran into a little boy, six or seven, coming back from school, with his book-bag slung over his shoulder—like me, when I used to walk home from Bennett School in Charleston.

I stopped him to practice my Chinese. He was learning Standard Mandarin, so I could understand him.

"*Lao Mei ding hao!*" He started off—"Americans are the best." Many local people would sing that out, with a big "thumbs up" whenever we appeared in public—we were fighting the Japanese, we had money to spend, we were popular.

I asked him what he was studying. "Chinese," he said.

"It's hard for us to learn," I said. "Especially the tones."

"Tones?" He put his close-cropped head to one side.

"Yes, tones. When you say *hao* third tone and *hao* second tone, it's really the same word, isn't it? Just the tone is different."

Again, he put his head to one side and began repeating those two words to himself: "*Hao; hao. Hao; hao.*"

Then he looked up with a big grin and said, "They are a little alike, aren't they?"

He invited me home with him to have tea. When we arrived, I had tea with his mother and grandmother, whom I could barely understand, until his father came home. His father, Li Zhi, turned out to be a captain in one of the many secret police agencies that surrounded us—this one belonged to the provincial warlord/governor, Long Yun.

Li Zhi told me that they were instructed to take every opportunity of making friends with American GIs, so he was very happy that I had come to make friends with them.

Well, of course, I hadn't. But he dogged my footsteps, and my buddies', as long as we were in Kunming, and was a sinister nuisance.

On the next morning, still in first flush of excitement at finally being in China and able to use "my language," I drove into the bustling city of Kunming. In those days, it was a quiet, beautiful old town with no end of unique scenic spots, a stunning lake and graceful mountains in the distance (a far cry from the grungy commercial city and the shrunken, heavily polluted lake of today).

I was attracted by a little gang of newspaper boys—ragged trousers, barefoot, Chinese cousins of Huckleberry Finn.

I nudged the jeep over and parked in front of them, and they immediately swarmed all over the car, each thrusting his papers at me.

"*Lao Mei ding hao!*" and up-thrust thumbs all round.

"*Dou you shenme bao?*" I asked. "What have you got?"

They had the local Nationalist Party paper, as well as the national one; the commercial journal; a Catholic daily; the Nationalist Army paper… and, I discovered that buried underneath all the others they were peddling the forbidden Communist journals, the *New China Daily* and *The Masses* magazine. They seemed to feel safe showing me their secret wares, since I was a foreigner. And they were tickled pink when I bought both of the forbidden Communist publications.

I found out later that the Communist Party of China had a secret deal with local warlord Long Yun (later an official with no authority in the PRC government) under which Long allowed them to circulate their paper in Kunming, but *sotto voce.*

Finally, the whole gaggle of kids piled into the jeep and they directed me to the Confucian Temple Park—Da Guan Yuan—with its thriving market for fruits, vegetables, and sweetmeats, and we had a ball, roaming the park, chattering, and eating.

I took them back to where I had picked them up. From then on, we were fast friends, helping each other in various ways during the two months that I was stationed in Kunming. Actually, it was these ragged kids who introduced me to the underground workers for the CPC in Kunming—which changed my life.

But there was a little *entr'acte* that was highly instructive for me, long-term.

One day, my jeep was parked at the curb, and the little newsies were crowded around, chattering away as usual. As I was getting ready to leave, I happened to open the glove compartment and found that my big GI flashlight had disappeared. It had been there that morning, so I knew what had happened.

"Look," I said, "do you think this is right? We're all good friends, just sitting here talking, and somebody filched my flashlight. Is that the way friends treat friends? Whoever took it, please ask him to give it back, no questions asked."

There was a great hubbub, like they were debating, followed by some pushing and shoving; finally, they pushed a tiny little boy to the front. He was in complete rags, standing there, hanging his head. He fished in under his rags and slowly produced my flashlight, which he handed back to me.

I was moved beyond words. A simple act of human love and trust, bonding across seemingly unbridgeable gulfs. I hugged him and hugged him, and then put him in the front seat as we all went off for goodies to the Confucian Temple.

Sometimes, I would look at them and wonder about China's future. I thought of one of my favorite passages from Shakespeare—Romeo to the Apothecary:

*Art thou so bare and full of wretchedness, and fear'st to die?*
*Famine is in thy cheeks,*
*Need and oppression starveth in thine eyes.*
*Contempt and beggary hangs upon thy back.*

I did not know it yet, but these boys and those like them proved that they were not afraid to die, and thus did they accomplish the revolution.

*Sidney Rittenberg* *was the only US citizen to join the Chinese Communist Party in the 1940s and spent sixteen of his thirty-five years in China in prison. He now teaches China Studies at Pacific Lutheran University in the US and runs Rittenberg Associates, Inc., which assists companies seeking to do business with China. He is the coauthor, with Amanda Bennett, of The Man Who Stayed Behind.*

# SIMON LEYS
*The Hall of Uselessness*

*Everyone knows the usefulness of what is useful, but few know the usefulness of what is useless.*
– Zhuang Zi

I was born and grew up in Brussels. I had a happy childhood. To paraphrase Tolstoy: all happy childhoods are alike—warm affection and much laughter. The recipe seems simple enough. China was in no way—nothing at all (alas!)—an element of my childhood. There was no scope to study Chinese history or politics, or the Chinese language, at school.

I first visited the People's Republic of China with a group of students in 1955. The Chinese Government had invited a delegation of Belgian Youth (ten delegates—I was the youngest, age nineteen) to visit China for one month in May that year. The voyage, smoothly organized, took us to the usual famous spots, climaxing in a one-hour private audience with Zhou Enlai.

My overwhelming impression (a conclusion to which I have remained faithful for the rest of my life) was that it would be inconceivable to live in this world, in our age, without a good knowledge of Chinese language and a direct access to Chinese culture.

After completing my undergraduate degree, I started learning Chinese. Since, at that time, no scholarship was available to go to China, I went to Taiwan. I had no "career" plan whatsoever. I simply wished to know Chinese and acquire a deeper appreciation of Chinese culture.

Loving Western painting, quite naturally I became enthralled with Chinese painting (and calligraphy) and I developed a special interest for what the Chinese wrote on the subject of painting: traditionally, the greatest painters were also scholars, poets, men of letters; hence the development of an extraordinarily rich, eloquent and articulate literature on painting— philosophical, critical, historical and technical.

We are often tempted to do research on topics that are somewhat marginal and lesser-known, since, on these, it is easier to produce original work. But one of my Chinese masters gave me a most valuable piece of advice: "Always devote yourself to the study of great works, works of fundamental importance, and your effort will never be wasted." Thus, for my PhD thesis, I chose to translate and comment on what is generally considered as a masterpiece, the treatise on painting by Shitao, a creative genius of the early eighteenth century; he addresses the essential questions: Why does one paint? How should one paint? Among all my books, this one, first published forty years ago, has never gone out of print—and, to my delight, it is read by painters much more than by sinologists!

The virtue and power of the Chinese literary language culminates in its classical poetry. Chinese classical poetry seems to me the purest, the most perfect and complete form of poetry one could conceive of. Better than any other poetry, it fits Auden's definition: "memorable speech"; and indeed, it carves itself effortlessly into your memory. Furthermore, like painting, it splendidly occupies a visual space in its calligraphic incarnations. It inhabits your mind, it accompanies your life, it sustains and illuminates your daily experiences.

Traditionally, Chinese scholars, men of letters, artists would give inspiring names to their residences, hermitages, libraries and studios. Sometimes they did not actually possess residences, hermitages, libraries or studios—not even a roof over their heads—but the existence or non-existence of a material support for a Name never appeared to them a very relevant issue. And I wonder if one of the deepest seductions of Chinese culture is not related to this conjuring power with which it vests the Written Word. I am not dealing here with esoteric abstractions, but with a living reality. Let me give you just one modest example, which hit me long ago, when I was an ignorant young student.

In Singapore, I often patronized a small movie theater which showed old films of Peking operas. The theater itself was a flimsy open-air structure planted in a paddock by the side of the road (at that time, Singapore still had a countryside): a wooden fence enclosed two dozen rows of seats— long planks resting on trestles. In the rainy season, towards the end of the afternoon, there was always a short, heavy downpour, and when the show started, just after dark, the planks often had not yet had time to dry; thus, at the box-office, with your ticket, you received a thick old newspaper to cushion your posterior against the humidity. Everything in the theater was shoddy and ramshackle—everything except the signpost with the theater's name hanging above the entrance: two characters written in a huge and generous calligraphy, *Wen Guang*—which could be translated as "Light of Civilization" or "Light of the Written-Word" (it is the same thing). However, later on in the show, sitting under the starry sky and watching on screen Ma Lianliang give his sublime interpretation of the part of the wisest minister of the Three Kingdoms (third century AD), you realized that—after all—this "Light of Civilization" was no hollow boast.

The Hall of Uselessness pertains to the period when I was studying and teaching at the New Asia College in Hong Kong in the early 1960s. It was a hut located in the heart of a refugee shantytown on the Kowloon side (Diamond Hill). To reach it at night, one needed an electric torch, for there were no lights and no roads—only a dark maze of meandering paths through a chaos of tin and plywood shacks; there were open drains by the side of the paths, and fat rats ran under the feet of passers-by. For two years I enjoyed there the fraternal hospitality of a former schoolmate, whom I knew from Taiwan—he was an artist (calligrapher and seal-carver) sharing a place with two postgraduate students, a philologist and a historian. We slept on bunks in a single common room. This room was naturally a complete mess—anywhere else it would have resembled a dismal slum, but here all was redeemed by the work of my friend: one superb piece of calligraphy (in seal-script style) hanging on the wall—*Wu Yong Tang*, "The Hall of Uselessness." If taken at face value, it had a touch of tongue-in-cheek self-deprecation; in fact, it contained a very cheeky double-meaning. The words (chosen by our philologist companion, who was a fine scholar) alluded to a passage from *The Book of Changes*, the most ancient, most holy (and most obscure) of all the Chinese classics, which said that "in springtime the dragon is useless." This, in turn, according to commentaries, meant that in their youth the talents of superior men (promised to a great future) must remain hidden.

I spent two years in The Hall of Uselessness; these were intense and joyful years—when learning and living were one and the same thing. The best description of this sort of experience was given by John Henry Newman. In his classic *The Idea of a University*, he made an amazingly bold statement: he said that if he had to choose between two types of universities, one in which eminent professors teach students who come to the university only to attend lectures and sit for examinations, and the other where there are no professors, no lectures, no examinations and no degrees, but where the students live together for two or three years, he would choose the second type. He concluded, "How is this to be explained? When a multitude of young men, keen, open-hearted, sympathetic and observant as young men are, come together and freely mix with each other, they are sure to learn from one another, even if there be no one to teach them; the conversation of all is a series of lectures to each, and they gain for themselves new ideas and views, fresh matter of thought and distinct principles for judging and acting day by day."

I hope I have remained faithful to the memory of The Hall of Uselessness—not in the meaning intended by my friends (for I am afraid I am not exactly of the dragon breed!), but at least in the more obvious meaning of Zhuang Zi, quoted above. Yet is this second aspiration more humble, or more ambitious? After all, this sort of "uselessness" is the very ground on which rest all the essential values of our common humanity.

Looking back at those some twelve years, during which I lived and worked successively in Taiwan, Singapore and Hong Kong (plus six months in Japan), it was a happy period of intense activity—living and learning in an environment where all my friends became my teachers, and all my teachers, my friends. I am fond of a saying by Prince de Ligne (a writer I much admire): "Let each one examine what he has most desired. If he is happy, it is because his wishes have not been granted." For some years, I had wished I could study in China; but now, in retrospect, I realize that, had I been given such a chance at that particular time (1958-1970), I would never have been allowed to enjoy in China such rich, diverse, easy and close human contacts.

I did return to the PRC twice—first, for six months in 1972, as cultural attaché at the Belgian Embassy in Peking; second, for one month in 1973, as a member of a delegation from the Australian National University—and the experience is described in *Chinese Shadows*, first published in French in 1974.

My own interest, my own field of work, is Chinese literature and Chinese painting. When commenting on Chinese contemporary politics, I was merely stating common sense evidence and common knowledge. But at that time, this may indeed have disturbed some fools here and there—which, in the end, did not matter very much.

Do I have any regrets? Mine include—usually what we regret is what we did not do—sailing round Cape Horn and climbing Huangshan.

(These excerpts from Simon Leys' recent writings and interviews were selected and adapted by the editor.)

*Simon Leys, the pen-name of Pierre Ryckmans, is a scholar, novelist, and observer of Chinese culture and politics. He is the author of thirteen books including The Chairman's New Clothes, Chinese Shadows, The Death of Napoleon, The Analects of Confucius, and most recently, The Hall of Uselessness. He taught at the Australian National University and the University of Sydney. In 2004 he was awarded the Prix mondial Cino Del Duca.*

# DELIA DAVIN
## *Swinging Sixties in China (1963)*

I arrived in China in August 1963. I was nineteen years old and had
just finished high school in the UK. I was to teach English at the Beijing
Broadcasting Institute while my then husband W.J.F. Jenner, a graduate in
Chinese from Oxford, became a translator at the Foreign Languages Press.
Our journey seemed hugely exciting. We traveled to Moscow on a trans-
Europe express via Berlin and Warsaw, and thence on the trans-Siberian via
Ulan Bator to Beijing.

Our first stop in China was the Inner Mongolian town of Erlian, then
the site of the "break of gauge" where the broad track used in Russia and
Mongolia gave way to the standard gauge. Each carriage had to be lifted up
with a crane to have its bogies changed. This operation took a considerable
time, allowing the excited Chinese passengers, most of whom had been
working or studying abroad for years, the time to enjoy a proper Chinese
meal in the station restaurant. The next day the Chinese train attendants
vacuumed the floors, cleaned every surface in the carriage and hunted down
all the flies with swats to make the train fit to enter the capital. When we
finally arrived in Beijing it was quite a wrench to leave the reassuringly
familiar routine of train life and the attendants who had been proud of their
exotic British passengers.

After a formal welcome at Beijing station from the "leaders" of the Press and the Institute, we were driven to the Friendship Hotel, or "Druzhba" as it was often still called, a large residential complex that had been built for the Russian experts who worked in China. Although they had departed in 1960, the buildings still bore many traces of their occupation. The shops, dining rooms, clinic, swimming pool, club and theater were labeled in Russian although English, French, Spanish, and Japanese notices gradually appeared during the months we spent there. The scale of the architecture and even the furniture was large and clunky. We were lodged in two comfortable rooms with our own bathroom, much more luxury than we had expected in China and a considerable contrast with the furnished rooms with an outdoor lavatory that had been our home in Oxford.

Unfortunately we soon found that the comfort in which we lived was part of a systematic cosseting that tended to cut us off from the Chinese. In a petrol-short city where almost everyone rode bicycles to work and there were still very few cars we were expected to use the "Druzhba" taxis. It was only after many hours of argument that I was allowed to cycle to work and to take my lunch in the teachers' canteen there instead of being driven back to eat in a "Druzhba" dining room. The complex was guarded by the army and visitors had to be met at the gate and produce identity. We spent over a year there until we were finally able to escape to a hostel that belonged to the radio station, where our neighbors were mostly Japanese and Chinese. This building was just outside the old city and overlooked the old city wall and the moat, a much pleasanter situation.

The college in which I taught had been established in the Great Leap Forward. This meant that its buildings and facilities were pretty basic; the students for example had no canteen. They collected food from the kitchen in bowls that they kept in their desks and ate in the playground or in their dormitories. To their annoyance they were required to use spoons (like children, they protested) rather than chopsticks that might have rolled off their bowls when stored and thus been unhygienic. As the Institute was preparing people to work in the Broadcasting Authority, over twenty languages were taught including Swahili, Urdu and so on. When I arrived, an Indian teacher who had formerly looked after the English class was transferred to the Tamil class while his wife, who had formerly taught Tamil moved on to a newly enrolled group learning Malayalam. Both these colleagues generously shared their language teaching expertise with me. In one respect our Institute was privileged. We had inherited a collection of reel-to-reel tape recorders from the radio station to which we were attached. We used and reused precious imported West German tape. When a tape snapped we would mend it with sellotape. This was also imported and had to be collected from a technician who would carefully wind about an inch of it around my fountain pen—enough for two mends. I often wished I had brought some with me from England.

In the first year we used duplicated texts, many of which had originally been selected by Russian teachers of English. I found myself teaching extracts from *A Tale of Two Cities*, *Lady Windermere's Fan*, *The Scarlet Letter* and a translation of Gorky's *Mother*. A text on contemporary English life contained references to vacuum cleaners. My students could not begin to imagine what these would be like, so we went to the railway station to see them. The East German vacuum cleaners used on the Trans-Siberian trains were then, as far as I know, the only ones in Beijing. The station escalator was an added excitement. We also read Chairman Mao's account of his life as recorded by Edgar Snow in *Red Star Over China*. At that time the students knew nothing of the private lives of the communist leaders and were intrigued to learn that Mao had been married more than once. Later, as the Sino-Soviet dispute developed, our readings came under tighter political control. We were restricted to teaching texts from Chinese government publications including the polemics that the Chinese Communist Party was then blasting at the Communist Party of the Soviet Union. This was rather boring for the students who had to read and discuss the same documents in their politics class but it served me in good stead later when I taught this period of Chinese history.

My students had definitely been winners from the revolution. Many came from illiterate families and all felt that they would never have made it to university in "old China." Their lives were basic but they got enormous pleasure from the simple purchases they could afford from their stipends such as tiny tins of moisturizing cream, packs of pretty bookmarks or sugared dried peas that we ate at parties. Their food was simple—meals were predominantly steamed bread and cabbage—but for many of them an improvement on what they had eaten in early childhood. The students from the south longed for rice and were happy when it was available. Three students were of Hui nationality and ate only food supplied by the halal kitchen. Most of the people I taught were a year or so older than I was, but one was a mature student with three children. She had served in the Korean War and danced a "ladies excuse-me" with Premier Zhou Enlai—two claims to fame that impressed her fellow students equally. Of the thirteen in that first class all are still living except one whose health was compromised by poor nutrition and tuberculosis when he was a child laborer before 1949.

I often stayed on with my students after class helping them with their homework, chatting and doing physical training. This mostly consisted of running, which I was good at. However, we also practiced throwing dummy grenades and we were all hopeless at this. Indeed, the trainer informed us that our throws were so short we would have blown ourselves up had the grenades been real. In those days Chinese were strongly discouraged from associating with foreigners except as colleagues or students. I felt fortunate to be able to spend so much time with these idealistic, naïve young people and to learn so much about their childhoods, their families and their ideas and hopes.

The Foreign Languages Press where my husband worked was a more complicated place. His colleagues were older; many had belonged to the highly educated elite and had foreign connections. Nearly all expressed great enthusiasm for the revolution and the People's Government but their levels of sincerity no doubt varied. Some had already been in political trouble, many felt vulnerable. Nonetheless, this was a close community. Employees lived in

Press accommodation and ate in the canteen. They did exercises or played badminton and table tennis together during the breaks. Spring and autumn expeditions to the Western Hills organized by the trade union were highlights of the year as was the annual distribution of grapes and honey from land belonging to the Press. For us, yearning for greater integration into Chinese life, the Press provided a better compromise than the expatriate society of the Friendship Hotel. Our dearest friends were the literary translators Gladys Yang and Yang Xianyi with whom we spent much of our free time. They were immensely knowledgeable about what was going on in China as well as about Chinese history and literature and we learned a lot from them.

The Yangs' hospitable household allowed us to meet Chinese friends and colleagues outside our foreign ghetto. Through them we also became friends with people who had one foot in each of the sharply divided worlds of the Chinese and foreigners in Beijing. Two New Zealand Chinese brothers who had come back to China to help the new People's Republic in the early 1950s worked as proofreaders. They were often criticized for their "foreign" way of thinking, or even for walking like foreigners. Yet when they went to work in the countryside they were admired by the peasants for their Kiwi ability to fix broken-down machinery. A black American then working as a translator had been taken prisoner in the Korean War, and had opted to stay in China at the time of the ceasefire. He subsequently took a degree in Chinese at Wuhan University, married and had two children. By the time we knew him he was homesick for the United States. He could not take his family back to Tennessee however, because under his home state's anti-miscegenation laws, his marriage to a Chinese woman would have been deemed illegal. He had to defer his return until the ban on interracial marriages was held to be unconstitutional by the Supreme Court in 1967. By this time the Cultural Revolution was also making his life in China very uncomfortable.

Beijing in the early 1960s was heaven for cyclists. Although there was little motor traffic, all the major roads had broad cycle lanes shared by pedicabs, mule carts, and camels that carried coal into the capital. Traffic lights were worked manually and the roads were so quiet that they could be switched off altogether when the traffic cops went off duty at 7:30 p.m. We worked a six-day week but on Sundays we could spend happy hours in the Forbidden City, Beihai Park, the Summer Palace or temples in the Western Hills. There was little pollution and we enjoyed clear blue skies day after day. As there was minimal heating and no air conditioning, I found both the winter cold and the summer heat difficult. At least thickly padded clothing in the winter helped. Foreigners were such a rarity that even dressed in Chinese clothes we inspired interest wherever we went and often attracted crowds. Small children called out "*Sulianren*" (Soviet) after us. Later they got more up to date and substituted this with "Albanian" or even on one occasion after the Zanzibar revolution of 1964, "Zanzibari."

Many other areas outside the capital were closed to foreigners but we were able to visit major historic cities such as Nanjing, Hangzhou, Suzhou, Xian and Luoyang before modern traffic and multi-story buildings changed their appearance forever.

The timing of our stay in China was good—fortuitously, of course. When we arrived food was becoming more plentiful, rations were increasing, the range of consumer goods was greater and prices were falling. We did not know then how severe the post-Great Leap famine had been but we were aware that there had been serious shortages and hunger. Confidence in the Communist Party had certainly been rocked by the hard years but by 1963 it was returning, not least because people really wanted to believe that life would be getting better. To our distress the explosion of China's first atom bomb was greeted with popular enthusiasm. We put on our British Campaign for Nuclear Disarmament badges and refused to celebrate.

There were events and campaigns that in retrospect one can understand as harbingers of what was to come, although of course at the time we had no notion of it. The Four Clean-Ups Movement (*Siqing*) meant that my students were sent off to the countryside for a month abruptly and to the detriment of their progress with English. The Socialist Education Campaign not only affected our teaching materials, it meant that western classical music disappeared from Radio Beijing and the hours our students and colleagues spent in political study doubled. We were all bused off to watch an adulatory film on Stalin shown across two evenings. It lasted a painful eight hours if my memory does not deceive me. Liu Shaoqi's *How to be a Good Communist* was reprinted in Chinese and many other languages. Soon afterwards, the *Selected Works of Mao Zedong*, which had been unavailable, reappeared in the bookshops and his name was mentioned on the radio ever more frequently.

When I left Beijing in August 1965 to study Chinese at the University of Leeds I could never have imagined that it would be more than a decade before I could return, that meanwhile China would undergo the turmoil of the Cultural Revolution, and that many of my friends would be imprisoned or sent away from Beijing for long years. When I did return in 1975, Beijing seemed in many ways a duller and a grimmer place. Since then of course it has undergone still greater transformations. The ancient city and the young revolutionary society I knew have disappeared. But I do not forget those two years that gave me so many good friends and an interest in China that was to shape my whole life.

*Delia Davin taught English in Beijing from 1963 to 1965, and returned there from 1975 to 1976 to work as a translator. She taught at York University and at the University of Leeds, where she is now Emeritus Professor of Chinese Studies. She has written extensively on gender and population issues in China.*

## W.J.F. JENNER
*Translating in Peking (1963)*

There was something unreal about first entering China one night in August 1963 in the middle of the Gobi after a week on trains since leaving Victoria station. We had crossed the frontier at Erenhot, and a Chinese dining car had just been added to the train to replace the Mongolian one that the Chinese passengers had been carefully avoiding. Now they were piling into it for a cheerful meal, and we joined them to celebrate being in China at last.

The next morning Delia Davin and I—we were then married—set foot on the ground briefly at Datong. There was no time to see any more of the historic frontier city before the last, spectacular stage of the journey through the passes and the Wall into Peking (as Beijing was then called in English). Through the train windows we glimpsed peasants who might have come from illustrations to Zhao Shuli stories, then crowds on bicycles waiting at level crossings as the city grew closer. The excitement of being in China and seeing what I had been reading about for years was dampened when the welcoming party on the platform of the recently built Peking station turned out to be from *Peking Review*. A month or two earlier I had signed a contract at the Chinese Chargé d'Affaires Office in Portland Place with the head of the Foreign Languages Bureau to work in Peking for two years. It stated that my "concrete working post" would be assigned on arrival. I had naïvely hoped to be translating literature. This, I realized, was to be it.

At least I had got to China, something not easily done from England in those days. Soon after I graduated in Chinese at Oxford in 1962 my teacher, the fine literary scholar Wu Shichang, returned to the country he had left as an endangered liberal in 1947. As a member of the Institute of Literature of the Academy of Sciences—the Academy of Social Sciences had not yet been separated from it—he passed on the message that I would be glad to work in China. It was then all but impossible to go as a student from Britain, and I longed to get there. 1963 turned out to be just the right time to ask to go. Up till then only a few people with native or equivalent English had been needed to teach, edit or translate. Most of them had been taken on locally, but there were no more to be had. Previously they had been supplemented by Anglophone political trusties sent by foreign communist parties or their front organizations. Hardly any of these links had survived the Sino-Soviet schism, and the only foreign communists to stay on were converts to Maoism. So just when China's rulers wanted their voice to be heard around the world they needed people with language skills. As a young graduate with some knowledge of Chinese and no Soviet connections I was doubtless seen as useful, as were a number of other new arrivals from around the world.

Going to China was a big decision. It meant giving up the British government studentship that had started the previous autumn and would have funded at least two more years of doctoral research at Oxford on Northern Wei Loyang. But I wanted to experience a country I only knew from books and to be part of what was happening. The medieval studies would have to be fitted in when they could be.

First impressions of Peking were of a city that still had its moat and some of the city wall gate towers. There were hardly any cars, and some buses were still fuelled by huge bags of coal gas lying on the roof. Much was still moved around on pedal-powered carts. People walked slowly. One day that first autumn I saw coal being delivered by camels.

So began two years of the artificial life of a "foreign expert." For the first eighteen months we had to live in the *Youyi Binguan*, the Friendship Hotel (or "the Druzhba," as it was still often known by its Russian name), northwest of the city. It then seemed a huge complex with its grandiose accommodation that had been built to Moscow's specifications in the 1950s for the Soviet and East European specialists who were advising on the creation of the new Chinese state along Stalinist lines. "Foreign experts" were a Soviet category that had been introduced for them. I suspect that the system needed substitutes to keep going after the Russians and their followers had gone. It may also have been a matter of pride to pretend that even after the split China could still bring in expert foreigners. This probably explains why a year after graduating I was given this unmerited status. Besides, there was this huge and now rather empty hostel in which to put us "experts." Like many colleges and other new institutions created in the first years of the People's Republic it had its own self-contained compound in a belt of what was then vegetable-growing land outside the city, which was then much smaller than it is today. It then seemed rather a long way out of town, though it is now an unremarkable set of buildings in inner suburbia, dwarfed by nearby shopping malls.

Some of the *Youyi Binguan*'s buildings were now used for Chinese conferences, and some for us new post-Soviet foreign employees. It was sealed off from the world outside by army sentries at the gates. Apart from the staff who worked there, Chinese people were only allowed in with special permission. It was run by the Foreign Experts Bureau, which liked to keep short-term "experts" as far from ordinary life as possible. We could eat in its subsidized restaurants without having to bother with the ration coupons that everyone else needed. "Experts" were ferried to work by bus or car in the morning, brought back for lunch, then returned to the office for the afternoon before being shuttled back in the evening. On Sundays there was a bus into town for shopping. Sometimes the Foreign Experts Bureau or one's own work unit would lay on a treat, such as visiting a prison, or going to see Peking ducks lining up to have a blob of glob thrust into their beaks through a metal spout. Sometimes we were fed globs of official culture.

The biggest occasions were around National Day. Hundreds of experts and their keepers would be taken in a motorcade to the Great Hall of the People for an impressively choreographed banquet at which Zhou Enlai might be distantly seen. On the day itself you could watch the parade from a stand by Tiananmen and watch the spectacular fireworks in the evening.

The Foreign Experts Bureau also organized the annual holiday trip outside Peking. At a time when travel was extremely restricted for foreigners, with only a handful of cities for which the Public Security might grant a travel permit, the chance to see Xian, Luoyang and Yanan was too good to miss. When torrential rains washed away part of the Longhai railway we flew to Yanan from Luoyang in an ancient DC3. Another trip was to the then utterly delightful Suzhou, which had not yet lost the beauty of its buildings and its Ming and Qing rentier urbanity, and to Shanghai, physically little changed since the 1940s. Shanghai felt like a slightly outdated version of the modern world where people walked briskly instead of ambling as in Peking. No doubt these trips only showed carefully chosen appearances, but I am very glad to have had those impressions of what places once looked like.

What we got to understand about life in Peking was limited but well worth having. The Foreign Languages Bureau and Delia's employers, the Broadcasting Institute where she taught English, allowed us some contact with reality. We could buy bicycles (without having to wait years for a permit as our Chinese colleagues did) and make our own way to work and into town.

The Foreign Languages Bureau was a large Soviet-style outfit set up in the 1950s and expanded after the split with Moscow. The Bureau was a typical 1950s Chinese office building in Baiwanzhuang with its own compound behind it that had crowded accommodation blocks for some of its staff. Office hours were long but leisurely, 8 a.m. to noon, then a break for lunch and siesta of two hours in summer and one and a half hours in winter before another four hours in the afternoon. The office worked six days a week, but foreigners were given Saturday afternoons off.

The Bureau's staff all belonged to it. It was not just their employer:

like other work units of the time it controlled their lives. Pay was low and living conditions were basic, but in exchange it provided security from cradle to crematorium: wages even after retirement, some medical cover, and accommodation, even if only a bed in a dormitory for the unmarried. Leaving was all but impossible. Back then, before the lethal madness of the Cultural Revolution, this forced coexistence meant that people had to get on together. Because they were not free to change jobs and promotion was glacially slow there was no pressure to work very hard, compete or get ahead. There was little privacy or freedom. Avoiding political mistakes or anything that might get you into trouble in the next ideological campaign seemed to be the main worries.

Given the nature of the Bureau's work everyone was very well aware of the rules for dealing with foreigners. Conversations with us, except on safe subjects, were guarded. You knew that they had to be reported. While it did not matter to me what the authorities thought about my incorrect views I did not want to create awkward situations in which my colleagues might find it hard to trot out the party line. Most of them did not go out of their way to give political lectures.

*Peking Review* was in a newer building at the back of the compound. The magazine was hopeless as propaganda, though it did give foreign governments and other observers authoritative translations of the Communist Party's line as given out for external consumption. The people on the magazine were pleasant to work with, but they had little say on what went into it and were not allowed to make it interesting. It contained no journalism and bore no resemblance to a news magazine. The content was largely set from above by the Central Committee's Propaganda Bureau, and trusties fixed the English of key political texts before they were issued by the Xinhua News Agency. *Peking Review* had to print them without changing so much as a comma. Checking the English of other articles made few demands on me, and there was no scope for making them less boring.

Suggestions about improving the *Review* met with wry smiles. I was sure that some of my highly educated and intelligent colleagues who knew the outside world were well aware of the *Review*'s limitations. After the death of Mao one of them was to be a key player in setting up *China Daily*, which with all its shortcomings at least pretended to be a newspaper. Something unexpected could provoke more spontaneous reactions. The assassination of President Kennedy brought out a sense of superiority at the incompetence of American security and a joke about *Kennidi ken ni*, Kennedy biting the earth.

I was rescued from *Peking Review* by a misprint. One day I was given a cutting from the *People's Daily* to translate, probably to find out if I could. The piece itself was of no interest, but a character in it seemed wrong. Asking about this must have given me some credibility, and things started to look up. While still having to polish *Peking Review* articles I was also given a wonderful assignment: editing Yang Xianyi and Gladys Yang's selected chapters from Sima Qian's *Shi ji*. With the blind confidence of twenty-three I cheerfully thought I was improving their masterly work, and they were good enough not to take offense. (The book was to disappear, only to be published in Hong Kong in the 1970s before it finally came out in a Foreign Languages Press edition.)

Towards the end of 1963 I was transferred from *Peking Review* to the Foreign Languages Press, the part of the Foreign Languages Bureau that produced books. My office was now a small room in the FLP English Section in the main building. I was given an unexpected assignment, to translate the proofs of what purported to be the memoirs of Pu Yi. The plan was that the English version was to be brought out as soon as possible after the Chinese original was published in the spring of 1964, before there was time for any rival translation to appear. China was then outside international copyright agreements, which meant that the original was unprotected abroad.

For the sake of speed the book, *From Emperor to Citizen*, was brought out in two volumes. The first was by far the more interesting, going from Qing court politics in the decades before Pu Yi's birth to the Japanese spiriting him out of Tianjin to the Northeast. It came out in 1964. This was the volume in which the Press's editors unfortunately made some cuts. (The editors who made the big editorial decisions dealt only with the Chinese text and were above the level of the English Section. You had the impression that they had not been contaminated by contact with the outside world.) They left almost untouched the second volume, with its goody-goody, and probably too-good-to-be-true, account of Pu Yi's "remolding" in prison. Here more blue pencil would have been welcome.

The FLP's English Section was a good place to work and observe the Chinese cultural bureaucracy in action. The care taken over every publication was extraordinary. Everything was checked over and over again. Proofreading was done to a standard of accuracy that no Western publisher could match today. Zhou Jiacan, an excellent colleague in my office, oversaw my version of the Pu Yi book. He referred some questions not to the supposed author but to his younger brother Pu Jie. It was surprising to hear him refer to Pu Yi in phone conversations with Pu Jie as *huangshang*, His Majesty.

Pu Jie, it was hinted, was one of the book's real authors. I was also told that historians had provided many of the stories and gossip about late Qing palace politics and the fate of the reduced court that lived on in the Forbidden City after the fall of the dynasty. Lao She, it was said, had given the whole manuscript a stylistic polish. It seemed plausible that as a Manchu himself Lao She would have wanted the story well told.

The whole Bureau was bound by one decision that had been made early in the history of the PRC: to use a degraded version of Wade-Giles romanization for proper names (except where Post Office spelling was followed for some place names) in all English-language publications. This continued even after Hanyu Pinyin had been introduced. This choice had apparently been made on the advice of Stalin-era Anglophone communists who thought that aspirations and umlauts would stand between the West's toiling masses and the red sun rising in the East. So Chu had to stand for what in Wade-Giles would be *Chu*, *Ch'u*, *Chü* or *Ch'ü*, or in Pinyin *Zhu*, *Chu*,

*Ju* and *Qu*. This sloppiness was followed by all foreign news media in their coverage of China until China switched to Hanyu Pinyin for international use.

I was of course excluded from meetings in the section's large office and in the Bureau's large hall, and my colleagues were careful not to pass things on. It would have been easy to trace the source of any hot news that got out through me. But sometimes I got a sense of what was happening. After the United States started bombing North Vietnam in the summer of 1964 there was no mistaking the tension. The canteen was plastered with posters of solidarity with Vietnam, and one colleague remarked, in a tone more of resignation than of enthusiasm, that it all reminded him of the atmosphere before China intervened in Korea. Later the sense of imminent war with America faded away. As we now know, Mao was not going to take on the USA when his main enemy was the USSR.

I nearly always avoided commenting on Chinese politics. One big exception was when there was delight in the office about China's first atom bomb in 1964. You could understand it after all the years of living under the American nuclear threat, especially since the end of the Soviet alliance had removed one factor that might have inhibited Washington. But as a supporter of the Campaign for Nuclear Disarmament I could not help asking, "Who are you going to drop it on?"

The Press was helpful about slightly loosening some of the usual restrictions for foreigners. I was issued some grain coupons so we could buy food from ordinary stalls and restaurants around town. I could also eat lunch in the big canteen with my colleagues instead of going back to the *Youyi* or using the Bureau's "small dining room" that prepared better meals for top management and for the long-term foreign staff who lived in the compound. (Its cooks were among the few fat people to be seen in the city.) When the English Section went to stay at a commune to help with the wheat harvest, Delia and I joined them for one day. The short-bladed sickles looked almost the same as Han dynasty ones, and as there were not enough of them we pulled the wheat out by hand.

The Press also let us travel unescorted to bring my parents by train from Hong Kong with a stopover at Changsha. A side trip to Shaoshan, where the Mao pilgrimage industry had hardly started, included a walk up the hill of that name. As we climbed the path our local guide pointed out the spot where a villager had killed a tigress and her cub the previous winter.

Up till then I had avoided trying to contact Pu Yi, who seemed from the book published under his name to be a pathetic creature. He had evidently been a puppet all his life—of his mother, of the eunuchs, of his tutors, including Sir Reginald Johnston, of the Qing loyalist elders, of the Japanese, of the Soviet Union, and finally of the Chinese Communists. My lack of admiration for him went with a wish to avoid a monarch, even a twice-deposed one. It all gave way when I was thinking of something special for my parents to be able to talk about when they got home. I asked if they could meet him, and the Press laid it on for me.

The meeting took place in a National People's Political Consultative

Conference establishment in the western part of the old city where veterans of fallen regimes were kept to be extensively debriefed and put their memories on paper. A tall, gangly figure in a black woolen standard Mao-era outfit ambled into the room. He seemed far from being the new man of his ghosted autobiography: he could not even smoke a cigarette without getting the ashes all over his clothes. It soon became obvious that he was not able to answer any questions about the book. All I learned from the conversation was that he spoke with the thickest of slurred Peking accents.

Once the Pu Yi book was finished I was granted a very big favor. I asked to be allowed to do a full translation of *Journey to the West* and they agreed. I was to continue with the translation after returning to England, but in 1966, with a first draft of thirty-three chapters done, I was told to stop and return my copy of the typescript. I did stop, but I kept the typescript, which was just as well as their copy was destroyed in the Cultural Revolution. I also polished translations of bad novels, sometimes having to unpick and redo the efforts of incompetent others. One very worthwhile translation I edited was to disappear in the Cultural Revolution: the Institute of Archaeology's *Xin Zhongguo de Kaogu Shouhuo*, an invaluable survey of ten years of Chinese archaeology that was to have been published by Penguin in England.

Where real human contact with China came was through Gladys Yang and Yang Xianyi, the Bureau's star translators, and their family. I had met Gladys when she gave a talk in Oxford in 1961 during her first visit to England in over twenty years. Right from our arrival she had opened their flat in the Bureau's compound to us. I used to take my siesta on their battered sofa during the long office lunch break every day. Gladys had chosen to make her life in China at the worst possible time when she made the difficult journey there in 1940 to marry Yang Xianyi despite her English missionary parents' heavy misgivings. She was admirably unlike those other permanent foreign residents who parroted official propaganda. Her commitment to China was to people, country and culture rather than to the twists and turns of the party line. She cheerfully spoke her mind, an immensely refreshing relief from the preaching of true believers.

While Xianyi formally observed the rules on contact with foreigners by not saying many things he might have wanted to, he could express a lot with a knowing smile and silence. When he had to produce some required formulation it would come with a warning such as "Of course, we say that…" Though he had to be discreet about the present he was a marvelous and quirky guide to enjoying the riches of China's past.

Of their three children the oldest, their son Yang Ye, was already away at university as a student. He came back occasionally at weekends, avoided contact with foreigners apart from his mother, and loaded his bag with books in Chinese and English before returning to university. You sensed a searching and independent mind, but not the terrible future that was to end with his suicide after the Cultural Revolution. His sisters Ying and Zhi were much better at coping with their Anglo-Chinese parentage. While being firmly Chinese they were more relaxed, friendly and comfortable with foreigners, but their main concerns seemed to be coping with the demands of the fiercely competitive school system. The Yangs' flat was a home away from home for us. When in 1964 more young graduates came from England to work in Peking they too made their way to the flat for an escape from official China.

## Retrospect

Looking back, those two years turned out to have taught me a little about daily life in the offices of one of the capital's work units and about the look of the few places I was allowed to see, but not much else. I allowed myself to remain in the dark about much of what had really happened in the rest of China. To be sure, I was told there had been three bad years with food shortages. Even in Peking the hepatitis rate was still high because of malnutrition, but there seemed to be pride that China had come through and that even government officials had shared the hardships. Hunger yes, but famine no—this was what people said and what, alas, I accepted. The only villages I saw were prosperous ones near big cities. What was visibly true from the availability of goods in shops was that in those two years the economy was recovering from the Great Leap.

As for the political picture, some changes were visible between 1963 and 1965, such as the growth of the Mao cult and the drafting of demobilized soldiers into the office to strengthen political control. The bitter struggles at the top that are now well known were then well concealed, making Mao's regime seem unlike Stalin's in that respect. Even the fallen Peng Dehuai was said to be living in dignified seclusion somewhere in the western suburbs. It seemed like a very stable dictatorship. By the time I left in August 1965 it was evident that Yang Xianyi and the friends who visited him could feel that an unpleasant political campaign was in the wind, and they were resigned to being targets. What they expected was something like the Anti-Rightist Campaign, a movement run from the top that might well hurt them but would be under some kind of control. Nothing pointed to the chaotic violence of the Cultural Revolution that was only a year away. It was inconceivable that my colleagues would soon be killing each other, Zhou Jiacan would be dead, and the Yangs would be in jail.

Two years of living alongside but not in China were enough. In August 1965 we took the long train ride back to England to start at the Department of Chinese Studies in the University of Leeds, Delia as a student and me as an assistant lecturer. It was to be over thirteen years before I saw China and the Foreign Languages Press again. When I went back in the spring of 1979 the place looked almost unchanged but belief in the system and its claimed values had gone.

**W.J.F. Jenner** *taught Chinese studies for many years at the University of Leeds and the Australian National University. His books include* Memories of Loyang: Yang Hsuan-chih and the Lost Capital *and* The Tyranny of History: The Roots of China's Crisis. *He has also translated the Chinese classic* Journey to the West *and the ghosted autobiography of China's last emperor Pu Yi,* From Emperor to Citizen.

# LOIS WHEELER SNOW
## *Let the Devil Take the Hindmost (1970)*

China became part of my life when I met and married Edgar Snow. I had read *Red Star Over China* long before I knew the author but the years that followed were largely devoted to my acting career in New York. China was rather remote from Broadway. Through Ed, I developed close relationships with his friends and colleagues. Agnes Smedley showed me how to cook "oriental pilaf" (something she didn't learn in Yanan); Ed and Jack Belden speculated about events in China, past and present, over frequent games of chess in our home. I became friends with Mariann and Edmund Clubb, and Caroline and John Stewart Service. Owen Lattimore fascinated me with his tales about Inner Mongolia. There were also letters from friends in China, but reception was complicated by the US postal service's requirement that mail from Communist China be acknowledged in writing before it was delivered (probably having been opened and recorded—no doubt the same occurred in China). At home in the 1950s we saw our American friends targeted by the McCarran Committee, Joseph McCarthy or more discreet members of the US leadership. There were supporters, but people were afraid of losing their careers, their livelihoods.

From years of reporting, the name Snow was closely associated with news about Communist China, those two words a "red flag" to editors and publishers in general. Gradually Ed found it harder to get published. Because of my marriage, but also because of my support for civil rights and other causes, I became blacklisted on television, a main source of an actor's income. With reduced savings, two children to raise, alimony to be paid, an offer to Ed for a position with a school traveling in Europe and Asia became a temporary lifesaver. We rented our house, and the children and I accepted the use of a friend's summer home close to Geneva, Switzerland. After months abroad with the school, Ed received word from China that he would be welcome to visit. The State Department, and Secretary of State John Foster Dulles, reacted negatively but a persistent Gardner Cowles of *Look* magazine overcame the "impediments." In 1960 Ed flew, legally, to Beijing—a lone American journalist and a single one as well, the State Department having refused my request to accompany him. In 1964, Ed went back. Again my request was denied. In 1970 I didn't ask; I went with my husband, carrying a contract to write a book on Chinese theater from Bennett Cerf at Random House. I also carried worry. Ed had not sufficiently recovered from a serious operation in the spring. He was weak and fatigued but he was adamant: we were going.

My first glimpse of the country, entering through Hong Kong, was from a modern, air-conditioned train operated entirely by women. Serving us mugs of hot tea, they were as eager to talk to us as we were to talk to them. From the train window I watched leathery buffalo, elongated heron and shimmering green rice fields dotted with farmers, birdlike in wide winged coats and peaked straw hats. Ed was impressed by evidence of farm mechanization, new since his last visit. When we arrived at Beijing's airport, I felt the awe of entering the Land of Oz. Having heard and read about people in China who had participated in events that shaped the country from the 1920s to the present, I knew they existed but like Ozma and the Tin Woodsman—could they be real?

They were. During our five months in China, I met them in Beijing, Shanghai, Canton and other cities and rural areas as we traveled to many different parts of the country: old friends, Chinese and foreign, Long March veterans, once-upon-a-time "Little Red Devils" in the Red Army, women whose crippled feet had been bound, peasants in remote communes, factory workers, doctors (barefoot and shod), actors, ballerinas, musicians, women engineers, women film directors, Red Guards, coal miners in universities, intellectuals and university students doing unaccustomed manual labor far from city comfort. Ed, knowing conversational Chinese, could talk with many of them directly. In an account of his 1960 visit he said that he was not given any "clairvoyant power to enter into their private thoughts" and that "at formal interviews, there was generally an official or an interpreter present, and nobody bares his soul to either one, especially with a foreigner around." Nevertheless, he noted: "I think I know more about all these people than I could possibly have understood had I never returned to China." For myself, I felt that I was learning something each day. It wasn't Oz. It was a huge country still trying to emerge from the effects of the Cultural Revolution.

Admittedly, my first visit to China was a special one. It began early on with an invitation from Premier Zhou Enlai for us to accompany him to a ping-pong match between North Korea and China at the enormous Beijing gymnasium where, some months later, the China-US ping-pong matches created international excitement. At a pre-dinner gathering in the Great Hall of the People, prominent members of the political hierarchy included some whom Ed remembered from the early days in Yanan. We dined with Song Qingling in her lakeside Beijing home, where she greeted us warmly, Ed being an old friend. I saw her often on later visits. Zhou Enlai's wife, Deng Yingchao, concerned about Ed's health, kept in close touch. One day I received a gift of sunflowers from her garden (I planted the seeds at home when I returned to Switzerland). An uncomfortable moment was my first meeting with Jiang Qing whom Ed hadn't seen since 1939 when she had become the young wife of Mao Zedong in Yanan, the Communists' headquarters for ten years before they entered Beijing in 1949. Introducing me, Ed remarked that she and I had much in common: "You are both actresses." Jiang Qing's face froze. She practically spat out, "I am not an actress!" (I retired behind Ed.) Nevertheless, she was indisputably head of the new "revolutionary model" theater, therefore of great importance for the book I was to write.

Five revolutionary "model" operas and two ballets comprised the whole of the Chinese theater at that time and she, Madame Mao, was in charge. The plots were pure political propaganda, simpler than fairytales; the actors trained in classic Beijing opera adapted to a modern, if stilted, stage technique replete with stunning acrobatics. Heroes were indefatigably heroic, villains were fabulously villainous—quite a different approach for me, a member of New York's Actors Studio. There was also quite a bit of music, all Chinese; foreign composers like Beethoven and Mozart were politically taboo. Children's dances and songs made up a different kind of entertainment, the little ones well trained and adorable.

On October 1, 1970, National Day, I found myself on a balcony overlooking Tiananmen Square, Ed and I on either side of Mao Zedong. Nearby were Zhou Enlai, Cambodian Prince Sihanouk and a host of notables including Jiang Qing, Lin Biao with his wife, to name a few of special interest considering what happened to them later. Turning to Sihanouk, I said that I wanted him to know that many Americans were against the war in Indochina. He replied, "When you go back, Madame, please tell the American people that every time a bomb is dropped, more Communists are created."

Standing there I became aware of two particularly striking things (besides the fact that I was so close to Mao Zedong I could have touched the mole on his face). A vivid impression was the sense of worship rising from the mass of people below on the square, people screaming—just like with the Beatles, Sinatra, Michael Jackson—so it was with Mao Zedong. My attention then focused on a huge sign bearing the words, "People of the world unite to defeat the US aggressors and all their running dogs." Why were we there, two Americans, side by side with the Chairman, before millions of Chinese citizens—and that sign? Afterwards Ed reminded me that the Chinese never do anything publicly without a reason. One December night we were awakened by Nancy Tang, Mao's chief interpreter who, seeing a sleepy Ed, said "Please get dressed. The Chairman wants to see you." It was during that midnight to near-dawn "conversation"—as Mao termed it—that the significance of our presence on the Tiananmen balcony became clear. We were the signal that Nixon could come to China. It took some time for that to sink in at the White House.

All along, Ed was unwell. Weakened by the operation in the spring, he had insisted on going to China, ignoring or putting up with pain and fatigue. Our Chinese companions urged us to take a week or two relaxing at the seaside resort of Beidaihe. Ed declined, saying that it would take too much time. Fixated on getting to basics, he wasn't always patient with excessively long discussions of different versions of the Cultural Revolution. Once he slipped me a note on which he had written "Mao said Keep Meetings Short!" We spent a week at two of Beijing's prestigious universities, Tsinghua and Beida, listening to students and professors recount tales of Red Guard fighting and upheaval on campus during the height of the Cultural Revolution. Ed was concerned when people he had known were not forthcoming, justifying or covering up an unclear situation. Friends were evasive: when asked the whereabouts of a particular couple we had expected to see, the answer was, "They're taking a trip; they'll be back soon." Another revealing reply was "Better not bring that up." An old Chinese acquaintance politely declined an invitation to come to our hotel for a visit, though others did come. But discretion, and caution, was obvious. Not until later was the hidden underside of the Cultural Revolution fully revealed, and the reticence—even among friends—becomes understandable.

Concerned as I was about Ed's health and his determined efforts to get to the bottom of past and present events, I was excited by the China I was seeing: the Forbidden City, the Summer Palace, the Ming Tombs, and the thrill of actually being on the Great Wall. I walked the wide, triple tree-lined streets of Beijing teaming with bicycles, watched the Little Red Soldiers—boys and girls too young to be Red Guards—standing at street corners and shouting through a microphone: "Don't cross on red lights!", "Use pedestrian crossings!" On a free hour it was fascinating to wander around narrow back lanes whose walls protected courtyards and low-roofed homes. A two-hour drive to Miyun dam north of Beijing on a tree-lined, paved road (trees were everywhere) took us past fertile countryside, orchards, tree nurseries and into villages with brick or mud houses, a primary school, fat pigs, and electricity supplied by the dam, which meant water and irrigation for the formerly arid area.

I was impressed, too, by working women "holding up half the sky" (or trying to); by small village hospitals, in need of paint, serviced by a dedicated barefoot doctor; by fruit-bearing orchards planted in earth-filled holes handmade out of solid rock. Ed described it as: "the physical transformation of the ancient Chinese earth by collective toil for the benefit of the group and not just for private gain—in a land which was second to none in the pursuit of personal aggrandizement and the devil take the hindmost."

After visits to communes in Xian and Yanan, and a May 7th School where a Beijing professor was tending a strikingly clean pigsty, we were driven to Baoan, the remote village in northern Shaanxi province where Ed had been in 1936 when it became the Red Army base after the Long March. It had been a desperately poor place, with a few ragged peasants scarcely able to feed themselves or their naked, unschooled children. The autumn we were there, Baoan, a commune brigade, held some three thousand citizens. A "model" opera was playing in the large theater; the main street was lined with houses, cave homes dug out of the loess hills, a well-stocked general store, a handicraft shop, a power plant and a dentist's office beside a small hospital. Goats and sheep grazed on the hills. We ate in the open with the people, who had produced a special feast: corn on the cob, sweet potatoes, spicy chicken, melon and fresh fruit. Children ran about. People, young and old, gathered and stared. We and the village were on display. Baoan's general population looked amply fed and healthy. Still far from the amenities of modern life (I knew that by going to the "toilet"), they had pulled themselves up to achieve a decent, if frugal, standard of living.

We were the first foreigners to visit Baoan in thirty-four years. It was I who had asked to go there, eager to see where Ed had first interviewed the outlawed Red "bandits." It was no Potemkin village made up for an expected arrival. If I was inexperienced, I had a companion who, having spent years in China before "liberation" and months more in 1960 and 1964-65, could see changes that had often made immense differences. We were driven along a motor road that led us to Baoan from Yanan. Ed described the roadless badlands he had walked over many years before as: "steep and interminable unkempt hills, divided by ravines, dry except in flood, with only here and there patches of grain and tumbledown caves." He also wrote: "The countryside always had a better potential... part of that potential has now been realized, and the regenerated green-clad hills and narrow valleys are often breathtakingly beautiful."

I had picked up a few Chinese sayings, among them *zi li geng sheng*, meaning "self-reliance." The emphasis on self-reliance was born out of the struggle of a poor but proud nation to overcome the isolation imposed by Japanese invasion, the support America gave Chiang Kai-shek during the Chinese civil war in the 1940s, and the US economic blockade of many years following the Communist victory. It was how China sought to recover from such deprivation.

I concur with what Mark Selden wrote in this series about "the imperative to understand other countries in light not only of their own history and culture, but also of the workings of global power, particularly American power." On that first visit (there were quite a few more), whatever displeased me or made me uncomfortable was mainly due, I felt, to my totally different life experience. I hadn't grown up hungry or illiterate, had never worked long hours in a factory, never labored in a rice paddy or gone without needed medical care. As an adult I had expressed opinions freely, voted for my choices, protested publicly, and chosen my preferred career. Escorted through a rug factory where scores of women bent silently over work as we smilingly passed by, I was surprised to see one young woman deliberately staring at us with obvious hostility. I sympathized with her (I can still see that look). I had to remember what or where she might have been before the revolution: a child working thirteen hours a day and sleeping under the workbench, a famished prostitute roaming city streets, an impoverished mother of undernourished children, a foot-bound slave to a domineering mother-in-law? China had overcome much, and there was much still to overcome. Baoan was a good example.

There were other examples of overcoming, especially in the countryside. Differences were plentiful: medical care with barefoot doctors in remote areas; schools in communes; free education; free means of birth control; physical transformation of the ancient soil—and, as Ed pointed out, for the communal group, not for private gain. That was 1970. Yes, there had been the Great Leap Forward with its tragic aftermath, when hunger had once again been a scourge, but since then almost-forgotten places like Baoan and Shashihyu and others we saw had made noticeable progress.

If crop yields were sometimes exaggerated, women's roles somewhat overstated or statistics unproven, sturdy stone and brick houses, reclaimed green fields and orchards gave evidence that hard work had made life better than ever before. When we were shown the best homes, those of families with a bicycle, perhaps a radio or a sewing machine, they pointed to what could be a similar future for others less advantaged. It was apparent that some units and some people could move ahead faster because of their own skills or possibly simply by hook or by crook. Communism didn't guarantee equality or honesty any more than democracy does.

Early in the following year we were back together in Switzerland typing up months of notes, working on our books. Ed's health slowly deteriorated. He died on February 14, 1972, two months after major surgery and just before Richard Nixon became the first US president to visit Communist China. No one could have saved Ed's life. Desperate, I had sought help. Friends responded generously with messages of love, hope and offers of money if needed. Nixon, who for years had loudly proclaimed his hatred of China and who had played a prominent role in the McCarthy witch hunt, had his bags packed for the trip to Beijing. He sent a message referring to Ed's "distinguished career" and expressing hope for his return to health. (We didn't answer.)

Help came with a medical team—three doctors, four nurses, an interpreter—sent to our Swiss home by Mao Zedong, Zhou Enlai and their wives. They undertook the needed care, eased the pain, softened fear in the face of death. The difference was not better Chinese knowledge in treating cancer; it was in an attitude unlikely to be found in a busy hospital most anywhere. In our home, they had time and the ability to comfort, to care. Everyone in touch, friends nearby and abroad, our village neighbors, were affected by these men and women who had come to help. Our thanks poured out to them and to those who had made this gift possible, one I shall never forget.

Thus ended my first trip to China. Years have passed, people have died. In 1989 the Tiananmen massacre shocked the world. I broke with the Chinese leadership. I no longer visit, though my son and I made a special, and short, trip in 2000 to express sympathy and support for Ding Zilin and the families of all those who, while participating in a peaceful demonstration, were murdered or severely injured by soldiers of the People's Liberation Army following orders from the country's leaders. In 1949 Mao had said: "China has stood up." In 1989 Chinese citizens were shot down while trying once again to stand up.

Ding Zilin's teenage son was killed the night of June 4th near Tiananmen while he was searching for a schoolmate; his mother has courageously and persistently called for an investigation of the massacre—so far to no avail. We were prevented from seeing her and the treatment my son and I received was, to put it mildly, far from cordial. Tiananmen was an outrage. Since then, learning nothing from that horrendous crime, the Chinese leaders have stepped up their persecution of peaceful dissidents and outspoken activists, intensified human rights abuses and multiplied unlawful arrests, imprisonments and forced disappearances. There is an increasing gap between the newly privileged, mostly urban rich and the still needy poor, a flagrant misuse of the judicial system and an absence of previous guarantees of livelihood.

I strongly feel the Chinese leaders misuse Edgar Snow when they praise the man who, at personal risk, broke through Chiang Kai-shek's blockade and brought word of the outlawed revolutionaries to the Chinese people and the world. The government promotes Edgar Snow as a model. Any Chinese journalist knows full well not to write about whatever the government does not want investigated or revealed. In 1936 Ed made a trip to an area forbidden of access by the regime in power, that of Chiang Kai-shek. Doing the equivalent with the present government would mean years in prison. To protest peacefully is dangerous, as Nobel peace laureate Liu Xiaobo found out—eleven years in prison. Wei Jingsheng spent fifteen years behind bars and is now in exile. Wang Dan and other student demonstrators at Tiananmen were jailed and exiled. The Tiananmen Mothers, headed by Ding Zilin, are under direct surveillance and are not allowed to publicly mourn their dead. At this writing, the noted Chinese artist, Ai Weiwei, has disappeared. At present, if you were truly to emulate Edgar Snow in China you would be in deep trouble.

When giving consent for publication of *The Long Revolution*, which Ed had undertaken to write before he died, I wrote, "This is an unfinished work—a beginning punctuated by the abrupt ending that death decreed for my husband. In it are the seeds of a new relationship between the people of China and America. If we nourish them they will grow." That was written forty years ago. Today both countries are engaged in capitalist competition. "Let the devil take the hindmost."

*Lois Wheeler Snow has been an actress on Broadway and is a member of New York City's Actors Studio. She has worked with Martha Graham, Harold Clurman, Elia Kazan, Herbert Bergdorf, Arthur Miller, and Norman Rose. Her books include China on Stage, A Death with Dignity: When the Chinese Came, and Edgar Snow's China: An Account of the Chinese Revolution Compiled from the Writings of Edgar Snow. She is the widow of Edgar Snow, the author of Red Star Over China.*

# Motherland

## Motherland

# C.P. Ho
*China Through the Eyes and Ears of a Little Boy (1942)*

China came alive for me when I was a little over five years old. Before then, I had been told stories by both my father and mother of a faraway land peopled by the heroes and villains of *The Water Margin*, of acts of heroism and intrigue by lords and generals in *The Romance of the Three Kingdoms*, and of flights of fancy into India and back by a Buddhist priest accompanied by a pig imbued with just too many human frailties and a mischievous monkey bent on challenging authority and the order of things.

They formed the staple of my bedtime stories, told to me underneath a white mosquito net yellowed and blackened by kerosene smoke from an oil-lit lamp. Home was in Ipoh, capital of Perak state in tropical Malaya where the family engaged in tin mining. The business, begun by my grandfather, had prospered during the First World War when tin was an essential commodity. But with the Second World War looming in the distance, my father, a first generation overseas Chinese brought up and schooled in British colonial Malaya, firmly believed his place this time around was with compatriots on the mainland to fight Japanese aggression.

Thus it was that the family found itself in Hong Kong shortly before it fell to the Japanese on Christmas Day in 1941. Suddenly, after the din of machine-gun chatter, the screech of falling bombs and the screams of people running in the streets, China as my country became very real to me. The sense of belonging enveloped me and a sudden feeling of patriotism came over me. I felt Chinese, special and proud of it despite, or because of, all the stories I heard about how badly we were treated by the Japanese and even by the *hung mao kwai* (red hairy devils), colonial powers. It made my young blood boil to hear how "my people" suffered defeat and humiliation at the hands of the Japanese as I hid with my parents behind three thick mattresses thrown up against the windows of my uncle's second floor flat in Happy Valley in Hong Kong. He was a medical doctor and it was through his influence that my mother became a registered nurse and mid-wife.

In those days, my mother was a *tai tai* (a lady of means—she was, in fact, among the first batch to pass the driving test for a license in Hong Kong) with *amahs* (servants). She knew how to dance and play the guitar, but not to cook and it was therefore doubly heart-breaking to see her preparing for the journey into mainland China. But my father was adamant, so she hard-boiled eggs, made rice balls filled with meat and put strong milk tea into flasks. Then she spent long nights sewing gold bars into the seams of her cheongsams and blouses. Her needlework must have been excellent for her treasures proved to be our lifeline in the months ahead.

My anticipation of "Free China"—as any territory on the mainland not under Japanese occupation was called—mounted and my interest in the motherland increased. Ipoh in the Kinta valley where I was pre-schooled was populated mostly by emigrants from Guangdong province in south China and Cantonese was not a problem for me. Still, I was told to improve my vocabulary and intonation because I sounded too much like somebody from Nanyang (Singapore and Malaya).

Food became scarce in Hong Kong by January 1942, and the Japanese military wanted to get the population down to a manageable size. So they issued "repatriation papers." Armed with these, my father moved his family on foot and by sampan, from Happy Valley on Hong Kong Island to a small cluster of mud and straw huts in the midst of what might have been rice paddy fields near present-day Shenzhen. There was nothing there but a piece of neglected rural farmland. I saw no chickens or ducks, nor animals except for seven or eight men holding wooden sticks for weapons. They were more threatening than welcoming.

The journey had taken three nights and the best of four days but was rather uneventful except for my first two slaps by a Japanese sentry for not bowing, a circumstance quickly rectified by my mother who nearly tore off my hair by pulling it—happily, along with my head—down to knee level. I felt deeply hurt and silently vowed vengeance for such a national dishonor as having to bow to a person of another race, not out of love or respect but because of fear and force. Thus it was with swollen red cheeks and tears in my eyes that I set foot on really Chinese sovereign soil for the first time (Hong Kong was a British colony and under Japanese occupation at that time).

But the very next moment, young as I was, I felt the desolation and fear, interspersed with greed and envy, that greeted my small group. The men looked Chinese but there was nothing friendly about them. A child's feelings about such matters are instinctively right at most times. Innocently, I had thought all Chinese were in this together to fight the Japanese and were good and kind to one another.

Dusk turned to night before negotiations were completed and money changed hands to allow us to stay until the morning. My father did not rejoin us until after midnight. It turned out that he was talking to the bandit chief and explaining how, as an overseas Chinese, he had been encouraged by Singapore millionaire Tan Kah Kee, a friend to both Kuomintang leader Chiang Kai-shek and Zhou Enlai (later to become premier of the People's Republic), to return to help in national salvation.

For yet some more money, the bandit chief agreed to have us taken further north to Ping Shek (where we had relatives) and even provided a three-man escort and a sedan chair for my mother, who carried me in her arms. It was hot and humid though it was May, but I was beginning to enjoy the rural scenery when the trio stopped walking and, in effect, told my father: You are within sight of Ping Shek. We have done what Big Brother told us to do. Now hand over everything and we won't hurt you.

We were relieved of everything and my father even had his shirt and trousers taken away. It was luck—or as mother said, the gods protecting us—that she and I were not touched at all and none of the valuables carried by us was stolen. Even so, I posed the question: Why do Chinese rob Chinese? The answer from my father was: Not only do they rob but they also kill. There are good Chinese and there are bad Chinese. When you are older, you must differentiate between the two.

And to this day, I have been trying to do just that. It has been difficult. In those few years in the wartime China controlled by the Kuomintang, father had people come to our place. Conversations were normal when the subject matter was about the Kuomintang and Generalissimo Chiang Kai-shek. But the tone turned low and conspiratorial when the Communist Party or Mao Zedong was mentioned. Father had opened an eating place of sorts and most of his clients were students from Lingnan College which had moved inland from Guangzhou to escape Japanese occupation and interference.

I knew nothing about politics and cared less as I sat at the till. But I was fascinated by the cheongsams worn by some of the girls and my fascination with the form-fitting gown has remained with me to this day—a pleasant wartime memory, as opposed to hiding against a tombstone in an open grave as low-flying Japanese pilots grinned down at us, firing their guns and releasing their bombs.

Somehow, father and mother made ends meet until V-J Day (Victory over Japan on August 15, 1945). We found our way to Portuguese Macau and boarded a motorized junk for a 22-hour voyage back to Hong Kong (during which time I became so seasick I never was seasick again).

A little anecdote remains to be told. I attended my first primary school in "Free China." Classes began with morning assembly—hoisting of the Kuomintang flag, singing of the national anthem, the San Min Chu-i (Dr. Sun Yat-sen's Three Principles of the People) and bowing three times before a statue of Dr. Sun, founder of the first republic. The establishment of the second republic in 1949 by Mao Zedong put forward "The March of the Volunteers" as the national anthem.

Like me, David Chen, the long-time, well-known China editor of the *South China Morning Post*, also went to school in China. Before his death in 2010, he and I were firm friends in Hong Kong and we used to reminisce about those morning assemblies by belting out, in the closed confines of our rooms, both anthems. Somehow, we felt good singing them both. They were not anthems to us as such but songs of national salvation which helped the Chinese people pull through some of their most difficult times and take their rightful places in the community of nations, with dignity and honor.

*C.P. Ho was AAP-Reuters correspondent for ten years before his secondment to Hong Kong Television Broadcast (TVB) to set up its news and public affairs department and become the company's first assistant general manager. He currently sits on the five-member world board of governors of the International Social Service in Geneva and acts as chairman of its Hong Kong branch.*

## Liu Heung Shing
*From Anti-Four Pests Campaign to Democracy Wall (1953)*

As a Hong Kong-born Chinese who is a naturalized US citizen, it's hard to pinpoint my first trip to China; at least, one that I remember clearly, for my real first trip was as a toddler, in 1953 in the arms of my mother who carried me to her hometown of Fuzhou. Most likely I slept through most of that trip, or was just too young to take it all in. So I guess, the real instance of a "first trip" in the sense of this series, would be my first trip to China as a professional photojournalist in 1976.

Yet, I would like to think that the first few years of childhood left their mark on me for the good. That experience, however fragmented or vague in my memory, definitely prepared me for my eventual first trip back to the mainland as a photojournalist in a way that was more profound than I first realized. It allowed the perspective of an outsider looking in, while still being privy to the many experiences of an insider in those trying years.

As a child in Fuzhou, I was enrolled in the Guyizhong Primary School (near Fuzhou PLA Garrison Command). My years there—six in total—helped define the way I came to portray China later in my professional life. I recall going to the school every day by walking out of the courtyard house, which my grandmother had gifted to my mother as part of her wedding dowry. By early 1955, it had already been appropriated by the State as part of the landmark land reform policy. The head of the neighborhood committee, a Madame Zhou, moved into the house, where she occupied two rooms; the others were taken by local families. Our family was left with the main house and a courtyard garden in the back, which featured a beautiful Dragon Eye (Longyan) fruit tree. I learned later that we were fortunate to have escaped the fate of many landlords who had simply been shot or disappeared. We were spared because the State classified my family as a "peaceful landlord." My mother's uncle, Chen Bi, was a Minister of Communication under Emperor Guangxu (in 1894). The Chen family's land had been granted by the emperor, not gained through business dealing or renting to the peasants, hence the title "peaceful landlord."

This family background may explain why the PLA children in my class treated me with condescension. According to the prevalent political jargon, they were "red" and I was "black." I remember the red slogans on the schoolyard: "We must catch up with Britain and surpass America." Under the highly charged political atmosphere following China's incursion in Korea, where troops fought the US military to a temporary truce, students were required to perform manual labor every Wednesday to help build a stronger socialist state. Every week I collected stones for building the railroad. Under the spell of the Anti-Four Pests Campaign, I was energetically motivated to catch flies at home, which I collected in a matchbox for my teacher. But no matter how many flies filled my matchboxes, semester after semester under the column labeled "Political Behavior," she would only grant me a "C" on my report card. I felt the effect of apartheid in a classroom full of kids from the families of the nearby army officers. Those kids instinctually felt superior to the sons and daughters of any other social class. I didn't officially "fit" into any of the social classes.

Many years later, in Beijing, I met the famed PLA writer Bai Hua, who in early 1980 wrote the film script originally named *Ku lian*, which later became the film *Sun and the Man*. Through the film's main character, he expressed the common feeling of many mainland Chinese and those who were expatriated: "I love my country, but does my country love me?" This open question of unrequited love was severely criticized by Deng Xiaoping and the film was banned. In 1980, Deng launched the Anti-Bourgeois Liberalization Campaign. Deng had then recently shut down the Democracy Wall in Xidan bus depot, where petitioners from all over the country put up big character posters to protest the injustices of the Cultural Revolution.

Come 1960, my neighbors who "shared" our house in Fuzhou were all stricken by malnutrition, their arms and legs swollen—The Great Famine, which was the harsh result of the disastrous Great Leap Forward. One day in 1959 a pig was killed in our neighborhood, leading hundreds of people to queue to buy a portion. I waited half a day to buy two ounces of pork fat. I was told I was lucky that the butcher gave me the fat as it was deemed more valuable than the meat. One day after school, I saw a man on the street selling tiger meat, a striped tiger pelt dangling from a tree above the vendor. My father, who was the editor of the international news page for *Zheng Wu Bao* in Hong Kong, knew it was time for me to depart Fuzhou. Much later, my father one day came home looking very upset, saying his pro-Beijing newspaper editor had refused to print the news that the Americans had landed on the moon.

On one trip back, in the summer of 1968, my mother took me to Guangzhou to visit relatives. I vividly remember being yelled at by a barber in the Overseas Chinese Hotel who forced me to stand and recite one of Mao's quotations on the wall before he would give me a haircut. At 6 p.m. Guangzhou was already dark. We queued for almost an hour to get a table in a restaurant, of which the city had but a few. The waitress threw the chopsticks on the table and walked away. Everybody behaved in a manner that officials liked to call "vigilant." Why vigilant? The Chinese in that era literally seemed to see enemies everywhere. I was glad to return to Hong Kong, feeling utterly exhausted by the hysteria which I absorbed from people's body language and facial expressions.

Perhaps it was these bitter, sour memories of childhood that led me to develop an avid interest in newspaper reports about China during my studies in New York. I followed the Toronto *Globe and Mail*'s dispatches in *The New York Times*—the Canadian newspaper was the only North American newspaper to have an accredited journalist in Beijing at that time. At the university library, I read the little weekly pamphlet *China News Analysis* published by Jesuits who monitored radio broadcasts from the mainland. Among the Jesuits were the few westerners who specialized in Chinese dialects, including those who could understand Mao's strong Hunan accent.

As I later discovered on my travels through China, Hunan, the birthplace of my father, was the only place I required the services of an interpreter.

In 1976, after nine months of apprenticeship at *Life* magazine with Gjon Mili, who had earlier taught me at Hunter College (part of the City University of New York), I went to Europe and photographed post-Franco Spain, and to Portugal where Communist presidential candidates were campaigning in the countryside with peasants driving tractors but who stopped to listen and enjoy a picnic as they did so. In Paris, I went to Hotel Matignon to photograph newly appointed French Prime Minister Raymond Barre. As I came out of the metro near Saint-Germaine-des-Pres, I saw Mao's photograph on the front page of every Parisian newspaper on the newsstand. It was September 1976: Mao had died. I was on the first plane to Hong Kong, then to the mainland on assignment for *Time* magazine. Before I left for the border at Lo Wu, my uncle introduced me to Lo Fu, editor-in-chief of Hong Kong's *New Evening Post*. Lo, a respected Communist newspaper editor, well liked by senior Chinese leader Liao Chenzhi, provided me with a letter of introduction to the border authorities. In those days, one needed an introduction letter from an organization just to check into a hotel.

I walked across Lo Wu bridge past the PLA guards. Before boarding the train bound for Guangzhou, I was stopped at customs. The guard inspected my camera bag; three cameras and assorted lenses, forty rolls of Kodachrome film. I didn't have a journalist visa; he asked me what I planned to do. I said I was a traveler and presented him with the letter of introduction from Lo

Fu. He disappeared for a while and came back with another more senior customs official. I gave him the same answer. They asked me to sit and wait. Just minutes before the train departed, the junior man returned and told me to hurry up if I didn't want to miss the train.

The army-green train was staffed by young attendants who were friendly by the standards of the Cultural Revolution: at least they smiled at me as they poured hot water over a bag of green tea that cost five *fen* (cents). The seats were covered with white cotton covers. The train roared through the rural areas towards Guangzhou. The scenes outside the window were familiar, but what was missing were the announcements from the omnipresent loudspeakers mounted on every telegraph pole. I was not sure if this was in order to mourn the death of Mao, or for other reasons. Few missed the streaming exhortations to keep up the revolutionary vanguard or the recital of the day's editorial from the *People's Daily*.

In Guangzhou I checked into the Overseas Chinese Hotel, where the portrait of Mao in the lobby was now adorned with the appropriate black trimmings. It was still warm in September, but outside I was struck by how quiet it was on the streets as I rushed from the hotel to stroll the embankment of the Pearl River. People wore black armbands of mourning. Some silently read the newspapers posted on the roadside propaganda boards. Elderly people were doing *tai qi*. It dawned on me; something had changed in the people's body language. They had lost that "vigilant look." Even though overseas Chinese and foreigners usually attracted inquisitive stares they seemed to have no interest in me. I sensed China was going through a profound but as yet undefined transition. The death of Mao did not seem to sadden the residents in the streets of Guangzhou, unlike those seen in the official propaganda photographs which showed youths crying crocodile tears while holding small printed portraits of Mao. On the contrary, I felt people, clearly more relaxed now, were behaving as if they had been relieved of a huge mental burden that had been hanging over them. Perhaps it was my childhood experience that prepped me to observe these unusually calm faces. As I continued to photograph daily life on the streets, I decided that if given an opportunity, I would photograph China after Mao.

But immediately I became caught up with my attempts to get a flight to Beijing to photograph Mao's funeral. My repeated requests to the China Travel Service were denied. I learned later that few people were allowed to travel to Beijing as the authorities were poised to arrest the "Gang of Four" (Jiang Qing, Zhang Chunqiao, Wang Hongwen and Yao Wenyuan). The death of Mao was world news and I missed it: I would not let that happen again.

The opportunity would eventually come again two years later, in 1978, when *Time* magazine decided to send Richard Bernstein to open the Time-Life News Service bureau in Beijing, ahead of the Sino-US Diplomatic Normalization in 1979. I would be *Time*'s first contract photographer in China since 1949, fulfilling my wish to document China After Mao.

In Beijing I joined Richard Bernstein, Fox Butterfield, Melinda Liu,

John Roderick, Victoria Graham, Irene Mosby, Jay and Linda Mathews, Michael Parks and Frank Ching—the first wave of American foreign correspondents to be stationed in new China, six years after President Richard Nixon opened the door. The rest, as they say, is history.

*Liu Heung Shing shared a 1992 Pulitzer Prize for Spot News and an Overseas Press Club Award for his coverage of the Soviet Union's collapse. In 1989, his image of Tiananmen was awarded Picture of the Year by the School of Journalism at the University of Missouri and he was named Best Photographer by the Associated Press Managing Editors. His books include China After Mao, China: Portrait of a Country, Shanghai: A History in Photographs 1842 to Today, and China in Revolution: Nineteen-Eleven and Beyond.*

# Frank Ching
## *When the East Was Red (1973)*

Unlike many others, my first visit to the People's Republic of China was not as a member of a delegation of academics or students invited by Beijing. Nor was I among the tiny handful of journalists fortunate enough to have been allowed individual visits.

Indeed, the Chinese government was unwilling to give me a visa because I was a journalist with *The New York Times*. After China and Canada established diplomatic missions in each other's capital in 1971, I flew to Ottawa from New York to explain that all I wanted was a private visit but I was told that the Chinese embassy could not issue me a visa. The decision had to be made by the Foreign Ministry in Beijing.

Eventually, I entered China as a "Hong Kong compatriot" since I was born in the British colony and, while I had become a permanent resident in the United States, was not yet an American citizen.

I flew to Hong Kong from New York in 1973 and, as a first step, obtained from the British colonial government confirmation of my status as a "Hong Kong belonger," or a British subject who was born in Hong Kong. Then I approached the China Travel Service, a mainland governmental agency, and argued for my right to visit as a Hong Kong "compatriot." After repeated visits, my request was granted. I was issued an "Introduction for Return to Native Village," which enabled me to visit the mainland.

This was a time, in the wake of the Kissinger and Nixon visits, that Chinese-Americans and overseas Chinese were resuming contacts with their relatives in China. And, fortunately for me, a good friend of mine from New York, Danny Yung, was also traveling to China with his parents to visit their relatives in Shanghai. We traveled together to Canton (now Guangzhou), Shanghai and Beijing.

On August 1, 1973, I boarded an old diesel train that took China-bound passengers to Lo Wu, a town on the Hong Kong side of the border. For some reason, China Travel Service had arranged for me to travel third class. There, men and women clawed their way onto the train, passing goods and children through windows and often climbing in after them because the narrow entranceways were jammed. Many people carried shoulder poles from which dangled live chickens, baskets of food and other gifts for relatives in China. Even standing room was scarce. I gained a foothold on the bottom rung of a carriage and hung onto the handrail to prevent myself from falling off onto the tracks. In this fashion, I was slowly borne by the chugging train toward China.

At the border, we walked across a rickety wooden bridge that separated British-ruled Hong Kong from the Communist mainland. Once across the bridge, we were in Shenzhen, now a major city but at that time only a small village. All the passengers were led into a vast shed to be interviewed by immigration and customs officials.

I was interrogated by a man who questioned me at length on my background, my job, my relatives and my friends. He made me empty all my pockets. In one pocket, I was carrying the business cards of several people I had met in Hong Kong. My interrogator was extremely interested in all of them. He asked me about each of them and what relationship, if any, that person had with any of the others. He asked me about my parents and my brothers and sisters. He wrote down all the answers. Then he asked me the same questions all over again, in different ways. The interrogation lasted for over an hour.

Finally, he allowed me to go through to customs. There, Hong Kong newspapers I had with me were confiscated.

The train ride from Shenzhen to Canton was a distinct improvement over the ride to the China border. The train was the only air-conditioned one in China, and it traveled back and forth between Shenzhen and Canton, I suppose to give foreigners a good initial impression of China. I sat back in my soft seat and watched the green fields of Guangdong province roll by. The loudspeaker played "The East Is Red," a paean in praise of Chairman Mao Zedong that had virtually become China's national anthem during the Cultural Revolution.

When we finally pulled into the Canton station, loudspeakers thanked the passengers for helping the crew to complete their mission successfully.

The China Travel Service in Hong Kong had advised me to stay at the Overseas Chinese Hotel in Canton, but the young woman behind the counter there told me the hotel was full and refused to refer me to another hotel.

"Hong Kong compatriots usually stay with relatives," she said. "We only serve guests from overseas."

I then was forced to produce American identification and explained that, though a Hong Kong compatriot, I lived in New York. The change in the clerk's attitude was remarkable. A selection of rooms was available, she said. The best room, for ten dollars a night, had a bathroom, a telephone and an electric fan. I took it.

The next day, together with Danny and his parents, I boarded a plane for Shanghai.

The atmosphere in Shanghai was noticeably different from that in Canton, where service bordered on being surly. In Shanghai, as soon as we checked into the Park Hotel across from the People's Park, or what used to be the Shanghai Race Course, a waiter arrived with glasses of ice water to provide relief from the stifling heat.

I had the address of my uncle Qin Kaihua, my mother's brother, whom I had never met. He and my mother were never close. But this uncle was my only point of contact with my entire family in China.

When I arrived at his home, I tapped gently on the door, trying not to arouse the suspicions of the neighbors since having "overseas connections" was often a crime in China. A skinny, elderly man dressed only in shorts and an undershirt appeared. He turned out to be my uncle. I introduced myself as Qin Jiacong, the son of Zhaohua, and he waved me in.

I walked into a dingy room with a wooden bed, then through a doorway into a small sitting room. Shanghai summers can be very hot and my uncle switched on the electric fan and directed it at me full blast while cooling himself with an old-fashioned straw fan. He introduced me to his wife, Lin Yanzhu, and their 16-year-old daughter, Zhifen.

In the presence of these strangers I felt curiously at home. I told them about the various members of the family outside China and what they were doing. And before leaving, I invited them to my hotel for dinner the following evening.

The next day, the hotel's reception desk called to tell me I had visitors. I went down to the lobby and found an argument going on between my relatives and the hotel personnel, who insisted that each of them produce identification. They were told to fill in forms in triplicate, giving their name, address and place of employment, plus their relationship to the person they were visiting. Only after that were they allowed to enter the elevator and go to the dining room. After dinner, when I invited them to my room, the elevator operator refused to take them. In the lobby, we were informed that only parents or children of hotel guests were allowed in rooms; other visitors had to be entertained in the lobby. Eventually, after filling in another set of forms, my relatives were allowed up as a special dispensation. Not surprisingly, they never visited me again.

I also spent time with Danny's relatives, which included not only his grandfather but numerous uncles and aunts. Among the presents Danny's parents had brought with them was a bicycle, but there was a problem: how could the bicycle be transported from the train station to their home? I volunteered my services and rode the bicycle through Shanghai's streets to the grandfather's home. It was an exciting experience and made me feel like a local, especially when someone stopped me and asked for directions.

As for my own relatives, they made me welcome in their home and I learned things about China and my family that I had never dreamed of.

Before leaving Shanghai, I bought a birthday present for my aunt. I went to the Friendship Store and purchased a Chinese-made watch, one of the more expensive brands. I also gave my uncle some knickknacks that I had with me. In return, he gave me a small jade rabbit that had belonged to his grandfather, one of the few things of value that he possessed.

From Shanghai, we went north to Beijing, which was still called Peking at the time. The city was awe-inspiring, with the Great Wall winding north of the city and the vast Tiananmen Square in the city center, where Chairman Mao had reviewed millions of Red Guards at the start of the Cultural Revolution. Changan Avenue, or the Boulevard of Eternal Peace, was the city's main street, built in the 15th century and wide enough for more than ten lanes of traffic. The whole city conveyed a sense of history, of being the center of an ancient and still vibrant civilization.

I visited Tiananmen Square and marveled at its vast emptiness aside from the Monument to the People's Heroes, as well as the Great Hall of the People next to it, where all major meetings were held.

Danny and I also ate in a duck restaurant, where we enjoyed our first meal of Peking Duck in Peking.

I had relatives in Beijing too, but did not know how to get in touch with them. During subsequent visits to China, I discovered relatives in Shanghai and Beijing on both my mother's and my father's sides of the family, gradually building up a mental picture of the family I never knew in China.

Despite its brevity, the trip to China was exhilarating. After my return to New York, I wrote several articles about my trip for *The New York Times*, not about politics but about such things as how Chinese families cope with shortages and how increasing numbers of Chinese-Americans were returning to their ancestral homeland. After my articles appeared, I was contacted by the Nobel Prize-winning physicist Yang Chenning, who taught at the State University of New York at Stony Brook and who had himself been to China, and I paid him a visit.

The trip to China confirmed me in my journalistic career of China-watching. The following year, I moved to Hong Kong and, after China and the United States established diplomatic relations in 1979, I became the first correspondent in China of *The Wall Street Journal*.

That first trip in 1973 launched me on a quest for my roots. It culminated years later with my writing a book on my family history: *Ancestors: 900 Years in the Life of a Chinese Family*.

*Frank Ching* is the author of Ancestors: 900 Years in the Life of a Chinese Family, Hong Kong and China: For Better or For Worse, The Li Dynasty: Hong Kong Aristocrats, and China: The Truth About its Human Rights Record. He worked for The New York Times, opened The Wall Street Journal's Bureau in Beijing in 1979 and later joined the Far Eastern Economic Review.

## STEVE TSANG
*Awakening From a China Dream (1978)*

It was a beautiful hot August day in 1978 when I walked across the old
Lo Wu Bridge from colonial Hong Kong to "mother China." I was full of
excitement and wanted to run across the bridge. I could not wait to set foot
on the motherland, breathe its air, take in the scenery and get to know the
heroic people who "ended a century of humiliation."

When the slow train from Shenzhen to Guangzhou finally started to roll,
I stopped talking to my travel companion. I could not take my eyes off the
big window. I wanted to see everything that came my way—every dwelling
and every stranger working in the fields. Yes, I wanted to look at every blade
of grass that the train passed. I was ecstatic just to be in "mother China,"
something I had wanted to do for years.

Born to a refugee family in Hong Kong and having just got a place
to read politics, history and philosophy at the University of Hong Kong,
I was searching for my own identity and reacted negatively to the colonial
nature of Hong Kong. It was not because I or my family ever suffered from
British colonial rule. Indeed, freshly graduated from King's College, I was
a beneficiary of British colonialism. But, a late-teenager, I simply rebelled
against the very "colonial education" that made me a Chinese patriot. I was
also mesmerized by what I read of "new China" under Chairman Mao, who
had died only two years earlier. In those days Mao was a hero figure to me.

The intense excitement I felt for "new China" could be traced to the first visit I made to exhibitions in the "China week" events organized by university undergraduates earlier in the decade. Now I know how many of these young people were themselves infatuated with the distorted pictures that came out of the Maoist propaganda machine. But they excited me as a teenager. A colonial subject, I felt an underdog and identified with the Communists who, as underdogs, staged "the revolution that got the Chinese people to stand up." They inspired me to read as many books as I could find—in English as well as in Chinese—on "the Chinese Revolution" and the construction of "new China." Almost all the Chinese books, I found in the Chinese state-owned book stores in Hong Kong. I often skipped lunch and saved the money to buy such books, including *The Quotations of Chairman Mao*. My head was full of Maoist ideas of how the people of China who suffered from Western imperial exploitation responded to the selfless leadership of the Communist Party to wipe away a century of humiliation.

This trip to the mainland was the opportunity for me to get to know "mother China" and find myself in the process.

The travel arrangements for me and my friend were made by China Travel Service (CTS) in Hong Kong. I knew of no alternative as we were not visiting relatives and could not book hotels or flights directly from Hong Kong. We had wanted to fly to Guilin the same afternoon we arrived in Guangzhou but were told in Hong Kong that the earliest available flight would be on the following day. We checked in at the Overseas Chinese Hotel.

I could not stay and rest and insisted on getting to know Guangzhou as soon as we put our luggage down. So we did.

A block away we walked past a CAAC (Civil Aviation Administration of China) office and went in to see if there were any earlier flights to Guilin. We had no expectations—it just seemed silly not to check. We were in luck. The man at the counter said there was a flight leaving in just over an hour and if we could return to the office in ten minutes we could be on it. Jubilant, we paid for the new tickets immediately, ran back to the hotel, checked out and dashed back with our luggage to the CAAC office, where a mini-bus took us to the Baiyun Airport.

In the old Russian turboprop aircraft I noticed something unusual. What appeared to be white smoke came out from the luggage compartment overhead. It did not take long for us to work out that this was not smoke but cold air from the air conditioner. Strange as it was to us used to modern Boeing jets, we got over it quickly.

A more enduring source of concern was the presence of two young men sitting on two small wooden stools in the aisle—no seatbelts, of course. I recognized them from the check-in counter. They were denied their seats and told to return the following day but they pleaded for their seats. We checked in our bags, moved on and paid no more attention to them. Here they were on the flight, placed in the middle of a small aircraft as human missiles. One of them sat so close to me that we could talk. When asked, he said they had to get to Guilin that evening for some family emergency and had their seats confirmed earlier in the day. But they were bumped off the flight at the check-in counter as their seats had been reallocated. They thought some officials got their seats and were simply grateful that they were allowed on board after all. I thought there might be a different reason. Since we were told in Hong Kong that all flights were full that day and we were offered two seats seventy minutes before departure, at double the regular price, I strongly suspected that we, not some officials, were the reason for the hassle and danger these young men had to endure. Luckily, the flight was uneventful. But my eyes began to open.

When we arrived in Guilin we checked in at the hotel CTS had reserved—being a day early proved not a problem. It was a pleasant and friendly place where we were the only non-mainland guests. We made instant friends with a few people, which was gratifying. On the second day I enquired about taking a boat trip on the Li River to Yangshuo. The hotel could arrange it. But it was by then obvious to me that this would be a tour for non-mainland visitors. I chatted to staff working at the hotel and others and asked about how the locals travel by river to Yangshuo. There was a local scenic ferry that sailed up every morning but tickets were hard to come by. To be sure one could get a ticket (available only to locals), one would need to queue up before 6 a.m., and the pier or ticket office was half an hour's walk away from the hotel. It was too good an opportunity to let go. My friend and I went shopping—Mao suits and "Liberation" brand green tennis shoes. Appropriately dressed, we set off before 5:30 a.m. the following morning and queued up. When our turn came, I asked for two tickets. The man at the counter did not even look at me and, bingo, I got the tickets.

The environmentally unspoiled scenes on the Li River were breathtakingly beautiful and serene. I enjoyed them and happily engaged in conversations with the local people about the customs and specialties of the region. As a touristic experience it was wonderful.

But stamped deeper into my memory was the experience of being one of the locals for the day. The food available on the ferry was disgusting— I never thought Chinese cooking could look or taste so bad. The conditions on the lower deck were not pleasant to say the least. I did not actually mind as I wanted to be with "the people." What really upset me was when I discovered a barrier between the lower and the upper deck which was not penetrable. It did not take much for me to work out that the upper, and much more comfortable, deck was where I would have been had I arranged the trip through the hotel. It reminded me of the "no dogs or Chinese" imagery of pre-war Shanghai as the boat sailed slowly upstream. Was the selfless and egalitarian Communist Party that I so admired not supposed to have ended this? Was the ending of this not what the "Chinese Revolution" was about? How could the People's government treat its own people as second class citizens in their own land? My head started to spin.

Back in Guilin, we went one evening for soup noodles in a local restaurant which had all its big windows wide open. Just as we started to eat, young children gathered outside the windows. I was curious and asked what they were doing. "Hungry" they said. Some had their hands out begging. It was a group of about fifteen or sixteen, with the younger ones about five or six years old. The oldest, who appeared to be their leader, was a girl of about fourteen. With them staring, I did not feel comfortable eating. I took some money, around ten yuan or so, and handed it to the big girl and said clearly that she should go and buy something for everyone to eat. The girl took the money and started running. The other children followed her shouting "share it." I was furious, dropped my noodles and ran after her. It was a couple of blocks away before I caught up with the big girl and grabbed her by her arms. The smaller children gradually caught up too. I snatched the money back and handed it to a smaller child and insisted that they must all share it. This time they left slowly together, with a few other children holding the arms of the boy with the cash.

I was shocked. Had "new China" under Chairman Mao not eradicated the ills of "old China," including begging? Where did the hungry young beggars come from? Why did the big girl behave so badly? As I opened my eyes wider by the day, the more beggars I saw, and not only in Guilin.

A young man more interested in searching for his own national identity than enjoying the touristic experience, I came across other similar incidents that made me think and reflect on what I had read of the many great achievements of the Communist Party. They just did not hang together. I did not know what was wrong but I saw and understood enough to start questioning myself and doubting the books I had read.

A week later when my friend and I returned to the Sino-British border in Shenzhen, I had changed—and in a way that I had not thought possible a week earlier. When I walked towards Lo Wu Bridge I saw the Union flag flying high and a Hong Kong policeman in khaki standing guard and felt a great warmth, affection and reassuring easiness. I was going home. The week in China had far greater impact on me as a young man than I had imagined. I saw the reality on the ground. I talked to people with whom I had wanted to identify. I left acknowledging the "new China" I had imagined did not match the reality. Above all, I realized that I was different from the Chinese on the mainland. For the first time in my life I felt I was a Hong Kong person.

Returning to Hong Kong, I wanted to understand the differences between myself and fellow Hong Kong people of my generation on the one hand and the mainland people on the other. I could now see an irony that I missed previously. Despite the colonial trappings and arrogance, Hong Kong did not discriminate against its own citizens in the way that egalitarian revolutionary China did. I still disliked the colonial nature of Hong Kong but I started to reflect on how the supposedly slave-grooming colonial education I had was making me ask critical questions. I wondered about the discrepancies between Chinese government statements and the reality in China. I started to question how colonial Hong Kong could be so much better than socialist China in so many ways—above all, in how it treated its citizens.

My first trip to China was meant to be a young Chinese patriot's journey in search of his Chinese roots. What I found was a Hong Kong identity and the realization that I must learn about the history of Hong Kong if I wanted to understand modern China. This was the beginning of my interest in the history, politics and society of Hong Kong.

*Steve Tsang is Professor of Contemporary Chinese Studies and Director of the China Policy Institute at the University of Nottingham. After completing his doctorate at Oxford University, he stayed at St Antony's College, where he served as Professorial Fellow, Dean and Director of the Asian Studies Center for more than twenty-nine years. He remains an Emeritus Fellow of St Antony's College and is the author of five, and editor of ten, books.*

# DAVID TANG
## *The Best of Motherland (1979)*

When Xenophon, around 400 BC, led his army of ten thousand Greek mercenaries out from enemy territories, they uttered the now immortal words "The sea! The sea!" when they finally reached the shores of the Black Sea. Those were the words that came to mind and the excitement I felt when I cast eyes on the ocean of clouds on my first visit to China, after climbing the mighty Yellow Mountains (Huangshan) and waking up at a monastery.

It was unusual to choose Anhui as the destination for my ethnic homecoming, especially when I had no affinity with the province. But it happened that the legendary Ho Yin asked me whether I would like to go with him and his family to China, and I was not about to pass up what I knew would be an extraordinary sojourn. After all, in 1979, it was far from fashionable to visit China. We in Hong Kong were still in the grip of the British colonialists, and the turmoil of the Cultural Revolution had only just subsided a couple of years earlier, with the trial of the "Gang of Four" still another couple of years away. We territorial Chinese were still apprehensive of mysterious motherland. But the Ho family, whose young son Edmund eventually became the first Chinese Governor of Macau, was exceptionally close to the mainland and represented, if nothing else, a comforting sense of security, which we now take far too much for granted.

So I went, and it was wonderful encountering Ho Yin himself, who was a walking legend of swearing! But he made it sound all very natural, and could have easily been a very successful standup comedian. I don't think I could have smiled or laughed or enjoyed myself more than listening to his conversations and many amusing tales. But he was too fat and unfit and blind to climb the Yellow Mountains, so the few of us were led up by a diminutive but feisty Mrs. Ho and her two sons.

Our ascent took all day, and we were continually overtaken by the local mountain people carrying heavy provisions on their backs, ridiculing our urbanite constitutions. Thankfully, the scenery was so beautiful that our pace provided us with opportunities to admire Chinese nature at its best. No wonder the Yellow Mountains have historically been the inspiration of many poets, particularly Li Bai, and painters. If there were to be a quintessential ink painting of a mountain in China, the likelihood is that it would be an evocation of the Yellow Mountains—with all the extraordinary Yingke Pines punctuating the ridges of their many peaks.

I remember being told that the highest peak was Tiandufeng and I was determined to get up there, which indeed the two Ho brothers and I did. But it was dark by the time we reached the summit and we were relieved to find a very modest but welcoming monastery where, exhausted, we had a light supper before going to sleep. The moment of waking up to the sound of the cockerels, coming out onto the balcony and seeing the ocean of clouds, is the indelible memory I have of my first real contact with motherland. It was like a moment of warm embrace after many years of separation. As I watched the drifting clouds, I also noticed the sun rising, almost as if it couldn't wait, warming the bubbling vapors and dispersing them to reveal the surrounding peaks, which seemed to rise from an ocean floor towards the blue sky. All the pines appeared like bonsais, as if they were sculpted to stir our Chinese roots within the natural and beautiful bosom of China. Even though the place was silent, I could hear the imagined sounds of a *guqin* playing in the background of my mind. For a few moments, I just stood there taking in an experience which I knew would always remain with me, the fondest memory I could have had from my first encounter with motherland.

I was secretly contemptuous of all my friends in Hong Kong who were still rather skeptical about visiting China. It's all very well for nearly all of them now to declare themselves patriots or admonish those who are not patriotic enough, although they are precisely the lot who harbored suspicions and didn't even have the guts to find out more about the fast-changing China that they should have embraced as their own country without hesitation. So in my Chinese world, I felt I had done something which so few from Hong Kong had ever ventured to experience.

We continued to climb other peaks and spent two more days up and down, up and down, that extraordinary repository of giant stalagmites, soaking up the crisp and refreshing air of the mountains, and eating and drinking as simply as monks or country folk, who seem to have all the right ideas about living a life of contentment without the distraction of the materialism that saturates vulgar urbanites. It was a perfect lesson in pastoral harmony, which those of us who live in the cities forget far too easily. And it was a useful reminder of the vast rural population that underpinned the whole country.

After these few days of absolute bliss, we went on to Hangzhou, which is probably the most beautiful city in China, with its famous West Lake surrounded by weeping willows. Again, there was a wonderful sense of nature that is virtually unique among cities in China. And so I was glad to have had my taste of China through its green and verdant aspects, and not by the sharp contrast of concrete blocks and impersonal boulevards and the choking atmosphere of soot that have come to characterize virtually every other city in China. I was indeed lucky to have been first introduced to the best of motherland. As they say: "You haven't been to China if you have not climbed Huangshan." And how lucky was I to have gone there on my first visit.

*David Tang was born in Hong Kong, and was educated locally and in England. He read philosophy at university, went to Law College and has taught at Peking University. He worked in the oil and mining industry before starting numerous businesses of his own: Shanghai Tang, China Club, Pacific Cigar, and China Tang. He is the author of An Apple a Week and A Chink in the Armour.*

# After Nixon

**After Nixon**

## Roderick MacFarquhar
*A Long Wait for the PRC (1972)*

I first applied for a visa to the People's Republic of China (I say PRC
because I had visited China with my parents as a child) in 1955, as a fledgling
journalist covering China for the London *Daily Telegraph*. On the few
occasions I visited the PRC mission in London, I was always told that they
had not heard from Beijing; I had visions of an exhausted Chinese courier
trekking across Siberia en route to London with the reply held in his cleft
stick. Seventeen years later, I finally got that visa.

The occasion was a goodwill visit by UK Foreign Secretary Sir Alec
Douglas-Home to mark the elevation of relations to full ambassador status.
Britain had recognized the PRC in 1950, but the Chinese government had
not agreed to an exchange of ambassadors at that time. Finally in 1971, the
two governments negotiated an end to this stalemate. The process had been
marred by Prime Minister Heath's fury at the lack of advance warning about
plans for the Nixon visit which he felt undercut the British negotiators, but
agreement was reached, and Sir John Addis took up his post as the first UK
ambassador in early 1972. A scholarly diplomat, Sir John had compiled the
book *Communist China, 1955-59: Policy Documents and Analysis* while a
fellow at Harvard's Center for International Affairs in 1962-3, but because of
his diplomatic status, the credit for authorship was assigned to John Fairbank
and Robert Bowie. Sir John is better remembered for his considerable

expertise in Chinese porcelain, some of his collection now being housed in the British Museum.

The Home mission was designed to set the seal on the new relationship and it naturally attracted a large group of journalists, including my late wife Emily MacFarquhar, the China specialist on *The Economist*. I was a research fellow at the Royal Institute for International Affairs—no longer a journalist, no longer the editor of *The China Quarterly*—but the Institute's director, Andrew Schonfield, paid my way to go as the "correspondent" of the Institute's monthly magazine *The World Today*, which actually had no correspondents. The Chinese duly gave me a visa, but on arrival in Guangzhou in October 1972, one of our minders from the Ministry of Foreign Affairs, later an ambassador to a major western power, looked me sternly in the eye and told me that since this was a goodwill visit, the Chinese had decided to admit anyone whom the British said was a journalist. In other words, don't try this trick again! Later we became friends after a Mao Tai *gan bei* contest which ended in a draw (seven all if I remember). Generally, the vibes of the trip, coming as it did after the Nixon visit and China's entry into the UN, were very positive, but I don't remember learning anything new from our discreet minders about current politics.

We flew first to Shanghai where the entire delegation, including hacks (as British journalists are often described, even by themselves), was treated to a splendid banquet, with a large ice swan in the middle of the table. When I later remarked on this meal to a local in Beijing, he patronizingly replied that it was true that the Shanghainese did make their food "look" good.

We visited a suburban commune, clearly on the tourist route as the signs for the lavatories were in English, and Emily questioned the responsible cadre concerned about the wages and status of women. She was so excited at finally being able to speak the Chinese she had learned at Harvard and honed in Taiwan that she eventually became totally hoarse, and at subsequent sites, one or another of our colleagues would chime in with "Let me ask Mrs. MacFarquhar's question!" Later, at the Capital Hospital, she was treated—at her request—with Chinese herbal remedies, but since the doctors also insisted on giving her western medication, she was unable to gauge their effectiveness.

Other experiences in Shanghai included witnessing an operation with acupuncture anesthesia and visiting the setting for the CCP's 1st Congress, but our most interesting times occurred when we had some blessed free play and we wandered off with another journalist (whom we met next in 1979, transformed into an acolyte at the ashram of Bhagwan Shree Rajneesh in Pune, India). In back streets we found local citizens digging the crude air raid shelters which the party had ordered as a precaution against a Soviet surprise attack. It reminded me a bit of the shelters which inhabitants of Jinmen had under their houses to protect themselves against mainland shelling. Later we were taken to the far more professionally constructed shelters under Beijing.

In the capital, housed in the Beijing Hotel, the journalists were assigned to a fleet of cars, two to a vehicle, according to an order of precedence apparently based on the Chinese estimate of the prestige of each hack's publication. As just a notional "correspondent," I should probably have been in the rear car, but the officials relented sufficiently to let me travel with Emily. If I remember correctly, David Aikman, a British citizen but the employee of an American publication, *Time*, was regarded as an anomaly and therefore did bring up the rear.

In our hierarchical convoy, we went to another commune (named for North Korean dictator Kim Il Sung) and were driven a long way out of Beijing to watch army maneuvers, perhaps to rub in the point that the Chinese were determined to defend themselves against the Soviet "social imperialists." From that drive, I remember: a construction team beside the road with the obligatory red flags fluttering; the way in which truck drivers coming our way chickened us into accepting their right to the center of the road; in this barely motorized economy, drivers tried to stay in top gear at all times even when their cars were juddering to a halt. We also went to a May 7th Cadre School, where the displaced officials proudly claimed that they had built their camp without help from the local peasantry. On further questioning, it turned out that they had received considerable financial help from the authorities with which to buy materials.

We hacks paid a visit to the *People's Daily* where we were told that sometimes the *People's Daily* was a morning paper and sometimes an evening paper, a reflection of the need in those uncertain times to respond to sudden developments. And of course we were taken to the Great Wall, the Ming Tombs, and the Palace Museum. During the latter visit, I told an official that

I had just written a book entitled *The Forbidden City* (a coffee table book in a *Newsweek* series "Wonders of Man") and had an advance copy which I would like to present to the museum director. A day or two later, I was whisked back to the museum and received by a deputy director. He told me we were meeting in a room which had been used by the Empress Dowager for theatricals, but which from the sounds emanating from the walls seemed now to be a home for large numbers of mice. Despite this interesting tidbit, it soon became clear to me that the deputy director had a very shaky grasp of Chinese imperial history and must be a reliable political appointee. He probably had no interest in my book, but he accepted the gift nevertheless, so mission accomplished.

Zhou Enlai gave the delegation a banquet, shook all our hands—a *zongli hao* ("hello Premier!") from me elicited a sharp look but nothing more—and posed with us for a photo op. Years later I was told that the Chinese had expected Home to ask to see Mao and that they would have agreed, but the British never asked and so we were deprived of even a glimpse of the Chairman.

But politically, the high point of the visit for me was the 50th birthday banquet for Prince (as he then was) Sihanouk of Cambodia. At the last minute, a few of us managed to get invitations and we lined up in the Great Hall of the People waiting for the VIPs to arrive. Zhou Enlai entered with Sihanouk, then Jiang Qing with Princess Monique, followed by Vice Premier Li Xiannian, Foreign Minister Ji Pengfei, and a handsome, rosy-cheeked young man in military uniform who looked as if he had just stepped off the stage of a model opera.

The two women stood to one side while the four men moved round the circle of assembled ambassadors, shaking hands. I asked a Beijing-based (presumably East) German correspondent who the young man shaking hands was. He didn't know but suggested it might be the interpreter. The idea that the Chinese would so dignify a mere interpreter seemed absurd so I turned for enlightenment to a Chinese cadre. He said that it was Wang Hongwen. When I asked why the Shanghai chief PLA political commissar would be in Beijing, he said he didn't know. In fact, that was Wang's first public appearance in the capital and gave us China watchers a foretaste of what was to come.

After that, everything was pretty anti-climactic, though we hacks did give our minders a merry return banquet, the scene of that Mao Tai contest. But the day we left Guangzhou for Hong Kong, I got a further instance of the more relaxed atmosphere that had followed Mao's discomfiture over the Lin Biao affair. In Beijing, I had handed the stern minder a copy of my newly published edited volume, *Sino-American Relations, 1949-1971*. In Guangzhou, he told me that he had read Donald Klein's chapter on the shredding of the Foreign Ministry during the Cultural Revolution, and that it was out of date: fifty percent of the personnel losses had been made up and within another year, the ministry would be back to full strength. On that note of bureaucratic optimism, we left China. I never did "correspond" with *The World Today* but I did contribute a brief article on the visit to the *People's Daily* to *The China Quarterly*.

While preparing for my first visit to the PRC, I had remembered a short story (by Somerset Maugham?) about a criminal whose devoted wife had visited him in prison every day of his long sentence; but the day he was released, he walked out of the prison gate and straight past her. He had become sick of the sight of her. After years of studying the PRC, would I be totally turned off when I finally got there? Fortunately not!

*Roderick MacFarquhar is the Leroy B. Williams Professor of History and Political Science, and Professor of Government, at Harvard University. He has been Chair of the University's Government Department and Director of the John King Fairbank Center for East Asian Research. He was the founding editor of The China Quarterly. In previous personae, he has been a print journalist, a TV reporter, and a Member of Parliament in the UK.*

# Jerome A. Cohen
## *The Missionary Spirit Dies Hard (1972)*

I started studying the Chinese language on August 15, 1960 at 9 a.m. Confucius said "Establish yourself at thirty," and, having just celebrated my thirtieth birthday, I decided he was right. I would not be allowed to visit China, however, until May 20, 1972. For almost twelve years my study of China's legal system and related political, economic, social and historical aspects, had necessarily been second-hand, dated and from afar. It was a bit like researching imperial Roman law or deciphering developments on the moon.

Like many other American specialists on China, as a new era of Sino-American relations dawned in the early 1970s, I tried many ways to finally reach the Promised Land. The one in which I had invested the least effort was the one that panned out first. A phone call from the Federation of American Scientists, a group of liberal scientists seeking to initiate cooperation with China, suddenly brought an invitation to accompany its chairman, the distinguished physicist and policy advisor Marvin Goldberger, and its executive secretary, the dynamic political activist Jeremy Stone, on a several-week trip to promote the first scientific exchanges between our countries. The three of us were allowed to take our wives, but not our children.

So Joan Lebold Cohen, who had become a specialist in Chinese art on the faculty of the School of the Boston Museum of Fine Arts/Tufts University, and I shared this first trip to China just three months after President Richard

Nixon's famous China visit. We had been spending the academic year in Japan on my Guggenheim Fellowship, and we reluctantly left our three school-age sons in Kyoto under the supervision of our kind and competent housekeeper, Hatenaka-san.

We were guests of the Chinese Academy of Sciences. One of its able staff, Li Mingde, met us at the Hong Kong border and escorted us to Beijing's Minzu (Nationalities) Hotel. Excited to finally be there, I awoke early the next morning and decided to explore the neighborhood before joining my wife and colleagues for breakfast. The area was bustling with people rushing to work, leaving no chance to strike up a casual conversation. I tried to talk with people in the nearby market, which would have been difficult at any time, but especially at 6 a.m. I heard one vegetable-seller say to another: "He's a Frenchman," perhaps because Americans were few at that point and I had a mustache. After a while, since I was hungry and getting nowhere in my marketplace effort at cultural exchange, I decided to try my luck at a nearby "little eating place." As I stood in line, the man behind the counter seemed friendly and asked what I wanted to eat. I asked him to give me what those ahead of me were having: hot soy milk soup called *doujiang* and a long cruller called *youtiao*. Armed with these props, I took the fourth seat at a table for four occupied by three middle-aged workers. Everyone else in the room was watching but my new companions barely looked up. I was determined to get them to talk, but how to start? I remembered that foreign journalists who preceded me in China had told me that, every time they asked anyone about the mysterious fate of disappeared leader Lin Biao, the answer was always: "Have some more soup." So, instead of explaining who I was and how I got there or reminding my companions about Chairman Mao's emphasis on being at one with the masses, I stayed with what seemed a safe topic and said to the fellow on my left: "What's the name of this soup?" He didn't answer.

The room hushed, and tension began to mount, but I pushed on, saying hopefully to the man across from me: "Do you know the name of this soup?" He wouldn't answer either. At that point, as the sympathetic man behind the counter looked unhappy at the cool reception I was receiving, I noted a sign on the wall that said: "Heighten revolutionary vigilance. Defend the Motherland against spies." And standing in a corner staring at me with bulging eyes was a man who resembled a security officer about to make an arrest in a Jiang Qing opera. Meanwhile, the anxious man seated on my right was slurping his soup furiously in an effort to clear out and avoid the inevitable. He probably didn't want to be impolite like the others, but may have feared that, if he told me the name of the soup, the next question would be "What happened to Lin Biao?" In some desperation I persisted and said to him: "You must know the name of this soup." He looked at me and then at the soup and said what Chinese often say when they don't want to answer: "I'm not too clear about that!" At that point, hoping that the official route to cultural exchange might be more successful, I decided it was time to return to the hotel!

On that first full day in Beijing, I underwent an unexpected name change.

For twelve years my Chinese name had been Kong Jierong. My first Chinese language tutor in Berkeley, California, a learned former Beijing scholar, had given me this name. Kong, he had said, was the perfect family name for me since it sounded like Cohen and was the name of China's most famous sage, Confucius, who took a great interest in law. But in the China of mid-1972 Kong had become the enemy, the hated symbol of China's feudal past, and anathema to every upstanding revolutionary. I had inadvertently arrived in the midst of a nationwide campaign to wipe out the remnants of Lin Biao and Confucius. So my hosts declared that I should have a new, more proletarian name. They decided that Ke En would do nicely since Ke was an ordinary name of the masses and, together with En (they knew I admired Zhou Enlai), would sound even more like Cohen than Kong did and have a favorable meaning. I gave the matter little thought, but later, in 1977, when I escorted Senator Edward M. Kennedy and ten members of his family to China to meet Deng Xiaoping and other luminaries, Taiwan's *Lianhe Bao* (*United Daily News*) used my new mainland name against me, claiming that I had abandoned the name of China's foremost figure. Of course, outside the mainland, I have continued to be known by my original name, and recently, since the resurrection of Confucius in China, some mainland organizations and friends have adopted it in referring to me.

We spent our first ten days in Beijing, preoccupied with the usual introductory tourist sites and meetings devoted to persuading our hosts to send their first science delegation to the United States, which they did six months later. For me, two personal academic/professional meetings stand out. One was a four-hour chat with three members of the Legal Department of the China Council for the Promotion of International Trade (CCPIT). It was my only contact during the entire visit with people concerned with law. The domestic legal system had been a shambles and arbitrary even before the Cultural Revolution, and the revolution still had four more years to run when we appeared. Legal education had virtually ceased. Although the worst days of violence had long passed by 1972, struggles reportedly still occasionally took place in cities that were closed to foreigners. Yet China's international trade was expanding, raising legal problems that had to be handled, and business with the United States was gradually opening. So when I asked to meet legal experts, my hosts naturally turned to the CCPIT's Legal Department. The three people introduced, although they lacked formal legal education, seemed to be experienced, competent people, and I was destined to see much more of them when, beginning in 1978, China launched a serious effort to establish a credible legal system. The director of the department, Ren Jianxin, in the late 1980s became not only President of the Supreme People's Court but also, concurrently, head of the Communist Party's Central Political-Legal Commission, which controls the activities of all the country's government institutions for implementing the law. Tang Houzhi became China's best-known expert on international commercial arbitration, and Liu Gushu the leading specialist on patent and trademark matters and founder of an important law firm dealing with these problems.

The other meeting I recall well was with a large group of "America watchers" convened by the Foreign Affairs Association (*Waijiao Xiehui*), an offshoot of the Ministry of Foreign Affairs. They were familiar with my July 1971 article in the American journal *Foreign Affairs* calling for US recognition of the People's Republic and disengagement from the Republic of China on Taiwan. At least a few knew that I had chaired a Harvard-MIT committee that in November 1968 gave President-elect Nixon a confidential memorandum recommending that he send a close aide for secret talks in Beijing with China's leaders. That was the origin of Henry Kissinger's famous 1971 visit. Of course, my hosts, the "America watchers," wanted to discuss the problem of Taiwan and prospects for normalization of diplomatic relations between our countries, but they seemed most anxious about Senator George McGovern's chances of unseating Nixon in the fall presidential election. I was known to be an advisor on Asia to McGovern, although, since I had spent most of the year abroad, I did little for his campaign. At a time when China was looking to the US to be a shield against the Soviet Union, McGovern's pledge to cut the defense budget by one-third seemed very worrisome to my hosts. Also, it was obvious that the PRC had high hopes for cooperation with the Nixon administration, much of it based on the admiration that Kissinger and Zhou Enlai professed for each other.

I had agreed to talk with the group about these subjects if they would agree to also discuss problems of cultural exchange. I wanted an opportunity to let them know how this initial effort looked to their guests. Since they hoped to establish diplomatic relations with the US, I thought it useful for them to make their reception of Americans as smooth as possible. I especially wanted to ask about the most puzzling of our experiences—the subway, an experience that reminded me of the old jokes about the then new Moscow subway of the 1930s. When our escort inquired whether we would like to ride on the Beijing subway that had been under construction, I said that the newspapers had reported that it was not yet in service. Our escort said that it was already in service and that we could ride on it. At the appointed hour, while standing next to the track, we were given a long lecture about the history of the subway's development. During that time, only two trains came by, and neither had a single passenger. The next train, which we took through eight stations, also had no other passengers, nor did we see any people waiting at any of the stations. We were told they were all in waiting rooms, where conditions were more comfortable. When we got to the last stop, the Beijing railroad station, our escort still insisted that the system was in use. I embarrassed my wife by saying that we would like to wait a while for evidence that people really were using the subway. I had had doubts about some of the information we had been given on other matters and was disturbed that we could not successfully communicate about something as basic as whether the subway was in service. A bit exasperated with my determination to clarify an evident misunderstanding, my wife and a couple of others in our group went up the escalator to the main hall to wait. Down at the track, no trains came in for a time but finally one did appear with about twenty assorted workers, peasants and soldiers who seemed flustered when they encountered the escalator. With some satisfaction, our escort said: "You see, the system is in service." When I later asked the Foreign Affairs Association group about this mystery, our escort's leader, with the escort seated next to him, smiled and said: "It's very simple. Our subway is not yet in service."

Our escort had given me a more reliable insight into contemporary China earlier in the trip, as we viewed the beautiful valley of the Ming Dynasty tombs outside Beijing from a hilltop. By that time I felt we had become friendly enough to talk politics and even international law. Just a few weeks earlier, at a lecture in Tokyo to the Harvard Club of Japan, I had discussed the increasingly tense dispute between China and Japan over the eight piles of rock in the East China Sea known as Diaoyutai in Chinese. When on May 15, 1972, the United States surrendered administrative jurisdiction over these islets to Japan, Sino-Japanese relations deteriorated further, and even today the dispute continues to fester. When I mentioned Diaoyutai, my escort became uncharacteristically emotional. "China," he said, "will never allow the Japanese aggressors to occupy one inch of its sacred soil. We will fight them to the death." But when I gently informed him that Japan had assumed jurisdiction over the islets only the previous week, he suddenly resumed his usual relaxed manner and said: "Oh, well. There is a right time and place for everything. We are in no hurry. We can settle this matter any time in the next 500 years!" I had witnessed the two sides of contemporary China's politics—

nationalism and pragmatism—in short compass.

One question that overhung our first ten days was where we would go next. My wife wanted very much for us to visit the ancient capitals of Xian and Luoyang and their nearby artistic treasures. For days we waited for confirmation of this excursion. Finally, after dinner on our last night in Beijing, our escort came to our room and told us that it would not be possible. After he left, Joan expressed her anger at their rejection of her only request. I agreed with her view, while motioning to her to raise the volume of our continuing conversation about our disappointment. I assumed that our hosts might be monitoring our conversation and may well have been right. The next morning, just twelve hours later, our escort returned to tell us the exciting news that we could go to Xian and Luoyang. Moreover, at the farewell lunch that the famous poet-official Guo Moruo, then head of the Chinese Academy of Sciences, gave us that day, Guo, unprompted by us, said to me: "I understand that your wife is interested in ancient Chinese culture. So we will arrange for you to go to Xian and Luoyang!" That incident taught me a lot about the importance of using imaginative negotiating techniques in China.

One other question concerned us in Beijing—whether we would meet Premier Zhou Enlai. We were told that we might, but there was no word by the time we left the capital. Nor was there any information as we pursued the rest of our itinerary. Our travels proved pleasant and stimulating but plagued by the continuing "cat and mouse" games played by our local hosts to parry my efforts to learn basic facts about public life. An exchange in Shanghai conveys the flavor. I asked: "What are the names of your Shanghai newspapers?" "We have the *People's Daily*," I was told. I responded: "But that's your national newspaper. What are the names of your local papers?" Our host replied: "You wouldn't be interested." I answered: "Then why do you think I asked the question?"

We ended our travels by returning to Beijing in order to fly to Guangzhou on our way out of China. Our hosts seemed slightly embarrassed that there had been no confirmation of a meeting with Premier Zhou. Then, while en route, bad weather in Guangzhou required our flight to be diverted to the closed city of Nanchang, capital of Jiangxi Province. Because Nanchang was closed, we were kept at its airport until dark and then taken to the People's Hotel, which we were forbidden to leave. At 4 a.m., we were awakened to return to the airport before daylight to resume our flight to Guangzhou. In the interim, however, big news came from Beijing.

At 1 a.m., as we were fitfully sleeping amid blistering heat on our woven bamboo mats, there was a knock on our door. It was a telephone call from Professor Lin Daguang (Paul Lin), a Canadian friend who had previously been an assistant to Premier Zhou. Would Joan and I be willing to return to Beijing to meet Zhou? I said I would gladly return and would let him know about Joan. I also suggested inviting our companions on the trip, which he arranged. Joan, understandably, felt she had to return to Kyoto to look after our sons. The Goldbergers also had to go home, but the Stones were able to return to Beijing.

As Harrison Salisbury later commented in his book *To Peking and Beyond*, invitations to meet Premier Zhou were often issued at the last minute, and it was not unusual to bring guests back from all over the country. There was also sometimes an air of mystery surrounding these meetings. For example, I was told to wait in my hotel room from 5 p.m., after which I would be picked up and taken to a preliminary meeting with an unidentified person, to be followed by dinner with an unidentified group, but with a strong hint that Premier Zhou would be the host. The preliminary meeting turned out to be a private one-hour session with Deputy Foreign Minister Qiao Guanhua, a stimulating and self-confident interlocutor whom I enjoyed. I then went to dinner and met with Premier Zhou, Qiao and some of their principal aides, at least two of whom eventually became ambassadors to the US and heads of the North American section of the Foreign Ministry. Our interpreter was Tang Wensheng, known to many Americans as Nancy Tang, who had grown up in the United States while her father served at the UN. Although I had several short chats in Chinese with Premier Zhou, Nancy did the heavy interpreting for the evening. The main guests were Professor John K. Fairbank, America's senior China scholar, and his charming wife Wilma. Fairbank was my senior colleague at Harvard University, where I was then teaching in the Law School. The Fairbanks had been friendly with Premier Zhou in Chongqing during the mid-1940s before the Communist Party's 1949 victory in the Chinese civil war. Foreign correspondents Harrison Salisbury of

*The New York Times* and Richard Dudman of the *St. Louis Post-Dispatch*, and their wives also attended, as did Jeremy Stone and his wife.

Salisbury's book gives a long account of most of the conversation at our almost four-hour evening with Zhou and this group. I need not repeat it, although it was surely the high point of my first visit. Here I will mention only my most outstanding impressions. The deepest impression was left by Premier Zhou. He gave us an hour of discussion, sipping tea before dinner while seated in a circle. He was genial, informal, relaxed, humorous, yet serious and always guiding the conversation by asking questions. His first remark to me was: "Why didn't your wife come with you? We invited her." When I explained that Joan had wanted to join but was concerned about our sons, he quipped: "Oh, I forgot. In America, parents still have to look after children." Later, as we went in to dinner, he said to me with a smile and a bemused twinkle in his eyes: "I understand that you have done many books on our legal system." This showed the respect he gave his guests by learning their backgrounds in advance. Yet he said it in a slightly quizzical way that gently implied that perhaps I had made more of China's legal system than China had. After all, the country was then still in its Cultural Revolution!

What I remember most vividly from the pre-dinner conversation was the Premier's preoccupation with cancer. Zhou knew, of course, that the purpose of Mr. Stone's and my visit was to initiate cultural exchanges in the sciences. He seemed especially interested in inviting to China America's leading cancer specialists, in theory and practice. Since the Premier appeared so lively and healthy, it didn't dawn on me that he might be inquiring on his own behalf. I did think that he might be asking on behalf of Chairman Mao, whose health had reportedly been deteriorating and was the subject of much speculation at home and abroad, and soon after our meeting I wrote about this in an op-ed in *The Washington Post*. We later discovered that Premier Zhou had learned in 1972, the year of our visit, that he himself was suffering from several kinds of cancer, which ultimately caused his death in January 1976, eight months before the demise of the Chairman.

Broader cultural exchange was one of our dinner talk's main themes. Since Professor Fairbank sat on Zhou's right and I on his left, we were in a particularly good position to urge him to allow Chinese to visit and study at Harvard. Zhou deflected our efforts as well-meaning but premature. He seemed to think that brief visits could soon be arranged but that study might better await the establishment of formal diplomatic relations between our countries. He appeared especially worried that Chinese students might have unpleasant encounters with students sent to America by the Kuomintang government in Taiwan. He even asked me, as an international lawyer: "If our students debated on the same Harvard platform with students from Taiwan, wouldn't that be implicit recognition of a 'two China' policy and signal Beijing's acceptance of the legitimacy of the Chiang Kai-shek regime?" I assured him that academic debate among students had no necessary international law implications. At point, about an hour into dinner, perhaps to ease the pressure from Harvard, the Premier suggested that we take a five-minute break. In the men's room, as we stood at our respective urinals, Professor Fairbank, indicating that perhaps we had put too much pressure on the Premier, looked me in the eye somewhat sheepishly and said: "The missionary spirit dies hard!"

I had wanted to make one serious suggestion about international law to the Premier and his colleagues and waited most of the evening till an opportunity presented itself. I said that, having already entered the United Nations the previous October, China should move quickly to take part in all UN institutions, including the International Court of Justice (ICJ). That gave the Chinese officials their biggest laugh of the evening. They thought I must have been joking. Why, after all, would a revolutionary communist government want to participate in a bourgeois legal institution where its views of international law would not be accepted and it was sure to be outvoted? I explained that the world was entering a new era and China, having recently been acknowledged as a great power by being awarded a permanent seat on the UN Security Council, should obviously want to play a role in the application of international law by the ICJ. The People's Republic did not nominate its first judge to sit on the ICJ until 1984. Although Chinese judges have played a constructive role in the Court's work ever since, their government has only gradually expanded its confidence in the ICJ's deliberations.

After the memorable evening with Zhou Enlai, anything else that occurred in my first trip was inevitably anti-climactic. Yet the exchange of ideas at the dinner with Zhou encouraged me to offer one more suggestion on a very sensitive topic before leaving Beijing. We were meeting the next morning with Professor Zhou Peiyuan, then Chairman of the Revolutionary Committee of Peking University, or, as he preferred to put it to us, president of that illustrious university. Zhou Peiyuan, a University of Chicago PhD in physics and a former Cal Tech professor, had already spent a great deal of time accompanying us as the senior person responsible for our visit. His mission was presumably to get acquainted with and hear the views of his fellow physicist and sometime US government advisor, Professor Marvin Goldberger, the leader of our small delegation.

I wanted to express my concern for my friend and college classmate, John T. Downey, Jr., who had been detained in Chinese prison since November 1952, after his plane had been shot down over China on a CIA mission to foster armed resistance against the then still new Communist government. I had been trying for many years to obtain his release and had previously suggested to both the Chinese Ambassador to Canada (later Foreign Minister) Huang Hua and Henry Kissinger that this could be accomplished, to the satisfaction of both countries, if the US would finally acknowledge the truth of China's accusations that this had been a CIA incursion. I had also revealed the truth of the Downey matter in nationally-televised testimony before the Senate Foreign Relations Committee in June 1971 and in a *New York Times* op-ed. I did not want to leave Beijing without again urging consideration of this idea, and I took the meeting with Professor

Zhou as the best opportunity. Early the following year, six weeks after President Nixon discreetly conceded the truth of the charges against Downey in a press conference, Downey was finally released.

It turned out that Professor Zhou had an even more sensitive topic to raise with us, even in Professor Goldberger's absence. He surprised Jeremy Stone, a knowledgeable Washington defense expert, and me by asking what we could tell him about the so-called "smart bomb" that the US had reportedly begun to use in the Vietnam War. I, of course, knew nothing about this subject and didn't know whether Stone was informed. In any event, we told Zhou that if anyone in our group could answer the question it would be Professor Goldberger, who had already returned to the US. I'll admit that I was a bit naïve in feeling shocked at what seemed a blatant effort to turn cultural exchange into an intelligence operation.

Overall, Joan and I found our first trip to China enormously stimulating despite the evident limitations on cultural exchanges in both law and art. I felt that my research, and especially the year 1963-4 that I had spent in Hong Kong interviewing Chinese refugees, many of whom were former officials, had prepared me well for the visit. Every experience left me with vivid images. Joan, a professional photographer as well as art historian, was more struck by the drabness and austerity of contemporary life and the absence of amenities. After returning to Japan, we took our boys to see Charlton Heston and Ava Gardner in *55 Days at Peking*, a colorful film depicting the imperialist heyday of the Boxer Rebellion, which by coincidence was playing in Kyoto. As we left the theater, Joan said: "That's the China of my dreams."

Nevertheless, we both agreed with the humorist Art Buchwald that, after a stomach-full of China watching, an hour later you're hungry for more!

*Jerome A. Cohen is Professor and Co-director of the US-Asia Law Institute at NYU School of Law. He was formerly Associate Dean and Director of East Asian Legal Studies at Harvard Law School, and former Director of Asia Studies at the Council on Foreign Relations. He retired from the partnership of Paul, Weiss, Rifkind, Wharton & Garrison LLP at the end of 2000, after twenty years of law practice focused on China.*

# LEO F. GOODSTADT
*How News Was Managed During the Cultural Revolution (1973)*

In April 1973, I got a phone call from Xinhua News Agency instructing me
to apply for a visa to join a group tour of Guangdong. Xinhua was then a
very different organization. The "Gang of Four" were in power, and news
was more an export commodity to be managed and packaged rather than
professionally reported. And my "packaging" was to come undone, leading to
formal protests to Derek Davies, the *Far Eastern Economic Review*'s talented
but volatile editor, who had returned the previous month from such a trip
without provoking complaints.

Why I had been granted a visa so soon after Davies' tour, I could not
understand. I did not regard it as a sign that I was being taken seriously as
a student of Chinese affairs. In 1972, I had published a book about economics
and Mao Zedong, and the American edition was just out. But this had not
raised my status perceptibly, even at the *Review*. Here, I wrote about China
only in the absence of icons like Harald Munthe-Kaas and John Gittings who
had serious China-watching credentials, and while expecting the return to
Hong Kong of the redoubtable David Bonavia.

Unlike Davies, I would not be allowed to visit Beijing and the more
strategic areas of China. I would be confined to Guangdong province,
a restriction that I did not resent since it was well within my comfort zone.
There would be no culture shock. I knew that Cantonese and Cantonese

etiquette prevailed throughout the province despite the Cultural Revolution and the Red Guards' drive to purge the nation of the "four olds"—old customs, culture, habits, and ideas. And just as in Hong Kong, it would be almost impossible for people not to react kindly to any foreigner who, in Cantonese, tried hard to "follow the customs of the village," as the saying goes.

The big surprise once inside Guangdong was a strange feeling of familiarity and affinity. Everywhere we went, poverty was compounded by austerity. In the countryside, life was harsh and close to subsistence. In Guangzhou, food and clothing were subject to controls, and consumer goods seemed barely fit for use. At night, the streets were empty and virtually without lighting. But none of this seemed extraordinary to me. The parallels were striking with the Wales of my childhood and teens where austerity had reigned. British rationing of food and clothing was severe throughout World War II, intensified after the Allied victory in 1945, and was not lifted finally until 1953. Furthermore, the wartime blackout and an absence of civilian road traffic were what I had grown up with.

As for "modern" amenities, Guangdong's present was my not-so-distant past. The unavailability of indoor sanitation, bathrooms and even a domestic water supply on the Chinese mainland was a state of affairs to be found in much of Wales when I left home, and many houses had no electricity or even gas. Telephones were few in Welsh towns and villages, and private cars almost unknown.

All the same, Guangdong's poverty had a dimension that I had never encountered before. This was a pre-industrial society. Mechanical equipment of all kinds, vehicles and even tools were often ill-designed, clumsy to use and the products, it seemed, of cottage industry rather than factories. Mao Zedong had decided for strategic reasons that this coastal province should not be industrialized. The policy proved a great advantage when economic modernization began after 1978 because unlike China's northeast, for example, the provincial economy was not lumbered with obsolescent heavy industry modeled on the Soviet Union. But the immediate consequences for Guangdong were a dismal growth rate compared with the national average, and real poverty.

Now, almost forty years on, I have reread for the first time my 1973 articles on trading conditions at the Canton Trade Fair and life in a rural commune. They are professional enough but not especially memorable. I decided to compare them with the feature by the *Review*'s editor, recounting his own voyage round China the month before, which I find much better written. On display was Derek Davies' remarkable capacity to turn a week's visit into a compelling, far-sighted analysis of an Asian nation's current travails and its future prospects, identifying in particular the looming discontent within China's workforce.

Nevertheless, my coverage of Guangdong led to reverberations that lasted until 1998. The fallout began the day after my feature story was published. I came back to the office after lunch to find Davies puce with rage. I had, he said, destroyed the *Review*'s chances of ever opening a Beijing bureau. Chinese officials who had accompanied the tour, he went on, had just called to see him and protest at my reporting. They had alleged that I had tried to bring China into disrepute. They had warned him that my article bore no relation to what had been seen on the tour. Davies insisted that their charges could not be totally without foundation. After all, they had assured him that the photographs illustrating my article could not have been taken anywhere in Guangdong. They had probably been shot, they had suggested, in the newly-established Bangladesh (which I had never been to).

At this point, the complainants' case crumbled. The *Review*'s production editor, Hiro Pumwani, was able to retrieve from his filing cabinet the negatives of the rolls of 120 film, taken by me but developed at the company's expense. They were in continuous strips, which started with the British flag on one side of the Lo Wu crossing and the Chinese flag and PLA guards on the other. They recorded the train journey to Guangzhou, followed by pictures taken in sequence at each school, workshop, village and scenic spot we went to subsequently. And then the return journey to Hong Kong via Lo Wu. My article had been illustrated with genuine photos of Guangdong life.

What had caused such official ire? Although President Richard Nixon had dismantled the economic embargo in 1971 and transformed the Sino-US relationship with his personal visit to Beijing in 1972, the Cold War was not over yet. Chinese officials made considerable efforts to get the maximum advantage from foreign contacts. This process used to involve tests of moral fiber. From time to time, even in Hong Kong, I had been asked to meet this official or that who would upbraid me for a recent article. The dialogue rarely varied. I would be told that my account of official policy or economic performance was distorted. I would express my gratitude for this opportunity to learn what official speeches or statistics I had misconstrued. I would be told that my offense arose from my habit of quoting published material whose circulation overseas was not authorized. This showed a hostile attitude and lack of respect for China. Anything that it was proper for me to know about China I should seek solely in the *Renmin Ribao* or *Guangming Ribao*, *Hongqi* or Xinhua and the English-language publications intended for overseas distribution. It was hard for either side to take such an exchange of views seriously when Louis Cha's *Ming Pao* and its Hong Kong rivals were filled with incisive, "inside" coverage of mainland developments.

On our tour of Guangdong, the interrogations had become more personal. How, I was asked one afternoon, could I live with the shameful legacy of a father who had served for seven years as a professional soldier in India under British rule? How, I wondered, had this official obtained such an item of information. (It was ironic that, as I recounted earlier, an Indian colleague and his meticulous photo files was to provide the proof that I had been describing Guangdong.)

Round Two took place on the Sunday of our visit after I expressed a wish to go to Mass. I was told that China's Catholics had given up Mass in churches: each family celebrated its own Mass at home. An unlikely theological discussion ensued in which I opined that if Catholics were not permitted access to Mass celebrated by a priest, freedom of religion was not a flourishing feature of Guangdong life. For this, I was rebuked with the prompt reply: "You are trying to make trouble just like your mother-in-law when she came to Guangzhou with Hong Kong's Chinese Chamber of Commerce in 1954."

That verdict was something to be proud of. She had indeed refused during that visit to accept the propaganda line that the nuns who took in baby girls abandoned by desperate parents at a convent's doors later committed infanticide. Or that priests working with lepers and other outcasts were tools of an imperialist conspiracy. She was a woman I admired enormously: an accomplished businesswoman yet kind and caring to the distressed and deprived; irresistibly charming and possessed of strong principles. To be compared with her was an enormous compliment.

And yet, none of these exchanges as we traveled around Guangdong involved real rancor or mistrust. They were interspersed by serious discussions about Hong Kong-related matters. For example, a senior member of the official team took considerable pains to stress the special value which China's leaders attached to maintaining the effectiveness of the colonial administration. He recounted how he himself had conveyed reassurances from Beijing to the Hong Kong authorities at the height of the anti-colonial violence in 1967 that there was no intention of taking over Hong Kong. And an important channel of communication, he said, had been "Editor Davies."

In the 1970s, he continued, cooperation between the two sides would be even more important and he knew that I met senior Hong Kong government officials. I was not being invited to carry a specific message, it seemed, but I was being asked to convey friendly sentiments. Which I later did when I met the Governor, Lord MacLehose, during one of his charm offensives for the local media. He did not seem especially impressed, so there was no story for me there!

Yet, plainly my reporting had given offense. Otherwise why the mischievous allegations about the use of "Bangladesh" photos in a feature about a Guangdong commune? My article had been almost as predictable and routine as much of the reporting by visiting journalists. There was one difference, however. On rereading it today, I realize that twelve per cent of the text was devoted explicitly to recounting the serious poverty suffered by a model commune's families. In these passages, I was reporting the uncensored insights and experiences of a local cadre who could not bring himself to parrot propaganda.

He had begun his presentation to our group by declaring: "I won't speak Putonghua. I don't want to speak Putonghua." For me, it was like being at a meeting at home in rural Wales where a farmers' union representative insisted on speaking Welsh instead of English. Afterwards, I apologized to our host for taking up his time, which was a conventional Cantonese courtesy that anyone in Hong Kong would have expressed. In addition, I felt genuinely embarrassed. I knew how precious time is for farmers when work is heaviest.

We had taken him and other commune leaders away from the fields for almost an entire day, and I felt obliged to state my regret for imposing this burden on them.

The cadre said that he had indeed sacrificed precious time. But what bothered him most was the likelihood that none of us would take what he had said seriously. He had been told that the stories written by foreign journalists who had come to the commune in the past failed to acknowledge the persistent poverty with which it had to contend and the wretched conditions under which many of its members still lived. These visitors preferred to paint a pretty picture of life in New China, he complained.

I promised to prove the exception. My published account began with his admission: "'I ask myself how we survive on the earnings which the ordinary peasant gets on this commune.'" I went on to record how he "nudged me and pointed towards a small group… Dressed in tatters, the handful of men, women and children were Hakkas from the hills. 'These people are very poor indeed,' he continued. 'We try to help by selling goods to them at subsidized prices. But there is not a lot we can do.'"

This commune leader was scathing about one of the main features of life under Maoism: the "down to the country" movement which transferred seventeen million middle-school graduates from the cities to the villages during the Cultural Revolution. "Their efforts in the fields," my article said, "were described as 'a ballet dance' by a senior cadre, who said he would prefer not to see any more of them in his parish. They send far too much food back to their families in the urban areas. (Food in the rural areas, an official commented, is much cheaper than in the cities.) They reduce the rice ration available for ordinary commune members." Such accusations were not new, of course. In a contribution to a 1965 book, *Youth in China*, I had quoted similar rural sentiments reported by the official press during 1962-63.

While insisting on the paramount principle "obey Chairman Mao," this rural leader went on to brush aside the rhetoric of the "Gang of Four" and the "ultra-leftists." His own political strategy was: "First look after people's stomachs and their health, and then you will be able to touch their hearts and persuade them that cadres and the state care for them. Afterwards, you will be able to change their minds so that the people will recognize that their prosperity can only last and grow if the entire nation flourishes." He was expressing the sort of sentiments that were to get Deng Xiaoping dismissed from office in 1976 but gave him the credibility with the public at large to be restored to power and launch the 1978 reforms.

This man had serious moral courage. What happened to him subsequently I had no way of knowing. I was sure that he had discounted in advance the price to be paid for insisting on stating his views. But he did not strike me as an exceptional case. Similar encounters over the years with individual mainland officials and Party members whose pragmatism was inspired by ideals gave me confidence that Chinese people will always rise above the failings of their rulers and find their way to a better life despite the most unfavorable obstacles.

My attitude was neither naïve nor unduly sentimental. Anyone closely involved in Hong Kong's Chinese world could hardly avoid knowing the personal costs inflicted by the political upheavals of the Maoist era. In my extended family, there was a revolutionary guerrilla hero who had fallen into disgrace during an ideological purge—fortunately to be restored to an honorable career after the demise of the "Gang of Four." There were the Catholic relatives from Shanghai who spent over twenty years in labor camps for refusing to repudiate their religious convictions. There were the "New China" manufacturers and professionals—especially my "mentors" among senior executives in the Bank of China group—whose children had gone back to the mainland for their education only to fall victim to the anti-rightist and every subsequent campaign because of their family links with Hong Kong. Ironically, it was this group which provided the antidote to total cynicism on my part. They had accepted their family sacrifices in the belief that revolutions cannot be "temperate, kind, courteous" and that a revolution is "not a dinner party, or writing an essay," so that innocent individuals must suffer for the greater good. It was not until corruption became rampant on the mainland once more after 1978 that these by now elderly men went from disillusionment to despair. Such an outcome was still unthinkable in 1973. And I was reassured that these friends, so dedicated to "New China," took no exception to my article regardless of official complaints.

As was to be expected, the officials did not make their complaints entirely in vain, even though their allegations were patently absurd. Derek Davies decided that Beijing's goodwill ought not to be jeopardized by allowing me to write up the rest of my adventures in Guangdong. In the process, he deprived me of a potential scoop that would have had some historical interest. Our party had been taken to Foshan where we were briefed on a pilot scheme to attract direct foreign investment that had recently begun. The previous year, Tianjin had been allowed to borrow foreign funds to modernize key manufacturing plants whose export potential would enable them to repay the foreign loan and still make a respectable profit. But Foshan had gone a step further, according to a senior city official.

In the winter months, we were told, a national leader—identification refused—had come south to Foshan to escape the cold. While enjoying its scenic and cultural attractions, the distinguished visitor had been told that its Song dynasty temple was a huge attraction for Japanese tourists, some of whom had expressed an interest in setting up production lines in the city. The visitor had thought this suggestion an attractive initiative as China was starting to rebuild its financial links with the outside world. Sometime later, the city's spokesman said, Beijing had approved an inflow of Japanese funding.

I picked up some low-level gossip that the mystery leader was in fact Mao's wife, Jiang Qing, on her way to her favorite holiday resort in Hainan (then still part of Guangdong province). A more likely candidate I personally felt was an obscure soldier, Bai Xiangguo. This career PLA political commissar had made "helicopter rides" from head of Shantou's Revolutionary

Committee in 1968 to the leadership of Guangdong the following year and to the post of Foreign Trade Minister in 1970. Here, he had become the globetrotting front man for a massive surge in China's imports. His shopping list included US Boeings and British Tridents, Japanese and German steel plants, record imports of grain and chemical fertilizers. In 1973, he handed over to Li Qiang, a career trade expert, and returned to the PLA. One of the unsung architects of China's future strategy of growth through foreign trade, he ended his military career in 1984 as a deputy director of logistics. But I was denied the chance at the *Review* to write up Bai and the pioneering "open door" experiment at Foshan, years ahead of the Shenzhen Special Economic Zone.

Another story that did not make it into print was the apparent disappearance of Guangzhou's children with disabilities. We had visited one of the city's secondary schools which we had been told was attended by all children in the district without any form of selection or discrimination. This sounded a very enlightened policy of inclusive education. What facilities and resources did the school have to care for special needs children, I wanted to know. The reply was that there were no children in the district whose vision, hearing, mobility or mental capacity was impaired. My wife was a professional social worker who specialized in rehabilitation. After listening to her complaints about Hong Kong's service shortfalls over the years, I had a fair recall of the statistics for the main disabilities per thousand of the population. So, I asked what had happened to the cohorts who must have been born with disabilities. The reply was an insistent denial that any special needs children could be found in the district.

That was a story that deserved to be followed up. Its explanation probably matched Hong Kong's historical experience. The colonial administration was insisting even in the 1950s that there was no need to provide for such children because those with disabilities were sent back to their parents' native villages in Guangdong. The border was steadily sealed off in that decade, which brought this practice to a halt. But Guangzhou perhaps was able to have such children transferred to the care of an extended family in the countryside. I was never to find out.

My 1973 trip resurfaced as a target for public criticism a quarter of a century later. In 1998, the late Choi Wai-hang, Chairman of the Chinese Reform Association, published an unflattering article about me. He had been detained without trial under colonial legislation in 1967. The *Review* objected vigorously to these detentions as a breach of civil liberties, with little success however. I came to know Choi personally through a family connection after his release. He was a very talented corporate executive and impressively adventurous as well as shrewd in his business projects as the mainland opened up to Hong Kong firms.

In 1998, he expressed regret about our acquaintance in a Hong Kong newspaper, explaining that he had always mistrusted me. What legitimate reason could there have been for the four volumes of the *Selected Works of Mao Zedong* on my office bookshelf, he inquired? This was a painful reminder to me of how limited had been the impact of my book about Mao's economics, whose starting point for me had been a laborious perusal of each of these volumes. Not by accident, I felt certain, among his other criticisms was an assertion that for nefarious reasons, I had urged him to get me a journalist's visa to report on the Canton Trade Fair. This newspaper piece took me back to 1973 and the fallout from my Guangdong tour.

There had been one more small reminder of Wales in the meantime. A good friend in the Bank of China group told me when our families met for "tea" one weekend in 1973 that he knew that while in Guangdong, I had done my note-taking in Welsh not English. "Please remember, Mr. Goodstadt, that if we truly wanted to see what you had written," he said quite matter of fact, "you can be sure in China, we could find someone who can translate very accurately." That sounded like a promise of truly VIP attention!

*Leo F. Goodstadt arrived at Hong Kong University in 1962 and later became deputy editor at the Far Eastern Economic Review. He spent 1989 to 1997 as the Head of Hong Kong Government's Central Policy Unit. He has published five books: from China's Search for Plenty: The Economics of Mao Tse-tung to the latest, Reluctant Regulators: How the West Created and China Survived the Global Financial Crisis.*

# Ezra F. Vogel
## *China Before the Deng Transformation (1973)*

I first traveled to China as a member of the first delegation of the US National Academy of Sciences from late May to mid-June 1973. We traveled for three weeks in Guangzhou, Shanghai, Nanjing, Hangzhou, and Beijing and were hosted everywhere by scientists.

I had been hoping to travel to China ever since I began studying China in 1961, three years after my PhD. I was trained as a sociologist whose research was based on intensive interviewing. I believed interviewing was important to try to understand people's thinking; I was trained to think of the big picture of societies by Talcott Parsons and I tried to link the bigger picture with a deeper understanding of people first hand. I had interviewed Italian-American, Irish-American, and old-American families in Boston for my PhD thesis which I completed in 1958, and then I had interviewed Japanese families in Japan from 1958-1960. In 1961 I was selected by some of my former professors to begin a three year post-doctoral fellowship at Harvard to study the Chinese language and history; I was told that if it worked out, I might later have a chance to become the first faculty member to offer courses on Chinese society at Harvard.

Before 1960 some American universities offered courses on Chinese language, literature, and history, but almost none offered courses on contemporary politics, economics, or society. After the Korean War in the late 1950s, the "red scare" led by Joseph McCarthy caused universities to fear offering courses on Communist China. Some professors were afraid to show an interest in China; foundations offered no grants for studying contemporary China for fear of being criticized for being "soft on communism." By 1961 the influence of McCarthy had begun to fade and foundations were prepared to support some of us from various disciplines to get the background needed to start university programs on contemporary China. I was excited by the opportunity to study such a large and important society that was so little understood. I believed, as did many other American intellectuals, that the United States must open relations with Communist China, that we and the Chinese people needed to understand each other to have a peaceful world, and that I could play a constructive role in furthering our understanding of China to help pave the way for Americans and Chinese to work together.

When the Committee of Concerned Asian Scholars was founded at Harvard, I became a member and supported the activities. Like other members, I believed that the United States was wrong to attack Vietnam, and I believed our country should pull out of the war. I was close to the graduate students who were a few years younger than I like Jim Peck, Victor Nee, Richard Bernstein, Tom Eberhardt, Perry Link, Andy Nathan. I remember once driving seven Harvard graduate students in my station wagon to Washington, DC where we made the rounds of government offices to complain of the Vietnam War and urge a quick ending. But my father was a Jew who found opportunities in the United States while his sisters and their families perished in the holocaust in Europe, and I was more positive on America than some of my students. Also, I did not share the rosy view of life in Communist China held by many of the radical students. I had done interviewing of former residents of Communist China in Hong Kong from 1963-64 and for several summers after that. I had also read through a decade's worth of *Nanfang Ribao* to understand the changes in China from 1949 to the mid-1960s. I was familiar with the ideals that Communist leaders had enunciated, but I had heard tales of the many good landlords who were killed along with the bad ones. I knew of the Anti-Rightist Campaign of 1957. I had read of problems among the leadership—of Gao Gang, and the attacks in 1966-67 on Peng Zhen, Yang Shangkun, Lu Dingyi, Luo Ruiqing and then of Liu Shaoqi and Deng Xiaoping. I did not know many details of the failure of the Great Leap Forward, but I knew that there was widespread starvation and forced labor. And through interviewing in Hong Kong, I was aware of the tight control over citizens' lives. And yet I wanted Chinese leaders to succeed, to make life better for their people, and wanted to help bridge the gap between China and America. I was envious of radical students who had visited China before I had an opportunity; in discussions with them, some said "How could you know about China if you have never been there?"

The National Academy of Sciences, a private organization of scientists, had promoted exchanges with scientific organizations around the world. Their Committee on Scholarly Communication with the People's Republic of China had been established in the late 1960s in the hopes of promoting exchanges between scholars of China and the United States. A number of the senior American scientists had former students who had returned to China and held key positions in China's scientific institutions. The scientists were overwhelmingly natural scientists but there were a small number of social scientists among them. On this first delegation to go to China, over thirty natural scientists and their wives took part, as well as four of us in the social sciences and humanities: Eleanor Sheldon, president of the Social Science Research Council; Al Feuerwerker, a Chinese historian at the University of Michigan; his wife Yitze, a specialist in Chinese literature; and myself.

The meetings with Chinese scientific organizations were formal and polite. We visited universities and scientific institutes and received briefings. It was easy to sense that many Chinese scientists were eager to promote exchanges, that they were distressed at the poor state of facilities in China, and wanted to carry on ordinary scientific research, and yet they were very cautious in saying anything that might reveal their personal desires. We felt deep sympathy for the Chinese scientists, and we tried to take precautions so that they did not get into political troubles with their minders who had made their lives so difficult.

When we visited Peking University, we were received by the Revolutionary Committee. Zhou Peiyuan, the distinguished scientist who had been in effect the president of the university, welcomed us, but when we were all seated, he said he did not understand the political situation and called upon his colleague, a PLA soldier, who then recited the political line of the Cultural Revolution. His talk was full of political clichés, and we all felt sorry for Zhou Peiyuan who had to yield to people like this soldier who knew nothing about higher education and nothing about science and who behaved haughtily toward scientists who did not share the correct revolutionary perspective. We visited the factory where students did part time work. They were doing some simple routine work, and when an American physics professor asked about one of the machines they were working with, the answer was so simple that a member of our delegation later confided to us that it was at the level of an American technical high school. When we visited the Nationalities Institute, we were given general presentations but it was painfully obvious that the researchers had not been given a chance to do field work for many years.

At one city, we were received only by natural scientists; none of our welcoming committee was a social scientist. When I asked our guide if this meant that natural science was considered more important, he replied that social science was also very highly regarded. At the next stop a social scientist was included in the welcoming committee, but the poor man was so afraid of making an error that every time I asked a question he quickly changed the subject to talk about the weather or the scenery.

Our visit was heavily programmed. We were well-fed and stayed at hotels built during the Soviet period. I tried to find opportunities to take walks in the early morning before our schedule began. When I stopped people on the street, even to ask directions, the people were so petrified that they quickly evaded and walked away. One of the best chances to talk with people was after the formal briefings as we walked around in smaller groups to observe the university or institute where we were taken. Once when we walked around, a professor who had given us a radical briefing as a member of the revolutionary group came up to walk beside me. He had clearly picked me out. He began by asking me if I were at Harvard and when I replied that I was, he confessed that he had studied at Harvard and asked if I knew what had happened to one of his American friends. When I told him I knew the person and told of his whereabouts, he was deeply moved. When I returned to the United States and called his friend to convey the news, the American friend was so moved that I could tell he was choked up to hear that after decades of worry, his close Chinese friend was still in good health.

Some radical American students were disillusioned at the tight control and the poor conditions they saw on their first trip to China. I was not disillusioned for I had been prepared for what I saw by my talks with former residents of China in Hong Kong. However, I was deeply happy to be able to visit first hand some of the communes, neighborhood associations, and buildings that I knew about. Yet a few things surprised me. I had been told of the success of the campaign to wipe out the four pests and was surprised at the use of mosquito nets, which made it clear that mosquitoes had not been eliminated. I had not expected ordinary people to be so frightened of talking with foreigners. I had not expected to see campuses still in such disarray. I was surprised how dark the streets were at night. Bikes did not have bike lights. There were no regular street lights, only a single small light bulb every one hundred yards or so, even on busy streets in places like Guangzhou and Shanghai. The streets were filled with bikes but almost no motorized vehicles except the small number of cars owned by work units, tractors, and the open trucks. In the outskirts of some cities, I saw horse-drawn vehicles. Virtually everyone wore the same cotton dark blue pants and jacket so one could not tell status by clothing. There were virtually no little stores in which to buy daily goods. When we visited a Shanghai neighborhood association, the women who represented the neighborhood were plainly dressed but it was easy to see they were bright and could under different circumstances have been lively leaders. When we heard the Shanghai symphony play, they played simple marches and Cultural Revolutionary music, but they did it with such verve that one could imagine that the older members could play far more difficult classical music if given the chance.

When I asked guides at places like Mao's Peasant Institute questions that showed some familiarity with an earlier period, the guide was unprepared to answer; he had no knowledge of the period. Sometimes the political line seemed so far from reality that I could not resist asking mischievous questions that reflected my improper political training. When I noticed some perfume in a department store, I asked the guide if some people regarded perfume as a sign of revisionism; he answered "No. It depends on the purpose to which the perfume is put." "Do some people who hate imperialism," I asked a particularly politically correct guide, "feel it difficult to accept foreigners riding in such luxurious cars?" "No," he said, "they have been taught to believe in the friendship of peoples."

Our delegation was welcomed in Beijing by Foreign Minister Qiao Guanhua. The next day we were told to wait in our hotel rooms for we might be able to meet an important leader. We all waited impatiently in our rooms and then assembled in a waiting room where we waited some more. We were then driven from the Beijing Hotel in our cars, all numbered in order by the rank of our members, to the Great Hall of the People where we were received for over two hours by Zhou Enlai. We did not then know that Zhou already had cancer, but he looked thin; we did not then know he was under political pressure, but he seemed somewhat tense as he talked about the struggles between the two lines. Although we did not meet Deng Xiaoping, we heard that he had recently returned from the countryside to Beijing and there was an air of anticipation that he would be returning to an important position and that he was someone who was capable of bringing greater order to China. In May 1973 there was hope in the air that scientists and universities might again resume their regular activities, but scientific institutes did not really carry on much research until 1975 and universities did not really reopen until late 1977.

I was enormously grateful to have had the opportunity to visit in 1973. I was able to take many photographs that I could show to my classes on China that gave a first-hand feel of the place I was lecturing about. In later years, I was even more grateful that I had been given a chance to see China when it was so poor, when people were so frightened to say anything, and when universities were still under the influence of the Cultural Revolution. It made it possible for me to have a vivid sense of the progress that China made in later years and to tell those Westerners who later complained about limitations on free discussion in China how much change had taken place in the years after 1978.

*Ezra F. Vogel is Henry Ford II Professor of the Social Sciences Emeritus at Harvard University. In 1973 he succeeded John K. Fairbank as the Director of Harvard's East Asia Research Center. He was later Director of Harvard's US-Japan Program, the Fairbank Center, and the founding Director of its Asia Center. His books include Canton Under Communism, Japan As Number One, One Step Ahead in China and Deng Xiaoping and the Transformation of China.*

# Andrew J. Nathan
*Nan De Hu Tu (1973)*

In 1972, a man named Jack Chen showed up in New York. He was the younger son of Eugene Chen, who had been an associate of Sun Yat-sen's and intermittently foreign minister for various Kuomintang governments. Jack's mother was Trinidadian. He grew up there and did not speak much Chinese. At some point he had gone to China and made a career at the Beijing Foreign Languages Press. Then he came to New York, for reasons I think none of us in the US fully understood. (He and his wife, Yuan-tsung Chen, subsequently wrote several books that explained parts of their story, including how they suffered during the Cultural Revolution.) He became associated in some way, if memory serves, with Columbia University, and then later became an advisor or consultant with the Department of Education of the State of New York, helping to develop curricular resources about China. In that capacity, Jack arranged for a group of New York State college teachers to visit China in July, 1973.

The trip was called the New York State Educators' Study Tour and involved about a dozen of us from Columbia, Cornell, Hunter, the University of Rochester, and other institutions. Like all foreign visitors at that time, we were overwhelmed with curiosity. We were seeing in person for the first time a vast and strange society we had known before only from the outside. We were accompanied everywhere by guides from the national and local offices of the China International Travel Service, who smothered us with a protocol that bore a faint edge of hostility. We responded with a respectful attitude of learning from the Chinese about their country's wonderful advances and visionary experiments in human organization and economic development.

On the first day we crossed the short bridge between Lo Wu and what was then called Shumchun (now Shenzhen) by foot, seeming to leave the real world behind and enter, as I wrote in my notes, "a kind of poster art; the costumes, the signs, the murals, are all exactly as one has seen them in posters." We went to the second floor of a damp, airy, fan-cooled concrete building and sat in white slip-covered chairs sipping tea while our luggage was inspected. We met our national-level guides, had lunch with plenty of watery beer, and boarded a train for a two-hour ride through the emerald countryside to Guangzhou. The following day began a three-week program of visits to production brigades, factories, industrial exhibitions, neighborhood committees, department stores, schools, universities, and the occasional classic tourist site, moving from Guangzhou to Beijing, then to Shanghai, Hangzhou, and back to Guangzhou. At each unit we sat in an arc of chairs or around a table, received a *jiandan jieshao* (simple introduction) from a "leading cadre," took detailed notes, asked earnest questions, and walked through the facility trying to peer behind the façade of Maoist correctness for signs of real life.

In Beijing, we were summoned one afternoon to a reception hall in the Nationalities Museum to meet with Chi Qun, the deputy head of the Science and Education Section (*Kejiaozu*) of the State Council. After the fall of the "Gang of Four," Chi Qun was revealed to have been one of their top followers. According to my notes, he was a slight young man in a full Mao suit, a silvery watch, and plastic sandals. The notes continue:

> *There was much of the imperial in the manner in which we were received by Mr. Chi. The meeting had no date fixed in advance; it met in a place that one would not have expected it to meet in [a reception room at the Nationalities Museum]; all the trappings of power (the elegance of the setting, the waiters pouring soda, the large body of retainers, and even the Mercedes limousine) were present to awe the visitor. Mr. Chi affected imperial elegance as he languidly sat upon the couch and put in occasional questions ('is it true that Columbia is the biggest university in New York?') to set his visitors at ease. Our submissions (ideas about exchange programs) are accepted but no answers are given. We are not even certain with whom we are dealing. Questions will be passed on to the 'proper authorities,' but we are not to know who these authorities are, nor are we to confront them directly.*

Going around the circle of guests, Chi invited me to describe my research, which at the time focused on late Qing reform ideology. After hearing part of my presentation he interrupted me. "You may be aware," he said, "that there was an attempt to make reforms in 1892, but the Empress Dowager cut off the heads of Kang Youwei and Liang Qichao." Someone at his side whispered to him. Chi then resumed, saying that the reform took place in 1898 and that the Empress Dowager wanted to cut off the heads of Kang and Liang but since they fled, she cut off the heads of their followers instead.

In Shanghai we visited Fudan University. With elderly professors seated in a row in back, we were briefed by a young man identified as a "leading member" of the revolutionary committee. He told us:

> Before the Great Proletarian Cultural Revolution, the struggle of two lines was acute, especially in universities. This school was basically going the revisionist road. Before 1962 especially, the authorities of the university intended to turn it into a Moscow University of Asia. Teaching methods, texts, and school organization followed the Soviet system. This made it impossible to train intelligent proletarians. So revolutionary teachers and students rose up in 1965-66 in opposition, and following the teaching of Chairman Mao, called for a shortened period of schooling and an end to the dominance of the educational field by the intellectuals.

Upon leaving this meeting, I gave one of the senior professors a copy of the Columbia graduate school catalogue and a recent publication of mine, a small research guide entitled *Modern China, 1840-1972: An Introduction to Sources and Research Aids*. About an hour later I was surprised to be called out of my hotel room by one of our guides from the national guide team together with the guide who had conducted us around the university. According to my notes:

> They handed *Modern China* back to me. 'As soon as you left, Prof. Hu looked this over and he noticed this'—pointing to an entry entitled *Gongfei Qiejuxia de Zhongguo Dalu Fensheng Ditu* (A Province-

*by-Province Atlas of the Communist Bandit-Occupied Chinese Mainland)—a Taiwan-published item that I had listed in the geography section of the bibliography. 'Seeing such language he felt very angry and cannot keep the book.' I said, 'I am sorry to have caused Prof. Hu any unpleasant feelings. This choice of words is not mine, but is simply the title of an item which I thought had value, and so included.' 'We understand that'—here they nodded and assumed friendly expressions to imply that no fault was imputed to me personally. Next morning on the bus the guide from Fudan makes a point of sitting with me and making small talk.*

During a two-and-a-half hour train ride from Shanghai to Hangzhou I interrogated two of our guides.

*Is the man in blue riding the train a Public Security person? 'Yes.' Why? 'Because we still have class struggle, and this is an important communications route, so they ride every train. There are two sections in Public Security, the jiaotongjing and the minjing. They are armed. They help kids and old ladies, help people locate relatives, register births, deaths, and changes of residence, and are the people's friends, not oppressors.'*

*…'When you Americans ask where are the Liu Shaoqi elements in every unit, we must laugh, because there are no such things. Cadres are mostly good. We don't throw them out for one or two errors but help them mend their ways.'*

*...What will happen when Mao dies? 'He's still in good health, for one thing. Secondly, we are now strengthening proletarian dictatorship and have driven out Liu Shaoqi. The danger of capitalist restoration still exists, but can be avoided by efforts now underway.' But what if Mao had died in 1964, Liu would have been in charge. 'Yes, but he didn't die then.' Who will issue directives to solve problems? 'We have a Party Center, you know.'*

Arriving in Hangzhou, we were taken by bus to the center of town and allowed to walk around.

*Strolling, I stumble upon a series of about six freshly plastered dazibao (big character posters) on a wall. I get photographs of two only. There are about five older ones, already torn and unreadable. The thrust of them, as I hastily read them, was that the danwei of the Dianxinju (Post and Telegraph Bureau) contained a capitalist jituan which was not giving equal work for equal pay and was not following the policy of 'educated youth to the mountains and countryside.'*

That night:

*Mr. Huang phones [my hotel room] and asks to see me. He is acting as an intermediary for the Shanghai comrades [guides from the Shanghai office of CITS had accompanied us to Hangzhou]. Several of the broad masses have called the hotel to say that a foreigner with a beard and glasses and short pants took a picture of a big character poster this afternoon, and shortly thereafter two other foreigners came by and also took photos.*

*(So far as I know, this latter had not actually happened.) Since the matter discussed in the wall poster is an internal affair, some of the masses are opposed to our having these pictures and for the sake of future friendship and to make future US travel to China easier, the Shanghai CITS asks for my film, which they will develop and cut out the offending picture.*

*I explain that wall posters are a sign of democracy. I bring out Hongqi #6 (which contains an article) on unity and openness. (Huang laughs before I locate the spot on the page and says, 'I know what you are going to say.') I explain about preprocessing [when I purchased the film I had also paid for processing]. Huang says apologetically that it is not he but the broad masses of Hangzhou who want the film. I ask if I can just have a copy of the textual content of the picture. 'Not very practical.' My final question is only whether I can make the remaining 30 exposures on the film before handing it in. He'll ask.*

I had brought only thirty rolls of film with me, and had taken many photographs. I hated to waste most of a good roll of film. After a short delay, permission to finish up the roll was granted. The next day, my Columbia colleague Jim Morley and I took a walk in the hills around Hangzhou. I filled the film with pictures of the scenery and handed it in to Mr. Huang that night.

Three days later the senior guide accompanying us from the national CITS office, Mr. Yu, who seldom dealt with us directly, asked for a private meeting with the head of our delegation, Ward Morehouse of the New York State Department of Education. (Our group had been required at the start of the trip to designate a leadership structure so that we could fulfill the protocol requirements of our visit.) "Since it has to do with Nathan, he should leave," Mr. Yu told Ward. Ward resisted but eventually agreed, stipulating however that he would share with me whatever was discussed. Coming out of the meeting he told me that only thirty shots had come out when my film was developed, all of them scenes of our walk in the hills. The six shots of the wall posters were missing.

Next I was called in to speak directly with the number two national guide, Mr. Huang:

> *He accuses me of cheating them (pian). He says I must think the Chinese are not bright enough to know the difference between the beginning and the end of a roll of film. He rejects my offer that he can develop all of my film. He only wants the 'right' roll. He and Mr. Yu are very angry, especially Mr. Huang, who keeps waving the developed roll and pacing. He explicitly accuses me of trying to get away with handing over a wrong roll, of hiding the 'correct' roll, which they accuse me of knowing how to find among my films. Everyone [else in my group] comes up from waiting for the bus. Mr. Huang tells the whole story to them in agitation. Refusing the offer of all rolls, he stalks from the room.*

Ward, as group leader, had already protested the taking of my film during two of the many formal meetings we held with the guides to negotiate aspects of our program. His line had been that "the incident reflects unfairly on Nathan and the group as a whole since it seems to suggest that we have some less than honorable purposes in visiting your country." To this, Mr. Yu had responded, "As the representatives accompanying you for the whole trip we regard this as a small issue which never extended to the whole of the group. But I must say that I receive many foreign tourist groups but most are only tourist sightseeing groups. Very few are like this group. Of course this is a new experience for us, so in our work there will inevitably be shortcomings."

Now that a crisis had emerged, our group split. Several members urged me to stop playing games and hand over the right roll of film. Ward and my Columbia colleague Jim Morley, among others, accepted that I was telling the truth when I said that through some technical glitch—honestly one that was hard to explain—I didn't have any pictures of the wall posters. I have never known for sure why this happened. My best guess is that I had loaded the film improperly, so that it didn't advance when I moved the lever, but that some jostling had settled the film onto the sprocket by the next day, so that it started advancing normally. We all waited nervously to see what would happen now. My notes continue: "Next day, we leave by air for Canton (Guangzhou). Mr. Huang asks me to help hand out the boarding passes. The Shanghai CITS comrades seem neither to seek nor to avoid shaking my hand on departure."

The rest of our trip went without incident and a week or so later we crossed back into Hong Kong with a feeling of giddiness at its brightness and buzz.

All of us learned a great deal on the trip, about how various kinds of institutions functioned and about ideological conformity. But a note made in Hangzhou crystallized my most lasting impression:

> *This is the long-desired trip to China, but there is quite a sense of boredom and frustration in the group. Our rate of learning has plummeted as units and briefings begin to be repeats of basic types. Access to the populace is out because one simply cannot be inconspicuous. As we walk around, many compounds that we pass are out of bounds—PLA units, government offices, etc. Even the former Yueh Fei tomb, still called 'Yueh fen' on the bus stop sign, is now an 'exhibition on class struggle' and is for neibu canguan only—no foreigners allowed. The photo incident suggests how the society as a unit keeps its eyes on us. Nobody will talk freely. I, for one, am reduced to interviewing our more articulate guides for applications of the latest line to specific issues.*

*Nan de hu tu*, says an ancient piece of Chinese wisdom ("Where ignorance is bliss, it is a folly to be wise"). For me, making sense of this first trip to China became a project of many years.

**Andrew J. Nathan** *is the Class of 1919 Professor of Political Science at Columbia University, where he has taught since 1971. His books include Chinese Democracy, Human Rights in Contemporary China (coauthored), The Great Wall and the Empty Fortress: China's Search for Security (coauthored), The Tiananmen Papers (coedited), China's New Rulers: The Secret Files (coauthored), and How East Asians View Democracy (coedited).*

# Business

## Business

### THOMAS D. GORMAN
*From Pinko to Running Dog (1975)*

With a sense of great excitement, on an early morning in April 1975, I embarked on the full day, eighty-mile train journey from Hong Kong to Guangzhou, starting from the old Kowloon train station next to the Star Ferry, where the clock tower stands today.

After seven years of Chinese studies in the US, I was excited at long last to be going someplace where Putonghua was widely spoken. I had obtained an invitation to attend the Canton Trade Fair as a member of the American Chamber of Commerce in Hong Kong's delegation, despite being the assistant editor of a Hong Kong-based trade magazine.

Invitations were not easy to come by, especially for journalists; and visas were only granted to those with invitations. In Hong Kong, invitations were issued by the local arm of the Ministry of Foreign Trade, China Resources, whose offices were then in the old Bank of China Building on Bank Street in Central District, where portraits of Marx, Lenin, Engels and Stalin welcomed visitors from above a pair of ping pong tables—premises currently occupied by the China Club.

Traveling from Hong Kong to Guangzhou required boarding the early morning train from the Kowloon station, which brought you into Luohu (Lo Wu) in time to connect with the afternoon train to Guangzhou. No other transport connection was available. This was before the era of airplane, ferry, and highway links. The fastest way to get from Hong Kong to Beijing involved taking the train to Guangzhou, and an overnight there in order to catch a flight the following day.

After clearing exit formalities on the Hong Kong side of the Shenzhen River at Luohu, passengers walked with their luggage across the quaint, covered wooden bridge—with the PRC flag waving ahead and the Hong Kong flag flapping behind—and began entry formalities on the China side.

There was a distinctly slower pace on the Chinese side. Emerging from the covered bridge, it felt as if a giant stereo turntable had been stepped down from 78 rpm to 16 rpm. Not only was the pace different, but also the sights, smells and sounds. The Shenzhen River was not very wide, as rivers go, but crossing it at that point brought you into a very different world.

From the windows of the train station complex on the Chinese side one gazed out at a sleepy farming community, one corner of a People's Commune, with wallowing water buffalo, ducks dotting mulberry tree-lined fish ponds, rice paddies, and low brick buildings. This hamlet was the forerunner of Shenzhen, although it wouldn't be named Shenzhen for another five years or so. This was Bao An.

The advertising billboards near the Hong Kong side of the border were replaced by political billboards on the mainland side, with messages like "We have friends all over the world," "In agriculture, learn from Dazhai," "Dig tunnels deep, store grain everywhere," "Long live Chairman Mao," "Serve the people," etc.

There were many forms to be filled out. The tempo of inbound customs and immigration formalities was slow, but the reward was a sumptuous twelve-course Chinese banquet served to all foreign guests within the cavernous low-rise train station complex. After lunch there was time to relax in a room filled with plush antimacassar-backed armchairs with spittoons at their base, beneath a huge Chinese landscape painting captioned "The Welcoming Guests Pine Tree." Light blue enamel ceiling fans whooshed lazily overhead.

The spittoons, long since disappeared, were a unique feature of the design motif of meeting rooms. The standard spittoon had a white enamel finish with a stripe of bright red trim around its mouth and a cheery blue floral pattern circling its bulbous midriff. They were the bass note in the triumvirate of receptacles which awaited visitors in every conference room: spittoons, porcelain-lidded tea cups, and ashtrays. Local cigarettes featured copious quantities of red in their packaging, with brand names like Worker-Peasant, Red Lantern, Bumper Harvest, Unite, Glorious, Great Production, Great Leap, Hero, Red Flag, and Labor.

After lunch and the rest break (everything ground to a halt during mid-day nap time), came the two and a half hour train trip to Guangzhou, which delivered passengers there between 3 and 4 p.m. The view from the train windows was overwhelmingly agricultural: no paved roads or high-rise buildings, virtually no factories, and few mechanized vehicles.

At the train station in Guangzhou I was met by a representative of my host organization. Chinese people who had reason to talk to foreigners, and approval to do so, introduced themselves by surname only. Strictly speaking, the proper term of address was "Comrade," as in Comrade Li, Comrade Wang, etc.

Name cards were not yet in use among the Chinese side, ostensibly because they would have divulged an excessive amount of potentially sensitive information, such as names, addresses, and phone numbers. For ordinary Chinese to be accused of having unauthorized contact with foreigners (*li tong wai guo*) was a very serious matter indeed, which meant that the emphasis was on institutional rather than individual communications. Spontaneous street-level conversations with foreigners carried serious risks for local Chinese. The weather report was classified because it was deemed to be sensitive information of potential value to hostile foreign military forces.

All foreigners were mandated to stay in the Dong Fang Hotel. To find a friend or colleague in the hotel required checking the cork bulletin boards in the lobby, where each new arrival would post a business card with his room number scrawled on it. There were no telephones or air conditioners in the rooms. The best rooms, in the Old Wing of the Dong Fang, were more spacious and came equipped with a tent-like mosquito net which hung over the bed.

The telephone played virtually no role in doing business in China at the time. Instead, telex, telegrams and letters—all impersonally addressed to avoid getting the Chinese recipient in trouble—were the available communications conduits for the conduct of commerce. A private telephone was such a rarified, elite device that the telephone book was also considered a state secret.

China's total foreign trade volume was a pittance—her total imports and exports in 1973 were less than US$11 billion. That's roughly equivalent to the volume of her luxury goods imports alone in 2010—which represents a staggering degree of qualitative as well as quantitative change in less than forty years.

In 1975, all foreign trade and economic decisions were concentrated among a handful of high-level bureaucrats in Beijing, and implemented through twelve highly centralized, monopoly state-owned import-export corporations under the Ministry of Foreign Trade. Foreign trade was largely an extension of foreign policy, and viewed as a kind of necessary evil.

Foreign investment was taboo. Words like "advertising," "marketing," and "competition" were regarded with obvious disdain, trumped only by the ultra-sinister word "profit."

The Dong Fang Hotel during the trade fair housed a motley collection of people from every corner of the globe. Gaggles of folks wearing colorful native costumes shuttled between meals in the hotel restaurant and the sprawling trade fair complex situated across Xicun Road. The incredible diversity of the delegates was a bit reminiscent of the intergalactic bar scene in "Star Wars," except that bars were not permitted in China at the time.

Delegates were required to wear pink ribbons on their lapels, demonstrating they were authorized to enter the trade fair complex. The pink lapel ribbons added a festive, slightly comical touch, as if the wearer had won the competition at a county fair for growing the biggest pumpkin or baking the best apple pie.

After arriving in the Dong Fang that first afternoon, and filling out another small forest worth of forms, in a room dedicated to form-filling for foreigners, it was almost time for dinner. Meals were served at fixed times, with set menus. Good, cold Tsingtao beer was available; Coca Cola and coffee were not. Foreign guests were fed like kings and queens compared to ordinary Chinese people, who could be seen queuing at food shops around the city with ration tickets in hand.

Then it was time for an early evening. There was no place to go after dinner other than sit and talk with colleagues, send telexes, play table tennis or billiards. An upstairs dining room in the new wing of the Dong Fang was converted into an ersatz bar serving local beverages, which regulars affectionately nicknamed "The Purple Cockatoo," fantasizing about a far more enticing ambience than that which actually awaited them: hospital green walls, bright white lights, and plain cotton tablecloths.

So, that first evening I turned in early, excited about what the next day might bring. Finally, after all these years of study, my first full day in China lay just ahead of me.

My first trip to China had unlikely origins at an unlikely time: in the suburbs of Chicago, during the 1960s.

In the summer of 1966, the US and China were ensconced in a hostile, non-conversational relationship. China was in the early stages of the Cultural Revolution. American news media at the time referred to the mainland as Red China or Communist China.

Against that backdrop, that summer I received an IBM print-out from my high school suggesting that my second year courses would include Mandarin Chinese. For a high schooler in the American Midwest in the mid-1960s to study the language of Red China was considered weird at best, and possibly suspect. The anti-Communist witch-hunts of the McCarthy era were very fresh in people's memories.

One neighbor, commenting on my studying Chinese, asked me what I was going to do with that when I grew up: open a laundry, or a take-away joint? Another warned of possible communist brainwashing buried in the language texts. Some peers gave me nicknames which would be considered politically incorrect today.

I didn't realize that my study of Chinese was part of a new but temporarily short-lived trend. During the mid-1960s, more than three hundred American secondary schools (and a handful of primary schools) began offering Chinese language courses, mainly as a result of federal funds made available under the National Defense Education Act. NDEA provided funding for new programs in Chinese, Arabic, Russian, and Japanese studies, because these four groups were deemed most likely to be on the wrong side of future military conflicts with the US.

My high school was one of three in the Chicago area to get on the early Chinese language bandwagon. Within a few years, however, the NDEA funding for these programs had expired, and most of them were discontinued. My timing was thus fortunate. After three years of Chinese in high school, I became an East Asian Studies major at Princeton.

Imagine, then, my shock and awe that humid April morning in Guangzhou, when I was rudely awakened at 6 a.m., by piercingly loud, searingly shrill broadcasts from loudspeakers in the streets outside the window of my room in the new wing of the Dong Fang Hotel. What a way to start the day, with the latest thoughts of Chairman Mao recited by a high-pitched female announcer in a staccato style reminiscent of a dentist's drill. That particular morning, her focus was on denouncing Confucius, Lin Biao, and—much closer to home—American Imperialists and their running dogs.

I looked out the window to see a river of blue and gray Mao-jacketed bicyclists for whom this breakfast broadcast was a regular daily routine.

"Down with American Imperialists and Their Running Dogs!" (*Dadao meidiguo zhuyi jiqi zou gou!*)

There was some solace in the fact that I could understand most of the message, which proved my Chinese language studies had not been in vain. On the other hand, it was not exactly a welcoming message, especially given the method, volume and tone of its delivery.

Still only half awake as the harsh denunciation sunk home, I thought to myself: "I'm pretty sure I'm not an imperialist… but I'm not so sure what exactly constitutes a running dog."

The irony hit hard. A few years ago at home, I'd been teased about studying the language of Red China, marginally at risk of being labeled a pinko or commie sympathizer. Now that my journey had finally brought me to China, it seemed I was being labeled an imperialist running dog.

All meetings, with Americans at least, were scripted to begin with a critical political diatribe from the Chinese. Especially given the lack of business cards or job title information from the Chinese side, it was always a guessing game as to who the senior person on their side was.

Interpreters on the Chinese side were generally young and understandably lacking in international experience. Given the politics of the day and its impact on language instruction, they were more familiar with British than American English. Language misadventures and snafus were commonplace.

In one long, tedious meeting between my American Chamber of Commerce delegation and a fairly senior Chinese foreign trade official, our delegation leader rattled off a long laundry list of practical trade issues. The young Chinese interpreter rendered these into Chinese with a fair degree of fluency, although he was clearly becoming fatigued as the detailed laundry list dragged on through the afternoon heat and humidity. At one point the Chinese official said something to the effect that perhaps in due course the "relevant departments" might consider looking into the matter.

At this stage the impatient American interlocutor, fond of using big business slang, responded "That sounds fine, Comrade, but I sure hope someone's actually gonna put wheels under it."

The weary interpreter took that to mean that the American now had a proposal regarding the automotive industry. This elicited a barely tolerant grunt from the Chinese official, and from that point on, the conversation veered off into a series of non-sequiturs in the remote reaches of outer space. Both groups left the meeting in a state of puzzlement.

My return to Hong Kong after this first visit to China elicited a wave of curious questions from friends and associates, no doubt similar to what astronaut Neil Armstrong must have faced after his return from the moon.

I consider myself very fortunate to have witnessed that extraordinary stage of China's history first hand. I've lived in Hong Kong and continued my travels in China ever since that trip. Those early experiences have been very helpful to the process of appreciating the phenomenal changes in China since that era.

*Thomas D. Gorman has been a Hong Kong resident since 1974. His company, CCI Asia-Pacific Ltd., has published FORTUNE China under exclusive license from Time Inc. since 1996. He is the Chairman and Editor-in-Chief of the magazine, which is published nineteen times per year in print.*

## John Kamm
*Shanghaied at the Feather and Down Minifair (1976)*

I left America for Macau in August 1972, and by the end of 1975 I had lived most of the time in Hong Kong, but hadn't had an opportunity to travel to the mainland. My chance came in January 1976 when, as a freshly minted representative of the National Council for US-China Trade, I was asked to go to Shanghai to attend the China Feather and Down Garments Minifair put on by the China National Native Produce and Animal By-Products Import and Export Corporation (CHINATUHSHU). My visa only came through at the last possible moment, enabling me to make the flight to Shanghai from Guangzhou on January 6.

After crossing the border at Lo Wu, and waiting for several hours in the train station's dining area from which one could view a drab farming village (the future Shenzhen) in the distance, I and fellow trade fair attendees took the train up to Guangzhou. I was accompanied by a young American entrepreneur who had become a leader in manufacturing down garments, then quite the rage in America, and an Australian businessman and scholar and his wife. Upon arrival at the Guangzhou train station we hopped into grey Shanghai sedans for the run to the airport. We arrived at Hong Qiao Airport in Shanghai after nightfall, but there was no one to receive me.

Eventually Mr. Ma from the Shanghai Foreign Affairs Bureau materialized and I was taken to the Shanghai Mansions, the old Broadway

Mansions, where the trade fair was taking place. I was given an immense apartment with balconies overlooking the Whampoo, Suzhou Creek and the Bund. There was a big radio circa early 1940s in the living room.

The next day, January 7, I visited the trade fair itself, and registered with the liaison office. One of my jobs was to write an article on the minifair for the National Council's magazine, so I put in a request for an interview with the trade fair's leadership. My request received a cool reception. I was told to go to my room and wait for an answer. This was a sensitive time for people doing business in China, and minifairs, an innovation introduced as a modest reform in 1975, were under fire as examples of the "roots of capitalism" being introduced by Deng Xiaoping. I wondered if I would get an interview in Shanghai, or have to wait until I got to Beijing, where a Fur Products Minifair was about to open.

Rather than heeding the liaison office's instructions, I decided to take a walk along the Bund and up Nanjing Road. I have always visited bookstores on trips to China, and my first trip was no exception. I walked into the large Xinhua Bookstore on Nanjing Road, passing through thick canvas curtains meant to shield the building from the bitter cold outside. Upstairs I walked into the room that held internal publications sold only to cadres with the right documents. I was quickly and unceremoniously told to leave.

I wandered back to the hotel, stopping first at the office of the Hong Kong Shanghai Bank, located in a small building on a side street not far from the compound housing the Friendship Store and the Seamen's Club.

The compound had previously served as the sprawling British Consulate in Shanghai. I was greeted by the bank's British manager with more than the usual British reserve. He and his colleague from the Standard Chartered Bank were at the time the only resident foreign businessmen in Shanghai. Unfortunately they could not conduct business. They were in effect hostages of the Chinese government to insure that China's holdings with the banks wouldn't be expropriated. Their colleagues had in fact been detained during the early years of the Cultural Revolution. They couldn't leave Shanghai until new colleagues arrived to replace them. The fellow I met expressed relief that he would be ending his assignment later that year.

I decided to stop by the Friendship Store, a dreary place selling shoddy goods far below the quality found in Hong Kong's Chinese products stores. I then walked over to the Seamen's Club. In those days these establishments were the hubs of entertainment for foreigners in China. They served cold beer and one could almost always find a sailor willing to tell tall tales of his visits to China. I struck up a conversation with a young Hong Kong sailor who was working on a tramp steamer registered in Hong Kong and operated under the Chinese flag. Together we went back to the Shanghai Mansions where we had a simple dinner and played pool for several hours, drinking beer and eating peanuts. The young sailor told me of his life on a PRC-owned vessel. He complained about the incessant political study sessions he and his fellow seamen had to endure. I listened attentively. Apparently, others were also listening attentively.

The next day, January 8, I was advised that my request for an interview would be granted. I was told to come to a room on the top floor of the Shanghai Mansions at 10 p.m. I spent some time putting together my questions, and then prepared to join a tour of a Shanghai Commune. When I tried to sign up for the tour however, I was told that I was not welcome to join it. I protested to the liaison office to no avail. I headed out on another walk, this time witnessing the arrest of a Shanghai citizen by a police officer. The officer frog marched the young man down a narrow alley, attracting a throng of curious onlookers.

I went back to the Shanghai Mansions, had dinner, and waited in my room for the interview. At the appointed hour I went to the assigned room and found about two dozen cadres waiting for me. The interview was a formal affair, no smiles or words of greeting. I was told the ground rules. I would first ask all my questions. Thereafter I would be given a brief introduction to the trade fair. No further questions would be entertained. I must have asked thirty or so questions, after which I was given the brief introduction. Few if any of my questions would be answered. The "brief introduction" started out with words of praise for the wise leader Chairman Mao Zedong and the correct policies of the Chinese Communist Party. I was then given the bare bones facts of the trade fair: how large the exhibition space was, how many provincial animal by-products branches were in attendance, how many traders from which foreign countries were in attendance. That was it.

I tried to slip in one more question. In 1975 China agreed for the first time to sew into garments intended for export the labels of the western company that had ordered them, according to their specifications. This was a welcome reform as Chinese labels like Peony, Snowflake and the like didn't appeal much to American and European consumers. Suddenly, at this minifair, traders had been advised that this policy had been cancelled. No more foreign labels would be sewn into Chinese-made garments. There was much unhappiness about this sudden change, and I wanted to ask a question about why this step had been taken. I never got a chance to do so. I was cut off and reminded that there would be no more questions and told that the interview was over.

Shortly after I returned to my room the phone, an old black apparatus with a solid feel, started ringing. It was the young sailor I had befriended the night before. His voice was shaking, and I guessed he had company sitting nearby. Obviously distressed, he told me that he was leaving Shanghai early, and that I was not to try to contact him. He told me he would always remember our friendship. He rang off. A cold shiver ran up my spine.

I went to bed, but had trouble falling asleep. In the early hours of January 9, I heard a great commotion taking place on the barges on Suzhou Creek below me. Loud voices and the sounds of fighting. I dozed off and when I awoke I saw the streets lined with military vehicles, and all the barges gone. In the distance I could hear the somber music of a funeral dirge. I left my room and encountered an elderly floor attendant. "What has happened?"

I asked. He told me that Zhou Enlai had died. He was weeping.

I and other trade fair attendees went to the liaison office to find out more. The officer solemnly announced the premier's passing, and then told us that "the Chinese people will turn grief into strength" and that they would carry on the great traditions of the revolutionary leader. There would not be interruption to the trade fair. Business as usual.

I went down to the lobby and ran into my Australian friend and his wife. They had just had a harrowing experience. They had gone for a walk and saw crowds of people reading the newspapers which had been posted on wooden bulletin boards. They were reading official news of Zhou's death, and the couple decided to photograph the scene. Bad move. In those days it was against the law for foreigners to purchase or even read local newspapers like *Wen Wei Bao* and *Liberation Daily*. The couple were swiftly taken into custody by the local neighborhood revolutionary committee and held in a small room until the police showed up. They were interrogated and lectured at length. Their actions were unlawful and violated the terms of their visit to China. They were eventually escorted back to the Shanghai Mansions.

A small group of us decided to try another restaurant for lunch, having sampled just about everything on the Shanghai Mansions' menu. We walked to the Peace Hotel and took the elevator up to the dining floor. Sitting down, we noticed that the waiters were wearing black arm bands. One of the young men came to our table and explained: "We have been told not to commemorate Zhou Enlai's death, but we are doing so anyway. We are not afraid. Let them come and try to make trouble."

The next day I flew to Beijing where I attended the fur minifair, and visited one of the model communes on the city's outskirts as well as, of course, the Great Wall and the Ming Tombs. I also took part in the funeral of Zhou Enlai as a member of the American delegation. Diplomats were all dressed in black, thin clothing for the bitter cold. China would be visited with much more sorrow that year: the campaign against the right deviationist wind; the Qing Ming protests and the deadly response; the July earthquake in Tangshan; and much joy when the "Gang of Four" was overthrown in October. I witnessed all of those events, making six visits to the country that year.

Upon my return to Hong Kong after attending Zhou's funeral I was asked by a friend at *Ta Kung Pao* to write a eulogy for the recently departed premier. I did so, and the piece ran under my Chinese name given to me by a teacher in the United States: Kang Youhan. The eulogy was full of praise for Zhou. A few days after it appeared my friend told me that the article had been removed from the *Reference News* edition published in Shanghai. My friend suggested that I adopt a new name for any future Chinese language articles I might write. I adopted the name Kang Yuan, and have kept it to the present day.

## Postscript

More than 30 years later, I took members of the board of The Dui Hua Foundation to Shanghai. We went to the restaurant at the top of the Peace

Hotel, and there I recounted the story of the defiant young waiter. Across the room I spied a man of roughly my age who was now the manager of the restaurant. He looked familiar, and I asked him to come to our table. He complied, and we quickly figured out that he was that young waiter I had encountered in January 1976. In excited voices we relived what had happened. Misty eyed, he asked me a favor. Would I be willing to come back and talk to his young charges? "Young people have no idea how we lived then. And they aren't interested. You can help. Please come back." I agreed to do so, but when I returned a few months later the restaurant was closed for renovation. I subsequently found out that Mr. Zhang the manager had retired.

*John Kamm is an American businessman and human rights campaigner who has been active in China since 1972. He is the founder and chairman of The Dui Hua Foundation, a non-profit organization dedicated to advancing the protection of universally recognized human rights in China and in the United States. He was awarded the Department of Commerce's Best Global Practices Award by President Bill Clinton in 1997 and the Eleanor Roosevelt Award for Human Rights by President George W. Bush in 2001. In 2004, he was awarded a MacArthur Fellowship.*

# HELMUT SOHMEN
*Realizing a Pipedream in Thirty Years (1981)*

Having lived in Hong Kong for four years (1970-1974), my wife and I moved to Bermuda and then London on company assignments; then, charged with new responsibilities, we returned to Hong Kong in early 1982. One year earlier, in 1981, I had visited Beijing for the first time in the company of my father-in-law Sir Y.K. Pao and other members of my wife's immediate family. The policy of opening the country to the outside world had only recently started. China still gave the impression of uniformity, inadequate infrastructure, and control. The Mao-style uniforms were much in evidence with both men and women, and the army of bicyclists was the second major impression. Cars were definitely scarce. Today, of course, China builds many millions a year.

I arrived from Paris on flight AF188 at 16:35 hours on July 3. Emerging from the aircraft into the summer heat, I encountered a gentleman half-way down the airbridge in shorts, sandals, and a short-sleeved white shirt, holding onto an old briefcase. He said my name and I thought at first he was a driver sent to fetch me. I followed him to the immigration and baggage hall in the old terminal where we collected my suitcase. Inspection procedures were informal but certainly more thorough than today. When we got to the outside and into a waiting car, I realized my first mistake: the kind gentleman was not a driver but the Deputy Managing Director of the shipbuilding section of the Sixth Machinery Ministry. He clearly was educated and spoke passable English. I quickly dropped any preconceived ideas I had about the country and its residents.

I was driven to a state guest house in Beijing which, I learned later, had served as the Italian legation in pre-war times. Two PLA soldiers guarded the main entrance gate: unaccompanied individual entry and exit—I was to discover quickly when I tried to leave the compound for a brief walk— was not allowed. The safety of VIP guests was obviously of paramount importance. The house was old-fashioned but roomy and clean and reasonably cool. Staff was very much in sight at all times since bedroom doors remained unlocked. Staff duties seemed to include 24-hour service, including restoring to shelves items that had been thrown into the wastepaper basket. The hot water piping was antiquated but in the summer proved to present no real problem. The family had dinner on the premises, like in Hong Kong more food than one could eat.

The immediate reason for the trip was the groundbreaking ceremony, held the next morning, for a new hotel in the city, to be called Zhaolong Hotel to honor Sir Y.K.'s father, Pao Siu-long. Funds for the construction had been made available by Y.K. Pao to the Central Government to assist with early efforts in promoting tourism. The principal person officiating at the ceremony was Madame Chen Muhua, a formidable lady who subsequently became Governor of the People's Bank of China. The construction site, at a street junction in Chaoyang District, was a mud field rather unkind to normal footwear. A sea of ragged blue, red, yellow and white flags affixed to bamboo stakes in a fairly random order surrounded a clutch of shovels at the periphery, eventually used to turn over lumps of soil. Apart from the attending party, a small group of rather bored onlookers from the neighborhood had assembled to watch proceedings. They could hardly imagine the transformation that would take place at that street corner and in the District generally over the next twenty years. Neither would most of the visitors.

In the evening we were invited to a banquet in the Great Hall of the People which, especially then, took one's breath away given the grandeur of the approach via Tiananmen Square and the size and furnishings of the building itself. Cavernous meeting rooms, large murals, heavy sofas, incessant tea service imposed themselves on the visitor. I did not keep a record of the personalities in attendance, nor was I able to follow the conversations in Mandarin. Jet lag and the liberal portions of Mao Tai being poured no doubt created an exotic atmosphere conducive to personal relaxation. On subsequent trips I perfected the art of keeping the liquor down, so much so that later I was often asked to become the official toaster for groups in whose company I found myself traveling in the country. I also learned later that not every cup being consumed at these official get-togethers actually was Mao Tai, with the hosts sensibly trying to stay more sober than the visitors.

The following morning we were given a drive to the Ming Tombs on the way to the Great Wall. Restoration of the latter had only just begun, and the trip there took quite some time through a few local villages, avoiding bicyclists and the multitude of overloaded three-wheeled light tractors belching black smoke. For the first time in my life I experienced vehicles on two narrow lanes pretending there was a third lane for overtaking. A few hawker stalls along the entrance to the Wall were reminiscent of Shau Kei Wan in Hong Kong. The short walk then possible on the Wall was overshadowed by the guide's description of its history and the scale of achievement it represents; in 1981 the reality was not even a well-organized construction site. The mythical statues on the pot-holed road to the Ming Tombs looked rather forlorn in the midst of untended greenery; impressive but isolated. None of us imagined that the area would be graced by a golf course not all that many years later. Back to Beijing for an informal dinner.

A new dawn brought a morning visit to the Forbidden City—nothing compared to the masses of tourists now visiting this center of China on a daily basis. The guide moved us quickly through the courtyards and palaces for a superficial impression, creating the urge to come back and linger in the corners, absorb the perspectives, think of the history of this incredible place and the people previously inhabiting it. The reason for the rush was a scheduled appointment with China's leader Deng Xiaoping at 10 a.m. The slacks, short-sleeved white shirt, and easy smile came as a surprise when greeting the famous statesman. Deng Xiaoping was small in stature but big in his radiance as a personality, a man who knew himself and what he wanted, always curious, always argumentative, always probing. I was given a smart lady interpreter to help me follow proceedings, which consisted mainly of the dialogue between Y. K. Pao and Deng Xiaoping, with an occasional interjection or response to questions by others in the room. Many years later I met a lady in Hong Kong at a reception given by the Bank of China. She happened to be the wife of the bank's manager and cheerily asked if I remembered her from Beijing. She had been the interpreter and I felt honored.

From Beijing we traveled to Shanghai on July 7. The city looked stuck in time, barely reflecting its glory as China's commercial metropolis before the Great War of which old photographs gave adequate proof. Overpopulated old houses, inadequate drainage systems, narrow alleyways, and tired-looking commuters in jam-packed buses created a depressing image. Even the majestic buildings along the Bund looked neglected and worn out. Yet a dinner with Mayor Wang Daohan—the first of many over subsequent years—provided an uplift. Clearly the idea of reform and renewal had taken hold in China already, and plans for urban improvement and the resurrection of the city were being discussed. The constant pace of change keeps accelerating, especially in Shanghai, culminating in the 2010 World Expo. The next day we also visited Jiaotong University, to which Y.K. Pao would ultimately donate a new library, before setting off on a sightseeing trip to the canal and garden city of Suzhou in Jiangsu Province on July 9.

A first trip to China is unforgettable for all visitors. A visit before modernization had fully started was particularly memorable as it has allowed comparing old with new, giving a yardstick to measure the speed of progress, and a chance to marvel at what collective effort chasing ambitious targets can achieve in just one generation. China has become a global model. The country has of course not yet solved all its problems, and new ones are emerging all the time. But China is well on the way to realizing many of the things which in 1981 looked to be no more than a pipedream.

*Helmut Sohmen is an Austrian lawyer who came to Hong Kong from Canada in 1970, when he joined the World-Wide Shipping Group founded by Y.K. Pao. He became Chairman of this large shipping enterprise in 1986 while also serving in the Hong Kong Legislative Council. He was a non-executive Deputy Chairman of the Hongkong and Shanghai Banking Corporation, and International Chairman of the Pacific Basin Economic Council.*

# William H. Overholt
*Through a Glass Darkly: Assessing China's Early Reforms (1982)*

My first trip to China came about in an interesting way. When the Chinese set up their UN mission in New York, the PLA officers stationed there immediately started creating a network of knowledgeable people to talk with. Since their priority concern was their warm war with the Soviet Union, they first contacted Donald Zagoria, an expert on the Sino-Soviet dispute. They asked him to introduce them to someone from the Hudson Institute and he introduced me. They asked me to introduce someone from the (hard line anti-Soviet) Committee on the Present Danger, so I introduced Don Brennan. Don introduced Eugene Rostow, who introduced James Schlesinger.

We had periodic lunches and dinners at the Mission, across the street from Lincoln Center. These meetings were straight-talking, informative and fruitful. After I moved from Hudson Institute to Bankers Trust, they invited me to bring a friend from the bank. I brought the head of the International Department, David Sias, and when they heard he was coming they had the Bank of China representative in Washington, DC fly up for the dinner. With military intermediation, we resolved our local frozen assets problem. Bankers Trust had held US$500,000 of frozen Chinese assets in a checking account since 1949, in percentage terms the most profitable account in the bank. The Chinese wanted their money back with five percent simple interest—about US$1 million. As a banking matter, this was an almost incredibly modest demand, but Bankers Trust's lawyers said it was illegal to pay any interest at all on a checking account. The Chinese said we should have moved it to a savings account. The lawyers responded that it was illegal to move frozen funds to a different account. The Chinese said, no business until you repay us with interest. Impasse. Over dinner, I noted that, while it was illegal to pay interest on a checking account, it was common practice in US savings banks to offer a new customer a toaster for opening an account. In lieu of a toaster, how about US$1 million as an incentive for the Chinese to open a new account with us? We went back to the bank and came up with three options for them, of which the million dollar "toaster" was the least lucrative. But they had been instructed to come back with one million dollars, so they stuck with the least lucrative option. For the first few years, being bankers for China was incredibly frustrating for my colleagues; later, when, thanks to a brilliant dealmaker named Peter Kwok, we became for a number of years the most profitable foreign bank dealing with China, the million dollar toaster proved to be one of Bankers Trust's best investments ever.

At another dinner, in 1979, the most friendly general (technically they didn't have ranks at that time, but we knew their jobs) pulled me aside and said they were going to have to punish Vietnam for what it had done to Cambodia. He said they would invade, go as far as a particular village (whose name I've long forgotten) and then withdraw. I sent a note to Mike Armacost at the Pentagon, who replied with a note that said, Bill, thanks, that was a really good memo. We now know, of course, that President Carter got this same information directly from an even better source, namely Deng Xiaoping. The Chinese did exactly what they had told us they would do, albeit at a horrific unanticipated cost.

Sometime after they got their network fully in place, they began inviting us to China in reverse order; we had to pay for the trip to China but they would take care of all the internal arrangements. Schlesinger was first and, as the most senior, was taken to Tibet. I couldn't go until 1982, when I, insufficiently senior for Tibet, was escorted around Beijing, Xian, Chengdu, Hangzhou and Shanghai.

When I finally got Bankers Trust permission to go to China, I kept asking my hosts for a detailed itinerary and, to my annoyance, kept not getting one. I didn't discover why until I got to Chengdu.

In Beijing, my hosts of course took me to the Great Wall, the Forbidden City, the Ming Tombs (then fully open to visitors), the Summer Palace and the Temple of Heaven, as well as, inevitably, the Friendship Store. The historical monuments impressed as much as they were intended to. Equally impressive, with a different valence, was the emptiness of Beijing's wide streets—almost no cars. Everyone wore the same blue/gray clothing, except that some adventurous mothers had started dressing their babies in bright colors, especially bright red. I took lots of pictures of these little bits of brightness beginning to shine through the dreariness.

Policy discussions were mainly in an unusual format. Each night, my escort throughout the trip, Colonel Wang, would knock gently on my guest house door after dinner and come in for an hour or two to educate me about Chinese views of the world. He was invariably pleasant and conversational. No intense controversies, no browbeating. Not much that I hadn't read back home, not much that changed my mind about things, but his tutorials were concise and pleasant and they crystallized and gave context to what I had read. Colonel Wang explained to me that his main interest in being my host was to improve his English, which was clear and understandable but quite hesitant. The counterpoint to his pleasant tutoring was my gradual realization that, if I asked a question of Chinese officials, I would get the same answer, using pretty much the same words, anywhere in China. Given the almost insuperable difficulties of communication throughout the country at the time, this was both a formidable achievement and a somewhat frightening one.

Since I now worked for a bank, I requested a meeting at Bank of China. Colonel Wang took me to see the head of the International Department. After pleasantries, I began a monologue about the wondrous, technologically sophisticated things Bankers Trust could do for Bank of China. He politely interrupted and said, actually the kind of banking assistance they needed was advice on how to cash a check when they go to New York. It's been a long way from there to today, when China has four of the world's ten largest banks.

I had told my hosts that I wanted to see a rural village outside each city we visited. So one day we drove outside Beijing to visit a happy, rotund, red-faced, prosperous-looking peasant in his pleasantly accoutered home with, for instance, a comfortable sofa and a television. The picture on his wall of him with a previous visitor, Richard Nixon, indicated that his comfortable home was a frequent stop on the Potemkin circuit.

In Xian, Colonel Wang took me to the usual spots: the terra cotta warriors; the park built for Tang Dynasty courtesan Yang Guifei; the spot where Chiang Kai-shek was kidnapped. Photographing the terra cotta warriors was prohibited, but I was determined to get some pictures and had some sophisticated camera equipment that I thought would do the trick for me. It didn't. The guards knew all the tricks. I bought some paintings of Yang Guifei, looking like a slim contemporary Beijing beauty, only to be disillusioned subsequently by the realization that Tang guys liked their beauties seriously hefty.

Outside the terra cotta warriors exhibit, there was a crowd of peasants vigorously marketing children's jackets, mostly bright red with green fabric frogs sewn onto them. Colonel Wang was mortified by what he saw as aggressive incivility on their part. I laughed, told him that people from capitalist countries understood and respected entrepreneurs trying to sell their wares, and bought jackets to take home to my daughters.

Colonel Wang took me to a ballet. It was based on a traditional Chinese story, and the dancers were conservatively clothed, but it was considered very daring. This was one of many little cultural breakthroughs and signs that people were pushing back the Maoist limits. I imputed great significance to the fact that Colonel Wang made a point of showing me some of these in each place. He showed me temples and cultural sites, showing me how the Red Guards had destroyed much of China's precious cultural heritage but that Zhou Enlai had protected one temple in each city and much else.

In Chengdu, we moved into the Jin Jiang Hotel. Kim Il Sung had just been there, so the place was all prettified. I had some laundry done; the hotel brochure proudly proclaimed its one-day laundry service. My shirts came back at the end of the day in a plastic bag full of soapy water. The one-day laundry service for this large hotel was provided by one shirtless, sweaty old guy in a room as hot as a sauna scrubbing the clothes of a huge number of guests against a washboard. He had been ordered to provide one-day laundry service and he did, no extra charge for the soapy water.

I also learned at this time why I hadn't been able to get my itinerary six weeks in advance. The hotel's communications with Beijing consisted of one telex machine, and the telex machine consisted of an ancient 1930s-style typewriter with a wire painstaking strung from each key. So primitive were communications that the senior army people making my reservations could not simply call up and make a reservation. They had to dispatch a letter requesting rooms; when they arrived in town, their local colleagues would take us to the available hotel. Quite a difference from today—Huawei trying to cut a major telecoms deal with Sprint and being stopped because our Department of Defense fears that the super-sophisticated Chinese telecommunications company could slip some sneaky software past US defenses.

In Chengdu I became particularly conscious of how foreigners got special treatment in a way that would be unacceptable back home. When we went to a restaurant for lunch, invariably every table was full. Colonel Wang would politely but firmly make a group of local people leave their table in the middle of their meal so that we could have a table immediately. For me, this was acutely embarrassing. Likewise, when we ate at the hotel, I was served a magnificent meal in the main dining room while Colonel Wang would disappear to eat somewhere else that, as I discovered, provided inferior food for local people. I began insisting that he eat with me, at my expense, and he complied a couple times but then I had to relent after he told me that he could get in serious trouble for doing so. I was simultaneously appreciative of how much my hosts were doing for me, distressed by what seemed to me to be the unfairness of these practices, and fascinated by the tension between the nationalist rhetoric that the communist revolution was obliterating the second-class treatment of Chinese and the reality that I experienced every day.

I continued to insist that, in each city, we should visit some rural areas. So one day we drove four hours outside Chengdu to a vast ancient waterworks that channeled the flow of rivers into an extraordinary irrigation system. The complex would have been an extraordinary achievement for modern engineers; I kept trying to think how one could do the differential equations to manage all the varying flows. But this had been created before differential equations existed.

Along the way, I would randomly demand that the car stop so I could get out and see a village that hadn't been pre-selected and prettified. Colonel Wang went along with this. Each time the whole village would turn out, curious about this strange Caucasian intruder, and extraordinarily warm in greeting the stranger. I took lots of pictures of smiling children's faces. People welcomed having their pictures taken—something I have always taken as a sign of their self-esteem. But my time in the jungles of the Philippines and the mountains of Korea allowed an instant recognition of how poor these people were. They were thin and a head shorter than their counterparts from the area today. Interestingly, they came across as both poorer materially and far more positive in their outlooks than the beaten down population of Shanghai that I was to visit next.

Colonel Wang made a point of taking me to one particular rural production brigade. This brigade had diversified into more than forty businesses, such as laboriously making bricks by hand. They then faced the question of how to divide the profits. So, they told me, they had invented the "socialist concept of shares," dividing the proceeds of each business according to how much each participant had contributed. I joked that in ten years I would come back and find that they had invented the socialist concept of a stock exchange. To my chagrin this joke turned out to be in very poor taste. The idea that what they were doing was related to that core capitalist institution, the stock exchange, induced fears of terrible ideological retribution and they made it clear that I had said something bad. (By chance, the Shenzhen Stock Exchange opened exactly ten years later.)

Back in Chengdu the Vice Governor of the province put on a dinner in my honor. This was indeed an honor for a young American scholar, because the province of Sichuan had about the same population as Japan and the Vice Governor was a busy man. But Colonel Wang had forgotten to bring a translator, an oversight that threatened to turn the dinner into a social disaster—and a personal disaster for him. So he became the translator. Through some gigantic effort of Maoist will, he carried it off. I was awed. From that day on, undergirded by the self-confidence derived from that dinner, Colonel Wang's English was lucid, confident and unhesitating.

Our final stop was to be Shanghai. But there was a problem. We were scheduled to be there over October 1, a holiday, and the hosts in Shanghai wanted to spend the holiday with their families, not catering to some foreign stranger. So they came up with the win-win solution of shipping me to Hangzhou for a couple days. Hangzhou was unspoiled then. My hotel beside West Lake looked out over a scene that had long inspired painters and poets; it was inspiring to me too, although I have an exceptional lack of talent for both painting and poetry.

The Shanghai Institute of International Studies asked me to give a lecture on North-South relations. I gave a very extensive lecture on why the Group of 77's agenda was untenable. For instance, the attempt to control commodity prices would be overwhelmed by market pressures so powerful that no imaginable system of stockpiles would defeat them. I thought I had done an utterly persuasive job of demolishing the conventional southern agenda, and looked forward to a lively debate. But the chairman just said, "Dr. Overholt, we disagree with everything you said. Now let's talk about Taiwan." It seems that traditions of lively debate were a bit weak. Years later I tried to look up Mr. Dong, my host at SIIS, and was told that he had first gone to work for CITIC and then migrated to Los Angeles to become a business executive.

My Institute host took me on a cruise of the Yangtze. I was an enthusiastic photographer and he encouraged me to take pictures but on that boat trip I was very circumspect. Finally I told him that my father had taken groups of students on exchanges to the Soviet Union, and the Soviet tour guides encouraged the students to take illegal cityscape pictures so that they could be charged, threatened and blackmailed later. Our Yangtze trip took us past lots of navy ships and I didn't want to be accused of taking the wrong picture. Mr. Dong said, we would never do that to you. He was right. They don't play the game that particular way. But at the time I decided not to take the pictures.

I was taken on a tour of a machine tool factory. They had the most modern equipment in the world for making machine tools. They were proud of their equipment and they were proud that they were exporting their products. But they had one set working, and the others were idle, apparently being kept for future cannibalization when parts where needed. The workers were relaxed, standing around chatting and smoking. The factory was a monument to wasted labor and capital, and it took only a few questions to learn that they were able to export only because of large subsidies. Combined with the extreme poverty of most Shanghai people, the waste of resources embodied in this particular source of pride was actually tragic.

We went to a music performance, with mostly modern popular songs from all over the world. People dressed up, with some of the men in western suits. Tailors had clearly hidden away their suit patterns from the 1930s and retrieved them, because the huge lapels and tight waists were right out of Al Capone movies. The audience was extremely enthusiastic about the foreign songs, but booed deeply at a performance of a traditional Chinese tune on an erhu. Colonel Wang was deeply disturbed by this disrespect. I was heartened by the enthusiasm for foreign things and by the fact that people had the courage to vent.

Colonel Wang summed up one of the cultural lessons of what we had seen in the different cities. In each city the badges of social status were different. In Beijing, the sign of high status was to have a new bicycle. In Chengdu, the key was interesting, high quality food. In Hangzhou it was your home that counted. In Shanghai, your clothes defined your social standing.

My predominant social image of Shanghai was one of very tired people. In the evening people would wearily trudge home from work, often substantial distances. In many cases a family owned one bicycle but both husband and wife needed to commute. So the husband would hold the bicycle, with his arms and the handlebars forming a big circle around the wife, who walked and tried to catch some sleep at the same time. Then they would change places and the husband would try to get some rest while walking home. Watching all the tired people, walking home in their drab clothing, was profoundly dispiriting. Going back to Shanghai in the 1990s, seeing the crowds of energetic people in colorful modern clothes enjoying themselves, lifted the spirit.

On the last evening, Colonel Wang and I talked after dinner as usual. In a reflective and somewhat despondent mood, he asked how old I was and I told him, thirty-seven. He said I was fortunate, because I was young and could still accomplish great things. I asked him how old he was. He said, forty. I said, you are also young and can accomplish great things. You are only half as old as Deng Xiaoping, who is transforming China. He said, no, when he was getting his education the Cultural Revolution came and the schools were closed for ten years. "Mr. Overholt," he said, "ten years is a long time in the life of a man." When the schools reopened he was told to get a degree in Albanian literature. If memory serves, he was actually sent to Albania for a while. His ordeals had damaged his health. "No," he concluded, "for me, finished."

That was a sad conversation, but it was also a conversation with a man, an army officer assigned to a propaganda task, who had against all expectation become a friend willing to confide deep feelings. It was an appropriate symbol for the visit. I left for wonderful, free Hong Kong with all sorts of complex and contradictory impressions of China: a majestic culture; authoritarian repression; drab uniformity; glimmerings of expanded cultural freedom; Shanghai weariness; rural Sichuan energy; world-class bad factory management; breakthrough economic decisions that would improve people's lives; revolutionary hypocrisy; pragmatic determination to do whatever was necessary to improve people's livelihoods; army officers responsible for enforcing autocracy but eager to showcase the break with Maoism; and the glimmerings of cultural freedoms and markets.

However confusing and contradictory, this was the same general pattern I had seen in Taiwan and South Korea a decade earlier. Within the pattern, what I had seen in the villages (not counting the Beijing one) was decisive: China's people were mainly in the rural areas and Deng was doing the right things to improve farmers' lives. I went back to the US and wrote, every six months, that China was following a strategy, emulating South Korea and Taiwan, that would improve people's lives and make China an important country again. Equally, I emphasized that Gorbachev, who was ignoring the lessons of the greatest economic takeoffs in history and making the tragic error of listening to Western advice, would destroy the Soviet Union. A decade later, at the suggestion of Ezra Vogel, I stitched my articles together into *The Rise of China: How Economic Reform Is Creating a New Superpower*.

*William H. Overholt is Senior Research Fellow at Harvard University's Kennedy School of Government. He was Director of the RAND Corporation's Center for Asia Pacific Policy and served as Head of Strategy and Economics at Nomura's regional headquarters in Hong Kong. He is the author of six books, including The Rise of China and, most recently, Asia, America and the Transformation of Geopolitics.*

# Opening Up

# Opening Up

## Morton Abramowitz
### *Watching China-US Normalization on a Fast Track (1978)*

I first went to China in 1959. Not really. In the American Embassy in Taipei, Taiwan was China and Beijing was on the mainland. The ambassador was very firm in preserving this distinction and so it appeared in all our cables, other communications, and staff meetings. One even got used to it, and given Taiwan's extraordinary economic growth in the early sixties right before our eyes, compared to the terrible things then happening in the mainland— I often wondered about it. Nevertheless by 1963, when I left "China" to join the American Consulate General in Hong Kong, the usage had become a little tattered; a public campaign centered on a counterattack against the mainland and the imposition of taxes for that purpose quickly had come to an unceremonious end. The future was clearer, but plenty still had to be done both in China and Taiwan

The American Consulate in Hong Kong was in essence the embassy in China in 1963. But the closest I got to China in daily life was the myriad of China product stores that proliferated in Hong Kong to earn Beijing badly needed foreign exchange. My job at that time was to cover the Chinese economy, particularly the foreign sector, and the stores, which I visited every two to three weeks, gave us some inkling of China as a producer—not very impressive basic stuff—and exporter. Countless refugee accounts, meetings with diplomats from Beijing, and of course the Chinese media helped fill out the picture. I also studied the agricultural situation, and the disastrous effects of the Great Leap Forward. We spent an enormous amount of time trying to estimate Chinese grain production and had endless controversies with Washington over the figures. Even if we got it right—the direction was easier than the figures—I never saw that it had much practical consequence for American policy at that time. More exciting was my last year in Hong Kong as the whole mission watched with fascination the incredible political events that started unfolding in 1965. I left Hong Kong for the States in 1966, the day Peng Zhen was removed as mayor of Beijing.

My first real visit to China came in May 1978 because of my position as Deputy Assistant Secretary of Defense for East Asia and Latin America (really) in the Pentagon's Office of the Secretary of Defense. I was mostly a potted palm in Zbigniew Brzezinski's very important trip to accelerate the normalization process with China. I was along to publicly convey the strategic aspect of developing Sino-American relations, particularly for the Russians. Crossing into Chinese airspace for the first time brought cheers from the delegation and a little dance in the aisle by Mike Oksenberg, who had worked so hard for that day.

My task was very specific: to brief the Chinese military on what we knew of Russian deployments and capabilities along their common border. And the US knew a lot—whether more than the Chinese I do not know, but I thought so. China had become one of my preoccupations in the Pentagon after the end of the Vietnam War. My staff and I had carried out a year-long reexamination of America's position in East Asia, including possible security relations with Beijing, which was widely read or briefed in the US Government. We also spent much time in helping shape the required drawdown of our military presence in Taiwan. Now in Beijing I was hoping, with Mike Armacost of the National Security Council staff joining, that we might have a modest first exchange of views with the Chinese military associated with my briefing. It was not to be. A senior Chinese military intelligence official listened with great interest to my presentation, pictures and all, but he said little and asked no questions. I tried to get him to ask questions and put a few to him. There was silence; his job was clearly to listen. After forty minutes or so I concluded my effort. We shook hands, he thanked us, and we departed. The US-China defense relationship had been cemented.

I was not invited to other formal meetings with the Chinese but shook hands with Deng Xiaoping and Huang Hua. (I met Deng again briefly in Thailand when he made a formal call on the Thai King later in 1978 and I was the US ambassador. Thai Prime Minister Kriangsak, in meeting the King with Deng, went down to a reclining posture to express the reverential Thai attitude toward the monarch. I watched with amusement Deng's clear amazement at Kriangsak's bow.) The three days of important meetings in Beijing were either small separate ones with Deng and Hua Guofeng that Brzezinski, Mike Oksenberg, and Ambassador Woodcock attended, or larger ones in the Foreign Ministry with Huang Hua including the State Department staff, notably Dick Holbrooke. But I went to our staff meetings and got reasonably caught up with the doings. I also participated in almost all the joint meals, where I met a number of then lesser ranking officials that I would again see in later years. The highlight was the meal Deng hosted at the Fang Shan Restaurant. The meals were excellent, mostly numerous courses all set down in rapid fire and accompanied with many *gan beis*, but the personal conversations with my neighbors were, not surprisingly, formal and stilted. Almost all were somewhat surprised by my affiliation. Our guest house was very comfortable, but we spent a good deal of time walking around the grounds so we could talk freely.

The most enjoyable times were actually the considerable sight-seeing the delegation did in those three days. It was after all the first time for most of us and, going around the Forbidden City with some great guides, history seeped in. We also spent a wonderful afternoon with an excursion to the Great Wall. Zbig had lots of fun with his Chinese hosts from the Foreign Ministry (translated by Shi Yanhua) in playing up the Russian angle. Once he stopped the group, peered northward, and said "Out there is the Russian bear and I am the bear tamer." Another time, as we approached a guard post he shouted to the Vice Minister: "Let's race to the guard post and first one there fights the Cubans in Ethiopia."

The visit was a milestone—the decision to normalize had been made and conveyed, leading to normalization at year's end. Brzezinski did an impressive job in generating the mission and furthering the normalization process, much to the consternation of the turf-conscious State Department. It was one of the real achievements of the Carter Administration.

I came away impressed with how far China still had to go, not remotely imagining what was in store. I was also impressed, after all the turmoil of the seventies, how well China played a weak hand. Lastly and more mundane— the bicycles awed me.


*Morton Abramowitz* *was the US Assistant Secretary of State for Intelligence and Research (1985-89), and President of the Carnegie Endowment for International Peace (1991-97). He has been the US Ambassador to Thailand (1978-81) and Turkey (1989-91). He is currently a Senior Fellow at The Century Foundation.*

## STEVEN W. MOSHER
*Witnessing Hell in China (1979)*

The year was 1978, and the diminutive dictator of China, Deng Xiaoping, had just begun to cautiously peek through the bamboo curtain that had long isolated Communist China from the rest of the world. Eager to feed on the abundance of technology, capital, and markets he saw flourishing there, he agreed to an exchange of scholars with the United States. This was a one-sided business from the beginning, and not just in terms of numbers. As the members of the US Committee on Scholarly Communication with the PRC dickered over the tiny roster of fifty American scholars who would on Deng's writ be allowed into China, the first of thousands of mainland Chinese academics and agents—it was often impossible to distinguish one from the other—began flooding into the US. That Beijing later accused me of espionage is not surprising, since so many of their supposed "scholars" were actually engaged in precisely that line of work.

The Committee finally decided that I was to be the first American social scientist allowed to do research in the People's Republic of China. I owed this unexpected honor to a certain facility in the Chinese language, which I acquired during a year at the Chinese University of Hong Kong, and also to certain ambitious professors at Stanford University, whose surrogate I was, and whose ideas about Chairman Mao's great experiment in socialism I carried, like retroviruses, within me. At the time Mao and Maoism remained objects of admiration, if not veneration, in certain circles, mostly academic. I and my colleagues were largely oblivious to the fact that Deng Xiaoping, to maintain himself and his comrades in power, was already hard at work constructing a Fascist dictatorship on the ruins of Mao's failed socialist paradise.

It would be an exaggeration to say that I went to China to join Chairman Mao's Red Guards, as the English journalist Malcolm Muggeridge went to Moscow intending to offer his services to Stalin to help build socialism. But I was favorably disposed towards Maoism all the same, having been taught by tenured professors, whose grasp on the truth I had no reason to doubt and whose ranks I hoped one day to join, that it had been a great boon for the peasantry. That few of these eminent pedants whose lectures I had attended and whose books lined my shelves had ever visited a Chinese village, or even spoken with a Chinese peasant, should have been, so to speak, a red flag. When I finally had a chance to ask them, San Gen, Ah Ming, and other villagers I came to know had an entirely different opinion of the commune system. I have recounted this story in my book *Broken Earth: The Rural China*. Suffice to say here that the villagers referred to the Chinese Communist Party itself as the *da dizhu*, or "big landlord." Given that Chairman Mao, in his carefully elaborated demonology of class enemies, reserved a special place in Marxist hell for "big landlords," this was a damning comment.

It was in March 1979 that I finally arrived, elated yet diffident, in the People's Republic of China. I was confident that my year-long stint in a

People's Commune would prove to be the adventure of a lifetime, not to mention provide the raw material for one—or several—books that would jumpstart my academic career. How could it not, when I was one of the first American sinologists in three decades to be allowed behind the bamboo curtain? From the point of view of sinology, the New China, as it was then called, was largely *terra incognita*. Still, I couldn't be completely sure that the gaping accounts of political pilgrims like Ross Terrill and others were not, to some degree, true. Perhaps I would find myself, after all, in a better world, where for the first time in Chinese history famine had been eliminated, free medical care provided to all, and the Confucian prejudice against girls and women eliminated. Who knew for sure?

So it was that I took up residence in the village of Xingcha in the Pearl River Delta of Guangdong province. This also comprised, along with several satellite villages, the eight thousand member Xingcha Production Brigade. The Brigade belonged to Junan Commune, and was itself divided into smaller "production teams." As these titles suggest, agricultural production was organized along military lines, with peasants expected to labor each day in the collective fields under the orders of commune cadres. The squalid reality of communal life, with its multiple privations and omnipresent regimentation, quickly disabused me of the illusions I had arrived with. Peasants sat down to meager meals of broken rice and salted vegetables not, as I had read, to heaping platters of pork, beef, and fish, which in fact could only be found at official banquets—but there, abundantly.

I was welcomed to Xingcha by Secretary Ho who, as the senior Party official in residence, effectively ran the place. Short and squat, he made up for his lack of height by his extreme breadth, possessing wide shoulders, thick, sinewy arms, and a broad face. Seated, as he was during official meetings, he made an imposing figure, but he was scarcely taller standing. Behind his back the villagers referred to him as "Toad." The first time I heard this nickname I laughed out loud, it so perfectly captured the man. He had a flat, expressionless way of watching you, not unlike a toad eyeing an insect it was about to devour. I have seen that same look of reptilian alertness on the faces of many PRC officials, bred into them by the necessity of enforcing unpopular policies on an often sullen population.

Secretary Ho was eager to help me, I soon learned, because of a certain directive that had come down from Beijing. Jointly signed by the Minister of Education and the Minister of Foreign Affairs, it declared that I was a "friend of China," and that officials at all levels of government were to "cooperate fully with my research."

He and I quickly formed a friendship of convenience, bound together as we were by reciprocal obligations. It was his job to keep watch over the "foreign friend," as I was referred to in officialdom, reporting my comings and goings to higher authority. For my part, he was the key to all the official documents, statistics, and directives I hoped to collect for the Hoover Institution of Stanford University. This was the assignment I had been explicitly given by Professor G. William Skinner at Stanford, whose understudy I was. By providing me with much of what I requested, Secretary Ho was able to report authoritatively on my activities up the chain of command, while I was able to obtain more and better information than I would have been able to manage on my own. So we both benefited.

We became partners in other ventures as well.

"Xingcha Production Brigade doesn't have a single truck to get our goods to market," Ho complained to me one day. "Chinese trucks are poorly made and hard to get." Eyeing me thoughtfully, he said: "We would like you to buy a Japanese-made one in Hong Kong, use it for the duration of your stay here, and then give it to us." He went on to say that he would advance me currency in renminbi for the remainder of my research expenses in China. I could then use, he suggested, the remainder of my research funds, held in a US dollar account in a Hong Kong bank, to buy a truck there and ship it into the country. Because it would be for my personal use, the standard import duty, a whopping one hundred percent of value, would be waived.

I agreed to this proposition, although I suppose it could be argued that it violated the foreign exchange laws of the PRC. I cannot say that I lost any sleep over the matter. The black market exchange rate between the renminbi and the US dollar, just like that between the renminbi and the Hong Kong dollar, was much more widely known and used than the official one. Only American innocents on guided tours, retired schoolteachers from Peoria and the like, would think of going into a People's Bank to exchange money, in effect donating half the value of their currency to the state. And even they would soon be enlightened by their Chinese tour guides, who were only too eager to profit from the *heishi*, or black market, in currency themselves. As far as importing the truck for my personal use, I did use it until it was time for me to leave the country, at which point I handed over the keys to Secretary Ho. So the letter of the law would seem to have been satisfied.

The Chinese government later accused me of espionage, claiming that I had used the truck to bribe Secretary Ho into giving me confidential documents. Beijing demanded, in typical Marxist cant, that I "confess" my "crimes against the people." I refused, of course, because it wasn't true. Had I not, Secretary Ho might well have gone to prison.

On the evening of March 7, 1980, Secretary Ho came over bearing the Party directive, marked "secret" as all such directives were, that would radically alter the direction of my life. "The Central Committee of the Chinese Communist Party of Guangdong Province has adopted a new policy," he said, in the tone of one sharing a confidence. I scanned Junan Commune Planned Birth Measures, as the directive was called, to learn that the provincial authorities had concluded that the population of the province was growing too rapidly... and had decided to impose a cap on population growth of one percent during 1980.

The last set of characters seemed to jump off the page. "A cap on population growth of one percent." I looked up questioningly at Secretary Ho. "It's very clear what you are ordered to do," I said. "But how are you going to do it?"

"It's very simple," he said patiently, understanding that I had no experience with the vast persuasive power of one-party dictatorships. "In my brigade there are about eight thousand people. At the end of the year there can be no more than eight thousand and eighty alive. Read the rest of the directive. Here's what the provincial authorities have told us to do. No women will be allowed to bear a second child within four years of her first. Third children will be strictly forbidden. Finally, all women who have borne three or more children by last November 1 are to be sterilized." He rattled off the new regulations matter-of-factly, not looking in the least abashed. I had begun to have a very bad feeling about what was about to unfold in the village.

"What I mean is," I responded, "It's already March. Nearly all the babies who are going to be born in Xingcha in 1980 have already been conceived... "

"We are launching a planned birth *gaochao*," he broke in. A *gaochao*, or high tide, was a kind of political tsunami that, like its seaborne counterpart, rises up suddenly and sweeps all before it. "We'll go from house to house, identifying all the women who are pregnant with illegal children. These will attend study sessions, where they will be told that, for the good of Junan Commune, they must get an abortion."

The *gaochao* struck the following morning. By midday, Toad and his underlings had rounded up several dozen pregnant women, whom he told in no uncertain terms to terminate their pregnancies. While some submitted after a day or two of lengthy "study sessions," others continued to resist his blandishments and threats. On the morning of the fourth day, the eighteen remaining holdouts were suddenly arrested and taken away to an undisclosed location. Their crime, the villagers were told, was that they were pregnant with "illegal" children.

I went after them, finding them locked up in a small room at the commune headquarters. The windows were shuttered and a guard stood at the door, presumably to thwart any of this sad, disheveled little group who tried to bolt. I thought the idea of escape ludicrous given that all the women were heavy with child and totally dispirited, sprawling listless and dejected on the short plank benches that were their only resting places. As my eyes adjusted to the dim light—a naked 25-watt bulb hanging by its wire from the ceiling provided the only illumination—I noted their grim faces and pained eyes, blood-flecked from lack of sleep and crying. It was like a scene out of Dante's Purgatory. Hell would come later.

A commune cadre, Wei by name, stood before these beaten-down creatures, scourging them with his voice. "You are here because you have yet to 'think clear' about birth planning," I heard him saying as I came in. "You will remain here until you do."

The unexpected arrival of the commune's "foreign friend" gave Comrade Wei pause, and when he began speaking again it was in folksy tones about how rich and powerful China would become if only everyone would stop having children. After a couple of minutes of this, however, he seemed to decide that my presence was no threat. Or perhaps he began to worry that, as "a friend of China" (for I had been so described in a communication from Beijing), I might report him for not carrying out the new party line vigorously enough. In any event, as I sat there in the perpetual gloom with my tape recorder running and my notebook open, he went back on the attack.

"None of you has any choice in this matter," he said slowly and deliberately. "You must realize that your pregnancy affects everyone in the commune, and indeed affects everyone in the country." Then, visually calculating how far along the women in the room were, he went on to add, "The two of you who are eight and nine months pregnant will have a caesarean-section abortion; the rest of you will have a shot that will cause you to abort."

Several of the women started crying at this pronouncement, and Comrade Wei, apparently deciding that his words had had the proper effect, sat down for a while. Other officials were soon at work on the women, softening them up further with alternating barrages of promises and threats.

But it was Comrade Wei who, towards the end of this cruel day, dropped the bombshell that would cause the expectant mothers incarcerated here to abandon all hope of resistance. "Do not think," he said, speaking slowly and with great force, "that you can simply stay here, eating the government's rice, until you give birth. We will not allow that. If you should go into labor before you give us permission to perform an abortion, we will simply take you to the clinic for the procedure at that time. You will go home alone." This death sentence was greeted by the women with open gasps and sobbing. The threat and the response burned into my mind like stigmata. "Agree to an abortion, or we will kill your baby at birth," I numbly wrote down.

My disgust over the mistreatment of these young women was already high, but it was a visit to the commune medical clinic that awoke me to the full horror of the situation. This rather primitive facility, with its seventy beds, had been hastily converted into an abortuary at the beginning of the *gaochao*, and now served as the government's killing fields. The doctor in charge told me that nearly all of the women confined there were within a month or two of term, and confirmed that, yes, they were terminating the more advanced pregnancies first. Comrade Wei's vow that no child would be born alive was obviously no empty threat.

The actual slaughter of the innocents was done assembly-line fashion. As soon as a woman was brought in, a powerful poison was injected directly into her uterus. Most babies died within twenty-four hours of receiving this lethal injection and were born dead the day following. Late in pregnancy the drug was proving less effective, however, and some babies didn't die as planned or, if they did, labor didn't follow. In these cases the doctors would open the woman up surgically and remove the now dead or dying baby. This is what Comrade Wei was referring to when he threatened the women with caesarean-section abortions.

My tour of the clinic ended in the operating room, where all such abortions were done. This room was constructed of the same gray concrete as the rest of the hospital but had large windows in each wall. The low operating table in the center of the room was already occupied. A short, stocky peasant woman in her early twenties lay on her back as a nurse busily painted her exposed, swollen stomach with a yellow antiseptic solution. An occasional curious face appeared surreally at the windows, only to be quickly driven away each time by shouts from the nurse.

The doctor followed, making a series of swift injections into the woman's abdomen. As he waited for the anesthetic to take effect, he explained to me that the woman had been given an injection of poison early the previous day, that it had been determined that the fetus had died, but that there were still no uterine contractions. Now, he went on, oblivious to the woman lying underneath his gesticulating, gloved hands, the fetus would have to be removed, thus and thus. The woman for her part stared fixedly at the ceiling throughout his verbal dissection, her body immobile. Only her laboring, calloused hands, clenching and unclenching at her sides, gave a hint as to her anguished state of mind.

The doctor made the first incision, drawing a bloody line across her lower belly with a scalpel. I turned to go, but the woman's broken cries drew me back and I watched, horrified, as the doctor soon pulled a tiny, limp body from her torn womb. The light seemed to fade from the room, as if it had suddenly been transformed into an antechamber of Hell.

Up to this point I had been pro-choice, yet I had now witnessed an actual, real-life abortion in all its gruesome detail. The act I had previously considered to have no more significance than a tooth extraction had turned out to be a capital crime, complete with a very dead victim and a grievously wounded mother. I became pro-life in a flash of recognition of our common humanity: a tiny son of Adam, and my brother, perfect in every detail of his anatomy, had been executed by government fiat. Population bomb or no, I could not but mutely mourn his passing.

I was led to inquire where his body and, for that matter, all the hundreds of bodies of his fellow victims, would be buried. The local gravedigger, I found out, was hard pressed to keep up with the constant stream of corpses. This harried man arrived at the clinic before dawn each day—he had been warned to come early to avoid public notice—pushing a little handcart. Filling the handcart with yesterday's harvest of sorrow, usually fifteen to twenty corpses in all, he would set out for the hills in the distance. There, after making sure that he had not been followed by some grieving family member, he would bury them all in a single unmarked grave. It occurred to me that these mass graves may someday be discovered by future archeologists who, horrified by this callous disregard of human life, may wonder what strange and bloodthirsty deity could have compelled child sacrifice on such a scale. Can they possibly comprehend how fear of a late 20th century phantasm called "overpopulation" could lead China's brutal dictatorship, one of the Baals of our time, to consign tens of millions of its own helpless subjects to the flames? I think not.

The tragedy of the abortions that the peasant mothers of Xingcha were forced to endure was given further poignancy by a quiet ritual that I happened to observe during *Qing Ming Jie*, the "bright and clear" festival which falls in early April. On this festival, on which Chinese remember their ancestors, I happened to visit a neighbor woman who had gone through a cesarean section abortion a month earlier. I found her standing before the high mantle on which rested the family ancestral tablets, chanting. Eight sticks of incense were smoldering away in a sand-filled urn in front of the tablets, one for each of the eight ancestors, male and female, in the previous four generations. Her chants consisted of prayers for the repose of their souls in the next world, and petitions for peace and prosperity for her family and herself in the present one. But instead of ending the rite at that point as I expected, she instead lit a final stick of incense. I watched, puzzled, as she bent down and placed it in a tiny cup decorated with red paper that stood in the corner of the room. She began chanting again, but this time her prayers were so broken by sobs and tears that I couldn't make out the words. After she had regained her composure, I asked her about that final stick of incense. She had been praying for "the unborn one," she explained to me, the child that she had lost.

As I took stock of what I had seen—the killing of full-term, healthy infants at birth, and the poisoning of viable unborn children in the last few weeks of pregnancy, the abortion of women against their will at all stages of pregnancy, the forced sterilization and contraception of women whose fecundity had been declared a danger to the state—the sense that all of this was truly wicked grew.

I left China in the summer of 1980 determined to bring these atrocities to the attention of the world.

## Postscript

Acting at the behest of the Chinese government, Stanford University carried out a five-year investigation of my China research. In January 1986, nearly six years after I had left China, the president of the university declared that I was no longer welcome there.

*Steven W. Mosher has been President of the Population Research Institute since 1995. His books include Hegemon: China's Plan to Dominate Asia, A Mother's Ordeal: One Woman's Fight Against China's One-Child Policy and China Misperceived: American Illusions and Chinese Reality. He has served as Director of the Asian Studies Center at the Claremont Institute and has been a commissioner on the US Commission on Broadcasting to the PRC.*

# JAMES MANN
## From Air Force One to Lao Gai (1984)

My first visit to China was different from that of many contributors to this series. I was of the second generation of American correspondents coming to live in Beijing. I had had no first-hand experience with China under Mao Zedong; I didn't set foot in the country until 1984, in the reform era of Deng Xiaoping, Hu Yaobang and Zhao Ziyang.

And I had the most bizarre introduction to China one can imagine: I first visited the country not by train from Hong Kong, not across the border at Lo Wu, not by a regular commercial flight to Beijing, but along with Ronald Reagan on his visit there in 1984. Or, to be more precise, on the press plane accompanying Reagan on his first and only trip to China.

I had already been assigned to take over the *Los Angeles Times*' Beijing bureau, starting a few months after the presidential trip. The newspaper figured that since Reagan was planning to visit, I should join the many hundreds of reporters accompanying him (including three other reporters from my own newspaper), and take the opportunity to see where I would live, where my kids would go to school, what I would need in Beijing. The editors may also have thought I'd get a chance to scout out what China was like. If so, that assumption proved comically wrong: a presidential visit to China or, indeed, any other country, has only the most fleeting contact with the country itself. What I did get to experience, for a few days, was the collection of assumptions, simplifications and clichés that affect American perceptions of China. Now, looking back at this trip, I think it was small wonder that my own particular interest as a journalist and author in the following years would be the American relationship with China.

My background had been that of a journalist, not a China specialist. Coming from a family of doctors, I had been crazy enough to start down that path myself, somehow gaining admission to medical school, before I asked for a year's leave of absence to try journalism. I loved it from the start and never looked back.

For the previous eight years, from 1976 to 1984, I had been covering the Supreme Court. The assignment was intellectually challenging, but had also become predictable. I was thirty-seven years old and was pretty sure I didn't want to do the same thing forever. I talked casually with my newspaper about taking a year off from the Court, applying for a fellowship somewhere. After a while, the editors had a counter-proposal: several foreign bureaus were coming open in 1984. The foreign editor, Al Shuster, asked if I was interested in one. I was; my wife and I had traveled a lot, had spent several months traveling overland across Asia in the 1970s. I wondered what bureau he had in mind. He threw out a couple of possibilities: Moscow or Beijing. I thought (rightly, as it turned out) that Beijing, then deemed a less important posting than Moscow, would allow more scope for broader non-daily stories, more reflective coverage and more time to travel around the country.

I chose Beijing.

The mammoth press coverage of a presidential trip abroad is a wonder to behold. Besides seeing China for the first time on the Reagan trip, I was observing the White House's overseas road show for the first time, too. It was as self-contained as you can imagine, if not more so. Sometimes, in places like the Middle East, the press plane is even in a different country from the president. Reporters sit in huge filing centers, usually in a large hotel, waiting for briefings and handouts. The traveling White House press corps has to grapple with brutal deadlines and exhaustion. On the other hand, the ordinary hassles a traveler faces are all taken care of: "Here are the badges you need... Put your suitcase in the lobby of the hotel in Beijing in the morning before you leave, and you'll find it in the lobby of the Shanghai hotel when you arrive at the end of the day." On a presidential trip, hardship travel is a 5:30 a.m. baggage call.

Of the many hundreds of reporters assigned to the trip, only a handful at any one time, perhaps six to eight, were part of a "pool" with the president. They typed up what they heard and saw, and then everyone else used their reports as the basis for their stories, each reporter adding in his own background, interpretation, descriptions or weather report. The pool traveled on Air Force One with the president; everyone else flew along in a separate plane, which on Reagan's trip was a Boeing-747 jumbo (or perhaps two of them). I worked in one of the pools, I think on the leg of the trip from Honolulu to Guam. A couple of Air Force One cocktail napkins were all the reporters got: we never saw Reagan on the flight, and I duly recorded this in my pool report, which was written on an Olympia typewriter and then copied for the use or uselessness of hundreds of other hacks.

We landed in Beijing, at the old airport, on one of those April days when it rains mud. The sky was a pale yellow-orange. The first stop was Tiananmen Square, where, in front of the Great Hall of the People, Reagan went to welcoming ceremonies: the girls waving bouquets and shouting *Huanying*, the twenty-one-gun salute. Some in the White House press corps made a great deal of this reception, interpreting it as an Important Sign of China's love for America or for Reagan or as an upturn in Sino-American relations. A day later, a reporter living in Beijing, perhaps from one of the wire services, told me the president of some non-superpower nation (was it Lesotho? Lichtenstein? Brunei?) had gotten virtually the identical welcoming ceremony, or a warmer one, in the same place the day before Reagan arrived.

We were taken to the place that would serve as our home for the next few days: the recently-completed Great Wall Hotel. For decades, visitors to Beijing had stayed in older hotels like the Beijing, Minzu and Qianmen. Now, the city had started to build a series of next-generation hotels: the Great Wall Hotel had followed on the Jianguo, to be followed next by the Jinglun (Beijing-Toronto). Our hotel seemed almost as if it were designed for the same purpose as the world-famous fortification for which it was named: to help keep foreigners out of China. Its cavernous new restaurants tried to serve an array of Western dishes—club sandwiches, French fries, spaghetti Bolognese—none of which tasted quite right and all of which left one yearning for real food, whether Chinese or Western. The press filing center was in the hotel. It became the venue for reunions of old friends arriving from different places: Rick Smith, a *New York Times* Washington correspondent who had served in Moscow, ran into Chris Wren, a colleague who had moved from Moscow to the Beijing bureau, and shouted out: *Tovarich!* Wren's response was in kind: *Tongzhi!*

The next day, I met Deng Xiaoping. Sort of. It wasn't exactly a one-on-one. I was standing on a row of bleachers, along with many other properly-badged journos, in the room where Deng welcomed the Reagans, husband and wife. Deng wandered over to the bleachers to say hello. What was my first impression? To borrow the immortal words of Richard Nixon at the Great Wall ("It really is a great wall"), Deng really was very short. He also, it turned out, had an impish sense of humor: in front of the assembled reporters, he turned to Nancy Reagan and told her that her visit was too short. "I hope you'll come the next time and leave the president home," he said. "You come just by yourself, independently…We won't maltreat you." Reagan had spent many decades and two careers handling that sort of patter. "It sounds like I'm the one being maltreated," he replied genially. Was this a Sino-American summit, or Jack Benny and Bob Hope? No time to find out further: the reporters were ushered out before the conversation could turn more serious.

That brief first glimpse of Deng was also my last one. Over the following years, living in and covering China, I never saw Deng again. In Beijing, I would be able to see once in a while the color of Hu Yaobang's (brown) socks, and the cut of Zhao Ziyang's many (grey) suits. More often, though, reporters in that era saw only the more limited wardrobe of the loyal, repeat-the-line Foreign Ministry press spokesman, Li Zhaoxing (whose haberdashery would improve over the following decades as he rose through the ranks to become Foreign Minister).

Over the following two days, I helped out in the coverage of the trip and dutifully attended the briefings, dinners and other events. Both the Chinese and the Americans wanted a smooth trip: for the Reagan White House, this was the year of a presidential election, and for the Chinese, the value of the trip lay in simply getting Reagan, one of Taiwan's strongest defenders in American politics, to visit the PRC. (In Honolulu, on his way to China, Reagan had crossed paths with his fellow conservative Barry Goldwater, who accused him of selling out Taiwan by making this trip. "I don't think I convinced him otherwise," noted Reagan in his diary.)

There is usually an attempt before summits like this one to produce some "deliverable," a specific agreement or series of agreements that can be signed by the two countries' leaders to demonstrate the talks have produced "results." On Reagan's trip, the deliverable was a nuclear agreement, signed in Beijing, permitting American technology to go to China; the deal would, it was hoped, open the way for Westinghouse to win the contracts to build Chinese nuclear plants. This was supposed to be the main "news" of Reagan's trip, and produced numerous front-page stories back home in the United States. Later on, Reagan's principal agreement in China turned out to be almost meaningless. It required congressional approval. Congress balked at the idea of giving China nuclear technology, because members of Congress—led mostly by Democratic senators such as Alan Cranston and John Glenn, supported by others like Al Gore and Joe Biden, with conservative Republicans like Jesse Helms joining in—feared that China was helping Pakistan's nuclear program, and that Pakistan might in turn spread nuclear technology to other countries. (Looking back, I can't imagine how they could have believed such far-fetched ideas.) As a result, Westinghouse didn't win those Chinese contracts.

At the opening banquet, in which Zhao hosted Reagan, I was seated so far from the head table it would have taken a ten-minute bicycle ride to get there. The People's Liberation Army played "My Old Kentucky Home" and "Home on the Range." The Chinese dinner partner on my right looked sufficiently distinguished to run a ministry, but turned out to be a telex operator. Meanwhile, I broke off from the official functions for the other purpose I had on the trip, a "look-see" to prepare for my upcoming assignment. I carefully checked out the schools, both Beijing International and The French School, because my daughter was then in a French immersion at a Washington-area public school. We eventually decided on the latter. I went to visit the apartment where my family and I would be living, in the diplomatic quarter at Jianguomenwai—a compound certainly not as shiny as the Great Wall Hotel, but just as separated from Chinese society and a lot more well-guarded.

In fact, the strongest impression I had throughout the trip was of how different China seemed from what was being written about it. By the mid-1980s, American newspapers and magazines were full of stories about how China was changing: new hotels, discos, golf courses. The stories were not inaccurate, but once there, you saw how marginal and fragile the innovations still were, how they were surrounded and overwhelmed by a different China that didn't appear as much in the American press coverage, a China that still remained untouched by westernization.

Reagan flew down to Shanghai, which in those days lagged far behind Beijing in new construction or new anything. It seemed as if it had been covered in a bell jar for more than a quarter-century. We stayed at the old Jinjiang Hotel, the place where Richard Nixon got drunk on Mao Tai, consuming glass after glass until past two o'clock in the morning, in celebration and relief on his final night in China.

One of Reagan's couple of events in Shanghai was a visit to one of the very first Sino-American joint ventures, the Shanghai Foxboro Company, which was making industrial-control instruments. "Business partnerships between Chinese and American companies are bound to succeed," Reagan declared with seeming certainty. I wasn't so sure. To me, the American head of the joint venture, Donald Sorterup, looked frustrated and lost. At the ceremony with Reagan, he admitted that the company's first year "has not been a totally calm journey." His evident discombobulation started me to wonder about the dynamics between the American business representatives and their Chinese counterparts. A few years later, this became the subject of my first book, *Beijing Jeep*.

Reagan was of course known as America's most successful anti-Communist politician, but by the time of this trip, it seemed far more accurate to call him anti-Soviet. He clearly wanted to make sure of China's continuing help and partnership in dealing with the Soviet Union and thus was eager for good relations with China's Communist regime. In Beijing, he twice reminded Chinese audiences that "America's troops are not massed on China's borders." Both times, China censored those remarks. He kept on trying. In Shanghai, speaking at Fudan University, he denounced the Soviet Union as an "expansionist power." This time, the speech was carried live, but not translated into Chinese.

He did also try to speak briefly about democracy and the values of free speech and freedom of religion, and these remarks, too, were censored. But in general, on Reagan's China trip, even the most obvious symbols of ideology were ignored or else converted for the audience back home into the terms of American politics, sports, commerce and advertising. Asked by some inquiring reporter whether he had ever been to a Communist country, Reagan's White House Chief of Staff James Baker replied, "I've been to Massachusetts." A deputy press secretary gave his Chinese counterparts baseball caps he had obtained from Nolan Ryan, then of the Houston Astros, that had red stars on the front. Red star over China—get it?

As Reagan was leaving Beijing, his motorcade passed through Tiananmen

Square again, where, in preparation for the May Day parade, China had put up large posters of Marx, Engels, Lenin and Stalin. Reagan's spokesman Larry Speakes said Reagan had seen the posters but belittled their significance. "He thought they were the Smith Brothers," Speakes said, referring to the bearded men on boxes of American cough drops. Later on, on the flight back over the Pacific, Reagan outdid him with a well-remembered line that again downplayed ideology: he referred to China as "this so-called Communist country."

Back home in the United States, I reported to my wife on the schools and housing and on the supplies we might need over the next few years. We bought boxloads of the items that were, at the time, not yet readily available there: a case of Pampers for the eighteen-month-old (not enough, and we would eventually have to beg departing parent-diplomats for more), boxes of canned vegetables, powdered milk.

I finished the Supreme Court term and said my goodbyes. "So you're going from covering the Supreme Court to China? That's quite a change," one justice told me. Then, flashing some unexpected wit, he mused, "At least, I hope that's quite a change." After a while, once in China, I realized that in one respect, at least, the two journalistic beats were similar: in both, a reporter in the 1980s had to keep an eye on the health of old men with life tenure or, in China's case, something close to it. In that sense, both places have gotten better. The Supreme Court now has three women and somewhat younger justices. China has managed to make the process of political succession considerably more orderly than it was—in fact, from the standpoint of anyone who believes in democracy, too orderly.

Several months later, I flew off to Beijing again, this time with family, and unpacked with them, first in the Jianguo Hotel and then in Jianguomenwai. Almost immediately after arrival, I was told the Foreign Ministry was offering a trip for reporters to visit Qinghai, which until that time had been a province closed to the outside world. One Australian diplomatic delegation had been allowed into Qinghai a couple of years earlier, and had reported seeing huge labor-camp facilities. I signed on. This was, in the 1980s, one of the last of the large Foreign Ministry-organized trips; China was opening up, allowing more latitude for reporters to travel on their own.

En route, we stopped for a day in Lanzhou, where we were taken to a large chemical factory. The air was smoky and foul. When it came time for questions, one of my colleagues asked for data on occupational safety and pulmonary diseases. The answer came back in a phraseology I had never heard before, but which would soon be familiar: "Since the Third Plenum of the Eleventh Central Committee..."

Once in Qinghai, we were taken to a factory that made carpets in Xining, the capital city. On them, we noticed, were labels that said, "Made in Shanghai." Later that day, leaving the city on a bus, we could see on the outskirts a large institution surrounded by high walls, with armed guards in a watchtower. On the way home, as we were passing it again, a couple of photographers called out, "Stop the bus, I'm feeling sick." Once outside, they began to shoot pictures. Suddenly, a local official supposedly from the Qinghai *Waiban* turned out to be a security official, and grabbed their cameras. "This is not a labor camp," Chinese officials told us. "It's a hydroelectric factory."

The following day, we were taken to the spacious, ornate Tibetan monastery at Taer Si, southwest of Xining. Chinese officials brought out a Living Buddha who had been released from prison a few years earlier. We asked him how long he had he been in jail—since the Cultural Revolution, we supposed? No, since 1958, since the time of the "crushing of the Tibetan rebellion," he said. He had been accused of "counterrevolutionary crimes," he said, and sent off to join the program of *laodong gaizao* (more commonly known as *lao gai*, reform through labor). And where had he been imprisoned? "Up the road, at the place they call the hydroelectric factory," he answered, knowing nothing of the incident the day before. In front of thirty people, a Qinghai provincial official whispered to the Foreign Ministry-assigned translator to say he had said that the institution in question was now a hydroelectric factory, not a labor camp. The Foreign Ministry translator refused. "He did not say that," he retorted, summoning forth both the spirit of apolitical professionalism that often prevailed in the mid-1980s and also the disdain of a Shanghai-born, Beijing-living Foreign Ministry official for the uncouth crudity of the backwards provincials.

After the isolation of the Reagan trip and the glitzy emptiness of the new Beijing hotels, I now felt that I had finally arrived in China itself, a place full of stories a reporter only rarely found out about and complexities an outsider struggled to understand.

*James Mann* *is author in residence at Johns Hopkins University's Paul H.*
*Nitze School of Advanced International Studies. He has written three books*
*about America and China: Beijing Jeep, The China Fantasy, and About Face:*
*A History of America's Curious Relationship with China. He is also the author*
*of several works about American foreign policy, including The Obamians:*
*The Struggle Inside the White House to Redefine American Power, published*
*in 2012.*

# Ian Johnson
*Deng's Heyday (1984)*

When I began thinking about writing this piece, my first trip to China in 1984 had seemed like a disappointment. Unlike today, this was the China of Great Events: the launch of bold reforms and an era of intellectual ferment unlike any since. Before arriving I had read about the foreigners who had come to China in the Mao era and seen nothing; I had fancied that I would do better. And yet I had spent most of my time tooling around the north of Beijing on a bicycle talking to a hodgepodge of foreign students and oddball Chinese. What had I really seen?

I softened my views after reading my diaries from that period, the first time I'd looked at them in a good fifteen years. I realized that if I hadn't experienced the sweep of events unfolding in Deng Xiaoping's China, my idiosyncratic experiences were in some ways a mirror of this time. Compared to today's budding superpower, this was a messier, odder China, like an old house full of memories that hadn't yet been spruced up for sale. It was also a country that was still really quite exotic in the best sense of the word: a place a long way from home, where one could get lost for months at a time and, despite one's best intentions, disappear from friends and family.

I went to China as a twenty-two-year-old senior at the University of Florida who had spent too much time working and too little time studying. Chinese was a lark: I had grown up in Montreal and knew French and figured

I would meet my language requirement by trying a non-European language. A note on a bulletin board alerted me to the fact that Introduction to Chinese needed a student to fill out its section. I decided that person was me and wasn't disappointed. I had a great teacher, the linguist Chauncey Chu, and his lectures on Chinese grammar made it seem like a fascinating puzzle. After one year, I eagerly signed up for another and then another. But by the spring of 1984 I knew all the uses of grammar particles like *le* and *ne*, but couldn't speak much Chinese. And I was sick of journalism, which I had been doing for four years straight to put myself through college. So I applied to a study-abroad program called AIFS and headed off that autumn to study at Peking University, or Beida.

There were only two of us in AIFS's China program and we basically were left to fend for ourselves. No one met me at the airport when I arrived—I had to beg a ride to Beida in the middle of the night—and no one helped me get registered; in fact, the university wasn't really sure what to do with me. I ended up in a tiny language class of misfits. My most memorable classmate was Sasha, a burly middle-aged Russian who never mastered more than a handful of Chinese words. The rest of the time he smiled pleasantly and nodded his head. Word has it that he was the minder for the Russian students, the first group to study at Beida since the Sino-Soviet split of the early 1960s.

But all of this turned out to be a blessing because I ended up falling in with a group of western graduate students who were infinitely more determined and savvy than I was. The key was my roommate, Lawrence "Chris" Reardon, a Columbia University graduate student researching the history of China's newly launched economic reforms. Chris and I both wanted Chinese roommates but the university had no intention of allowing us *laowai* to pollute the minds of the country's future elite. So we were stuck with each other. From my perspective it was the best thing that happened to me.

Chris didn't just help me with the logistics of life in China; he and other graduate students adopted me, even though I was far below them in every aspect. Through lunches, dinners and long evenings with these very focused Americans, Canadians and Australians, I began to understand something about China, from literature and linguistics to economic theory and politics. They lent me their books and organized their own trips around the city and country, which I joined. By the end of my stay, I realized that academics usually had a far better understanding of China than the Beijing-centric journalists I would also meet during my stay.

I was also befriended by a few eccentric Chinese. I say eccentric because you had to be a bit odd to make friends with foreigners at that time. Getting onto the Beida campus required signing in at the front gate and essentially admitting that you were going to see foreigners, which was potentially risky. China had only just begun to open up and given the xenophobia and brutality of the previous three decades of Communist rule, a prudent person would have avoided too much contact with foreigners.

This wasn't the case with Lao Zhang, or Zhang Anqing. He was in his early 60s, and I got to know him through Chris, who bumped into him at the post office outside the campus. Lao Zhang said he had been friends with the deposed emperor, Pu Yi, or maybe his brother Pu Jie. Or a cousin? Or was it that he'd walked past Pu Yi's house once? He was vague about the details but charming in an intense and unsettling way. He said he had learned finger painting from the royal household. He would come to our place for hours to talk and sometimes finger paint, usually blotchy pictures of shrimp. He would make smudges with his thumb and then, using a fingernail, etch long antennae.

It was clear that Lao Zhang had been through a lot. He had lived in China's oil center, Daqing, and during the Cultural Revolution had been severely beaten. We never knew how much to believe but he walked with a limp and his ear was badly scarred. And he did odd things like come by and sleep in our room for hours at a time. He didn't speak English but had beautifully precise handwriting and would carefully choose a few characters for me to look up, communicating through them complex ideas. Once he wrote the Chinese words *erzi huoche xinjiang bu huilai* or "son train Xinjiang not return." I thought about the implications of that for days.

Chris and I went with him on bicycle trips, once riding our heavy steel Flying Pigeon bikes fifty-five kilometers each way to the Marco Polo Bridge and then the Peking Man site at Zhoukoudian. Beijing was a much smaller city then and it was a trip through North China's parched countryside where we caught glimpses of Deng Xiaoping's economic reforms: free vegetable markets, small *getihu* (independent entrepreneur) businesses and snatches of colorful clothing that slowly were replacing the blue and green tunics of the Mao era. We ate in restaurants that required grain coupons and when one of my tires blew, Lao Zhang lashed my bike to his and the two of us rode on his several kilometers to the nearest village.

Lao Zhang also taught me lessons in how to skirt the military that still occupied most of Beijing's western suburbs. One day in November, he and I rode out to the Eight Great Sites, a complex of Buddhist monasteries and nunneries that had partially survived the Cultural Revolution. We rode along a country road and just before arriving at a corner, Lao Zhang pulled over, plunked his enormous fur hat on my head, pulled up my collar and said to ride with my head lowered. I did so and we passed the bored guards standing at the side of the road. Once past the guards he ordered me to look up— everyone would assume I was supposed to be there if I was there, he wisely said. Soon after we rode out of the military zone, I asked him why the area was restricted and he said that some military dormitories lay on that stretch of road, something of a disappointment as I'd assumed we'd slipped by a top-secret nuclear testing facility.

It wasn't the greatest subterfuge but it taught me about the paranoia of the state. I learned that restricted sites in China are often only out-of-bounds to people who look different. The people who devised these silly rules (some of which one still encounters in China) never seemed to consider that a blond-haired, blue-eyed person like me would be the last sort of person a foreign intelligence agency would employ to spy on the Chinese military. If you looked Chinese, you were a *neiguoren* and that meant you were okay. If you didn't, you were a *waiguoren*, often synonymous with being a problem. On a practical level, it was a lesson I'd draw on many times in the future when slipping past guards—big hat or hood, look down, walk briskly and act like you belong.

What I noticed most from the diaries is how much I was off campus on these endless bike rides. Beida at that time was in the suburbs, almost the countryside. Outside the west gate was farmland and we would bike every few days to the Summer Palace, Fragrant Hills or further afield. Haidian, now a busy commercial district, was a small town linked to the city by a two-lane street lined with trees, Baishiqiao Road—now a busy north-south artery. There were buses downtown but mostly we rode. At least once a week I'd ride the twenty kilometers each way to Tiananmen Square, the Beijing Hotel or the new Jianguo Hotel, which had a decent bakery.

Sometimes I was alone but often I traveled with friends like Chris or Bob Saunders, who was studying Beijing dialect, and Kim Besio, who was writing her doctoral thesis on *Dream of the Red Mansion*. We explored the *hutongs*, most of which are now gone, and I made my first forays to temples that would later mean so much to me, especially White Cloud Temple, the Daoist temple in the city's southwest. We ventured further afield to Luoyang, Xian, Hangzhou and Suzhou. And with government permission—much of China was closed off to foreign visitors and we needed a permit—we ventured to smaller cities like Datong and Shaoxing.

One of our favorite games was to use an old copy of *Nagel's Encyclopedia*, a Swiss guidebook written by French graduate students on the eve of the Cultural Revolution. It had essays on everything from Chinese chess to Daoism, but most importantly it offered interesting descriptions of sights that would later be attacked and destroyed in the Cultural Revolution. We ignored the local guidebooks or maps, which had only a handful of reopened sights, and used *Nagel's* to find dozens of temples, halls and palaces that officially didn't exist. Few were open to the public but we often could talk our way in—gatekeepers, we found, were happy to show off their grounds to earnest foreign students. It was a reminder of how weak China's cultural and religious organizations are; even today many temples and mansions are occupied by government agencies. Many others have simply been torn down.

Occasionally, we caught glimpses of bigger events. We saw Beida students protest the administration's decision to turn off their lights at 11 p.m. It seemed like a minor issue but for them was symbolic of their poor living conditions and lack of independence. They threw bottles—a homonym for the given name of the country's paramount leader, Deng Xiaoping—out of their dorm windows, a sign of the disgruntlement that would flare up five years later.

More memorable was the October 1 parade on Tiananmen Square for the 35th anniversary of the People's Republic. It featured the first military parade since 1960 and, despite some of the anger, students still called out *Xiaoping*, *ni hao!* (How are you, Xiaoping!) when he passed by in a limousine. Five years later, of course, the students and Deng collided and this almost naïve era ended in a bloodbath. But at this point Deng and the government were popular for having unshackled China and given people the first taste of prosperity in decades.

I wandered around Tiananmen Square, watching the spontaneous dancing, clapping, singing and shouting. It wasn't exactly Woodstock—alcohol was banned and the marchers were segregated by sex—but the feeling of elation was genuine. We were supposed to be grouped by our university departments, but order soon broke down and people mingled freely, singing songs and watching fireworks. I roamed the square until our buses left at 11 p.m., twelve hours after we had arrived. I was excited by what I had seen, writing "Chinese don't make good ballpoint pens or toilet paper… but they have a great country." I think this is one of the few insights from my diaries that still holds.

I also kept busy researching my senior thesis on North American journalism in China, biking down past Tiananmen Square to the Qijiayuan and Jianguomenwai diplomatic compounds to visit foreign correspondents. Among others, I interviewed Amanda Bennett from *The Wall Street Journal*, David Aikman with *Time* and Julian Baum of *The Christian Science Monitor*, as well as fellow Canadians Alan Abel of Toronto's *Globe and Mail* and John F. Burns with *The New York Times*. These correspondents candidly said they didn't travel enough outside Beijing and wrote too many of the same stories—

down to the same people and the same anecdotes. Much of this was due to restrictions journalists faced: they couldn't travel freely and had little access to information of any kind. They were also stuck in a cocoon of *ayis* and drivers, cooks and translators.

Compared to back then, journalists today are much more free and of course benefit from the Internet and social media sites. But it strikes me that many of the issues remain the same: too much time spent in one's comfort zone in Beijing, too many rushed trips to the provinces, and too many similar stories. If in the past a lack of information forced foreign correspondents to pursue the same leads, today the flood of information seems to create a pack mentality, with everyone trying to match each other and rush back to Beijing to file, if they even leave the city or their computer screens.

Another maybe obvious point is that this was an age of primitive telecommunications. We had no cellphones, no email and no Skype; all that was available was a landline to one special telephone room in the foreign students' dorm. This was a huge advance over having to go to the telegraph office, but making calls still required going to the phone room and ordering up a call. Receiving calls was tough because the person calling would have to know that you were in the telephone room. That meant I had on average one telephone conversation back home each month. The rest of the time I never touched a telephone, an amazing statement in today's networked world. Mostly I wrote letters, hundreds of them, and post cards. Six weeks into my stay it hit me how cut off I was when I woke up one day to realize

I'd forgotten my girlfriend's and my father's birthdays. I hadn't written or called. It was a terrible feeling but I had been immersed in China: I had been talking to my friends about China, meeting Chinese friends and studying the language.

This might sound a bit pat but I believe that the isolation made the immersion possible. I don't think it would have been the same if I'd have been able to have chats, Skype calls or cellphone conversations with my parents or girlfriend. Even today, I find I only get good material when I switch my smart phone into "airplane mode" and am forced to deal with the reality around me. The problem is this works for a day or so but inevitably the switch is flipped back and the babble of information restarts. I don't want to say I wasn't ever distracted back then but I was more focused on China than at any time in my life.

After looking through my diaries I see I did miss so much. I never talked to the Beida students to find out more of their grievances—it never even occurred to me that I, a journalist with scores of bylines under my belt, could go up and talk to Chinese people and write about them. I somehow had the sense I wasn't qualified to do so and that the gap was too large. How was I supposed to convey all this back home? I was years away from knowing how, or maybe from having the arrogance to think that I could.

But a kinder way of looking at it is simply to realize that our first encounters with China or any foreign country are rarely as grand as we hope. That is the nature of exploring foreign countries; all we can hope for is that our first steps are sturdy enough to carry us forward.

OPENING UP

*Ian Johnson* is a correspondent based in Beijing. He won a Pulitzer Prize in international reporting in 2001 when working as the China bureau chief of The Wall Street Journal. After the September 11, 2001 terrorist attacks on the World Trade Center, he ran a twelve-person investigative team on terrorism, and shared the German Marshall Fund's Peter R. Seitz Award. He is the author of Wild Grass: Three Stories of Change in Modern China and A Mosque in Munich: Nazis, the CIA and the Rise of the Muslim Brotherhood in the West.

# PORUS OLPADWALA
*Cities and Classes in Early Reform China and India (1985)*

I went to China for the first time in August 1985. Peking University had invited a Cornell delegation to consult on preserving the country's antiquities. Our host was China's foremost historical geographer, Professor Hou Renzhi.

I was more than usually excited at the prospect of the visit. Like my colleagues, I was inquisitive about a country about which I knew little. In my case, though, the little I knew had gone through three different iterations, two of them diametrically opposed. As a teen in Calcutta in the 1950s I was part of the neighborly good feeling of the Nehru-Zhou Enlai Hindi-Chini Bhai-Bhai (Indians and Chinese are Brothers) years. Not seven years later, in October 1962 and four months out of college, my friends and I were remotely contemplating volunteering in the China War when it came to its abrupt and ignominious (for India) close. The now-metamorphosed China as horned and fanged monster stayed with me through my corporate years in the next decade. That my employer for most of the time was the Indian associate of Jardine Matheson, whose assets the Chinese Revolution had expropriated, added to my distaste.

The pendulum started to veer back a few years later. Dissatisfaction with the social aspects of my corporate career had led to graduate study in international development in the US. China's development model is an important historical and theoretical moment in the history of socio-economic development, meriting study exclusive of preconceptions and conclusions. This is doubly so for India, for the two countries are the best, if not the only, true gauge of each other's relative progress. My investigations began uncovering the pros of Chinese development together with its cons, providing nuance but also confusion to my understanding. I was especially ready therefore to experience China for myself, even if only for a dozen days and in only two cities.

We crisscrossed Beijing for eight days, visiting sites from early morning till late at night. Touring the city, I found myself continuously and sometimes subconsciously comparing it to the Indian cities I knew. I found Beijing to be most unusual. For one thing, it was eerily quiet. It was surreal to see and to feel the bustle of a metropolis, but not hear it, because of scant motorized traffic. In the great thoroughfares massed pelotons pedaled away in silent flow. Smaller roads and *hutongs* were also uncannily quiet, devoid of the racket of ubiquitous two-stroke engines that fills every other byway in other less industrialized cities.

More unusual was the seemingly undifferentiated populace. Beijing looked to me an exclusively middle class city. We saw nothing that resembled destitution, even in the poorer areas, though clearly some citizens were less well off than others. Nor did we see wealth in the rest of the world's terms, though a glimpse of the newly opened Maxim's restaurant did hint at what was to come. Women and men dressed similarly in pants, blouses and shirts of muted colors—white and beige, khaki, grey and black. Whatever social difference that existed probably could only be discerned through the quality of cloth or cut, or the amount of wear on the fabric. There were fewer Mao jackets than I had expected but that could have been because it was a hot and sticky August.

There were other indications of broad middle class status. The most important was sanitation. Beijing was cleaner by orders of magnitude than any city in India or other developing countries I had visited. It was cleaner also than many US and European cities if they were considered in their entirety to include the poorest areas. Decent sanitation is both a prerequisite of and a sign of arrival into the middle classes and I was impressed by how universal was its prevalence in Beijing.

I also was struck by the absence of servility in the many service personnel we encountered. The custodians and dining room staff at the university guesthouse and cafeteria clearly did not consider themselves to be domestics or servants (as would be the case in India) and they were not treated as such. I was impressed that our drivers dined with us while on the road, even in upscale restaurants—an unusual occurrence in other less developed or even industrialized countries. (A quarter century later, in 2005, my wife and I invited our driver and our guide to lunch at a rest stop on the way back from the Great Wall. They declined our insistent importuning, saying that they were not permitted into our dining space, even as our guests, and would have to eat separately.) At one westernized restaurant our driver had difficulty figuring out the hierarchy of cutlery. In India and possibly other countries, a perverse intra-class snobbery would have had the wait-staff make him feel even more uncomfortable (what is an ignoramus like you doing in a place for *sahibs*?). Instead I watched in fascination as the waiters discretely helped the driver through his meal.

A variation of this theme was played out at the highest echelons of our visit. Thanks to Ed Bacon, we visited with Vice Premier Wan Li in Zhongnanhai. Ed had worked for American architect Henry Murphy in the early 1930s on projects that included Tsinghua University and the Harvard-Yenching Institute and Vice Premier Wan Li, who previously had been Beijing's deputy mayor, was an admirer. We were served tea and snacks not by liveried servants as would have been the case in India but by young people in beige trousers, white bush shirts and white gloves for whom clearly it was a day job and not servitude, and with whom the Vice Premier occasionally bantered.

The sense of an entirely middle class city extended also and ironically to that most bourgeois of middle class values—economic security and the dependable regularity of day-to-day existence. Most people seemed to have jobs to go to, even if they were uninteresting or strenuous; their essential health needs were met, however minimally; the children were in school; they were safe in their person and (what little they had of) property; they had opportunities for friendship and recreation.

It seemed to me an ideal period, the best of two worlds, with the worst of socialism slowly being discarded and capital's travails still some distance away. I sensed also that all who had come through the wrenching experience of the Cultural Revolution now just wanted some peace.

However, my colleagues and I rendered things differently. Where I saw almost everyone housed, they noticed the drabness of the housing; where I saw everyone clothed, they observed sartorial monotony; where I saw shops stocked with basics, they remarked on the lack of variety; where I saw people at work, they questioned the absence of choice in employment and opportunities for advancement; where I saw a partial acceptance of the system of government, they recognized only coercion.

It was clear that we were reacting to our own values, life experiences and *a priori* expectations of China. I had grown up middle class in Calcutta, but was surrounded by an incredible poverty that still persisted forty years later and which I found amazingly and pleasantly absent in Beijing. I always had been uncomfortable with the treatment of servants and so-called menial workers and it was refreshing to see such divisions substantially reduced. My father had been a small businessman and financial insecurity was a family norm. As a result I placed a premium on economic certitude and was appreciative of a society that made employment and basic needs a social goal.

Ed Bacon's reaction to China after an absence of a half century became critical to these exchanges. He became increasingly positive as the trip progressed, remarking mainly on improvements in infrastructure, hygiene and general orderliness. He was struck particularly by the absence of the deep poverty he had witnessed earlier. With the glaring exception of the destruction of the Ming Dynasty city wall, Ed also was impressed by Beijing's considerable attempts to preserve antiquities in the best way that a poor country could.

Possibly Ed's most common refrain was how much greener the city was. The local officials we met boasted that Beijing's goal had been to plant a million trees a year. Naturally we discounted the claim but Ed did say that the city was unrecognizably more verdant. On one occasion, viewing large swathes of green from either the Drum or Arrow Tower, Ed was reminded of a bus journey he had made from Shanghai to Beijing across the North China Plain. He recalled a slow and dusty trip over a landscape bereft of trees. Approaching Beijing, a very fine line had appeared on the horizon. As the bus drew nearer, the line became thicker and darker. Then it seemed to grow a few regularly spaced lumps. The line and lumps evolved into Beijing's old city wall and towers. It was as if the city had been in the midst of a desert. Now there were trees everywhere.

It transpired that Ed too had noticed the way service personnel were treated and was struck by the change from his first visit. He too commented on how our drivers ate with us even in the most expensive restaurants. His life in Shanghai had been different. Once he recalled—I sensed with not a little nostalgia—regular Saturday excursions on the Huangpu River with his Shanghai office colleagues. Servants rowed, cooked, served and cleaned while Ed and his mates lounged on deck with companions from what today would be called escort services.

At the historic sites, I found myself relating the period of the Chinese antiquities to what had been going on in India at the same time. Of the dozen major monuments we visited the oldest and the youngest provided the most intriguing connections. Lugou Bridge on the Yongding River west of Beijing is known more famously as the Marco Polo Bridge because the traveler wrote about it glowingly in his travelogue. It was constructed in the last decade of the 12th century at exactly the same time as one of India's most famous antiquities, Delhi's Qutub Minar, plus Marco Polo visited many cities on India's west coast on the same expedition on his way back to Venice.

We were at the magnificent eight hundred year old structure when a gigantic and very heavy piece of construction equipment similar to the tractors that haul rockets at Cape Kennedy started making its way across. There were new bridges on either side of Lugou and we asked why they were not being used. The answer was that Lugou was the only bridge strong enough to carry that massive a load! Some months later we received the happy news that the beautiful antiquity is now treated with the respect deserving of its age and provenance.

Our youngest site was the late-18th/early-19th century Yuan Ming Yuan gardens, destroyed in 1860 during the Second Opium War by a combined British and French force. The British had sacked Delhi just three years earlier and the man in charge of the Yuan Ming Yuan operation, Lord Elgin, moved to Delhi as Viceroy two years later in 1862.

One muggy August afternoon the Vice Premier summoned us to an audience. We went back to Zhongnanhai, this time to the official areas. The security was minimal compared to India where government offices at the time were sandbagged and bristled with guns (it was not yet a year after Mrs. Gandhi's assassination). At an internal gate a solitary PLA soldier in a dark green uniform got up from a chair under what seemed to be an army-issue garden umbrella and waved us through. It occurred to me as we drove past the languid sentinel that relative laxity in security at an important government site was only possible in an authoritarian state that otherwise had an iron grip on people and affairs.

The Vice Premier received us in the reception room made familiar from scores of photographs of Chairman Mao with visiting dignitaries. It was huge and mostly empty, except for an extraordinarily plush, sculptured beige carpet and a very large and exquisitely carved rosewood screen a few feet from one wall. We sat in front of the screen in the familiar inverted 'U,' with Ed and the Vice Premier in the center, and the rest of us strung out along the arms.

Wan Li clearly was delighted to meet the object of his admiration, but spent most of the time complaining about the horrendous traffic jams caused by Beijing's bicycles. He hoped to dispel the gridlock by replacing bikes with cars! Ed led us in spirited opposition but the Vice Premier was not to be moved. I suppose it was one of the few times that Ed was bested in argument.

Some of us went on to Shanghai for a few days. I had grown comfortable in Beijing because, for all its being different, it still was a Third World city roughly reminiscent of Delhi—many thousands of years old, sporadically the capital of an empire, and an administrative center with little or no business or industry. Shanghai on the other hand was uncannily like Calcutta, starting at the airport where a humongous altercation was underway involving porters, travelers and officials with no clear indication of how battle lines were drawn or what was being disputed.

Shanghai and Calcutta are young cities relative to their northern counterparts, both approaching 400 years in 1985. They sit at the mouths of their respective principle river systems—the Yangtze and the Ganges. They were created by foreigners—the English in India and a double fistful of Western countries in Shanghai's case. They were the driving forces behind their national industrializations and then the cradle and lifeblood of their countries' struggles against foreign domination.

All that I knew, but I was struck also by their physical similarities. Shanghai straddles the Huangpu River, a distributary of the Yangtze, in the same manner as does Calcutta the Hoogly, a distributary of the Ganges. Colonial era wharves, warehouses and offices lined both bunds. Many of the buildings on Shanghai's bund appeared to be mirror images of those that I had seen and worked in back in Calcutta and I fancied that some might even have shared architects. Jardine's China headquarters at No. 27 The Bund was particularly intriguing to me for its images had graced many a wall in No. 4 Clive Row, Calcutta. (Unfortunately I was not allowed in because it had become a government office.)

We spent two days at Fudan University where I gave a couple of talks on foreign direct investment (FDI). Since FDI's pros had begun to be a matter of faith in the Four Modernizations, I decided to dwell on its cons. The audience of professors and graduate students clearly was skeptical. Whatever credibility I retained was because I could back academic empiricism with personal examples from my experience as a businessman in a Third World country. At the end I was both exhilarated and depressed.

In the evenings we toured the Bund. Shanghai was considerably more crowded and poorer than Beijing but still not a typical Third World city to my eye because of the marked difference in public services and sanitation. One evening we were taken to dinner at a western-style restaurant overlooking the river. A European businessman was at the next table. I guessed from his accent that he was Dutch. He spent the evening berating his Chinese business collaborator about how inefficient, ignorant, backward and lazy the Chinese were and how the only way the country could progress would be to welcome unquestioningly the technical and managerial ways of the West. It was embarrassing even to overhear the tirade but there was no remonstration from the local official. Very few Indian officials I knew, private or public, would have accepted such a semi-public tongue-lashing without objection. I was surprised not to hear the hum of the Great Helmsman spinning in his grave at this negation of his goal of having the Chinese people "stand up."

Towards midnight on both evenings, after returning from the Bund, my colleagues and I wandered the *hutong* that backed up one side of Fudan's Yangpu campus. It was a very poor area with small, dilapidated shacks, some clearly self-made, and open gutters flanking the narrow lanes. The roadway was crowded with people, many of them sleeping outside. It was an area that might be a slum in other cities and probably was in the Shanghai of an earlier age. Yet clearly it was not a slum. The buildings were dilapidated but not ramshackle. The gutters were clean. There was very little refuse on the street. The lanes were well lit. Those who slept outside were not pavement dwellers without homes but neighborhood residents avoiding the stifling heat and humidity of their small homes, to which they would repair in the cold Shanghai winters.

Our last day we took a sightseeing trip to the garden city of Suzhou. The Venice of the East was every bit as delightful as its reputation. On the way in and out of Shanghai we passed through many kilometers of the city's agricultural green belt. As with tree planting in Beijing, I had taken Chinese claims regarding such belts with a pinch of salt. Once again, even if the reality did not quite measure up to the rhetoric, what had been achieved nevertheless was striking.

I left China more impressed than I had expected, mainly because of what had been done to improve the basics of life for larger numbers of people than in other comparable countries. I knew that a longer stay would shed a different light, as would travel beyond the two biggest and most important cities into the countryside. Most importantly, I had no personal experience of life in an authoritarian state. Political liberty, and freedom from the actions of capricious and unaccountable officials are essential to a decent life and these

I knew the citizens of Beijing and Shanghai did not have.

Nevertheless, I was confident in my specific comparisons about comparative living conditions in the two sets of cities, one of which I knew intimately. The poorest inhabitants of Beijing and Shanghai undoubtedly were better off than their counterparts in Calcutta, Bombay and Delhi. Just to begin, the Indian cities had from tens to hundreds of thousands of people who were homeless and lived on sidewalks, and some millions more lived in inhumane conditions in slums. Those slightly higher on the economic scale also fared better in China. Cramped tenements, sub-standard housing, inter-generational cohabitation and shared toilets are not the purview of socialism alone. These privations were also widespread in India. The difference in China's favor was the generally higher level of municipal and social services. The lack of potable water, decent sanitation, regular immunizations, preventive health measures and basic medical services made tenement life in Calcutta, Bombay and Delhi significantly more burdensome.

Still higher up the income charts, and particularly approaching the apex, the scales tilted demonstrably though not unequivocally in India's favor. Indian business elites and high government officials held a substantial edge over their Chinese counterparts because they were not subject to consumption constraints. But weak municipal services and the inescapable intrusion of deep poverty in all aspects of existence diminished the overall quality of life. The most opulent homes existed cheek by jowl with slums and slum dwellers. Municipal power was undependable and load-shedding or -sharing frequent and extensive. Of course the elite had their own diesel generators but these were expensive, noisy and highly polluting. With public hygiene undependable even in well-off areas, even the most sheltered families were prone to communicable diseases. Theft, burglary, personal safety and social unrest were constant worries. The elites had long grown inured to these conditions but their persistence nevertheless detracted from the day-to-day life.

The call regarding political liberty was the easiest to make and clearly favored India. Indian elites enjoyed one of the most genuinely open societies on the planet, with broad legal freedoms and effective protections. These rights and safeguards extended *de jure* to everyone else in society too but with diminished effectiveness at lower levels of income and class. Nevertheless, essential safeguards against serious political jeopardy including arbitrary arrest and detention were incomparably greater in India.

Differences were more muted where freedom from arbitrary petty harassment was concerned (obtaining ration cards, getting the proper rations, requesting permits) with social class making an important difference in both countries. Both nations had cumbersome bureaucracies, capricious officials and petty corruption. I knew from experience that India's elite had others to do the waiting and pleading and surmised that China's *nomenklatura* had similar arrangements. The less fortunate in both countries also shared a common fate, one much less pleasant that involved recurring waits, frustrations and humiliations. (Poor Indians did have one extra burden compared to poor Chinese. While both dealt with petty public officials,

Indians had to contend in addition with unethical and bullying private sector ones, e.g. landlords.)

These comparisons ultimately were tentative but I did come away with some firmer understandings. Societies may not be evaluated or compared except in disaggregated terms of social classes, constituencies and interest groups. Liberation in China favored the poor over asset-owning classes while India's independence from Britain had a roughly reverse impact.

Class gains and losses are not unambiguous. Reductions in political freedom, restrictions on choice of employment and sanctions on movement offset the material advances of the poor in China. The middle classes who forfeited property gained—however tangentially, disproportionately and unsatisfactorily—from civic improvements in the cities.

Attempts to assign net gain or loss at the country level suggests the adoption of a particular class or constituency perspective or the assignment, conscious or subconscious, of relative weights to the individual class and constituency interests that comprise the whole.

Last, it is more useful if like entities are compared. Early in modern China's development Western analysts compared it to Taiwan, Japan and Hong Kong and not surprisingly found the country wanting. A more suitable comparison in terms of geography, population, economy and history would have been India, in which case the results would have been more nuanced. (Interestingly, India at that same time was dismissed as a "basket case" and no attempt made to compare it to more advanced countries. It is almost as if the Western analysts in their desire to disparage Chinese socialist progress unwittingly and ironically paid the new way of life the backhanded compliment of holding it to a higher standard).

As I boarded my Narita-bound plane in Shanghai, I was already ready to return to China.

*Porus Olpadwala is Dean Emeritus of the College of Architecture, Art and Planning, and Professor Emeritus of the Department of City and Regional Planning at Cornell University. In an earlier career, he worked in India in the 1960s with the Indian affiliate of Jardine Matheson. He holds an undergraduate degree in accounting from the University of Calcutta, and graduate degrees from Cornell in business and planning.*

# MICHAEL S. DUKE AND JOSEPHINE CHIU-DUKE
## Spring Flowers and a Chilly Autumn (1986)

Our first trip to China began in August 1986 when we arrived in Beijing, where Michael was to serve as the Director of a United States study-in-China program. We lived at Peking University (Beida) for eleven months with one month's leave in Hong Kong. During the year, we traveled with our *Liuxuesheng banshichu* (*Liuban*, Foreign Student Affairs Office) guides through about ten provinces and twenty-some cities and towns. We had many interesting encounters with Chinese people, some of which we'll relate here.

After we settled down in the Shaoyuan dormitory for foreigners on the Beida campus, we set out to experience Beijing as the "common people" experienced it. That is, we took public transportation. It was very crowded and hot and a good way to lose weight.

Our first memorable encounter came when we went to eat at Donglaishun restaurant on Wangfujing, said to be a favorite of Premier Zhou Enlai. We made our way through a crowd of workers squatting on the street smoking, chatting and eating *baozi* and went up to the second floor, noting the beat up walls and cracked paint. We walked over to an empty table covered with chicken bones, dirty dishes and other scraps from the previous diners and stood there for a while waiting for someone to clean off the table, but no one did. Then Josephine saw some washrags on a cart, picked one up and started to clean the table. "*Ai ya, ta ziji yao ca!* She's going to clean it herself!" was the cry from all around. Then a server hurried over to clear the table. She quickly brushed all the bones and so on off the table onto the floor, narrowly missing my shoes. Not the Premier Zhou treatment, but we were "going deep among the people."

We ordered one catty of *jiaozi* and were rather surprised when that turned out to be enough to feed an army. While we ate, we were joined by two men in blue outfits who turned out to be peasants in Beijing on business. We struck up a conversation on this and that, and after a while the older man told us what he thought of Beijing. "The people of Beijing eat off the peasants, live off the peasants and despise the peasants. We should have another revolution to take care of them." After that, we were not surprised when we later learned that one celebrated writer, well known for her exposés of the hard lives of intellectuals during the Cultural Revolution years, argued that peasants should not be allowed to ride first class on trains because they are "too dirty."

As we left the restaurant, the peasant asked for my *mingpian* and I gave him my card. A couple of months later, he sent a letter asking if I would be willing to buy a truck for him. He would provide me the money and I could buy it at the much lower foreigners' rate! Unfortunately, I had to disappoint him.

A few days after Michael answered the peasant's letter, we learned that the film *Fu Rong Zhen* (*Hibiscus Town*) was going to be shown in the student auditorium at Beida. We were quite excited since we had read the novel and also because we really had been watching enough CCTV news every night, not to mention the endless protocol that we had to comply with. The auditorium was completely packed with students and perhaps some faculty members. When the bad CCP cadre in the film was persecuting the protagonists, I heard murmuring behind us saying: "*Zhe jiushi gongchandang*, This is exactly the (Chinese) Communist Party!" Toward the end when the bad cadre was losing out, loud applause suddenly burst out from the audience along with thunderous stamping of their feet on the floor. We joined them also applauding like crazy, but a deep sense of frustration filled the air.

1986 was a banner year for Chinese literature. Many now very famous writers published some of their best works that year. The intellectual climate was freer than it had been since 1949. Wang Meng, the Minister of Culture, organized the First International Conference on Contemporary Chinese Literature, and it was held in Jinshan, a suburb of Shanghai, in November. Josephine joined me on this significant occasion. One of the highlights of the conference was *People's Daily*'s investigative reporter Liu Binyan's critical speech in which he discussed the possibility of another Anti-Rightist Campaign. The campaign arrived in January 1987, but it was dubbed an "Anti-Bourgeois Liberalization" Campaign. The high point of the conference for us, however, came when Liu Binyan invited us to go with him to a university in Shanghai where he was scheduled to give a talk.

On our way, the taxi driver asked Liu about China's chances for real reforms. Michael was getting ready to take notes, but I interrupted and asked if the driver himself could offer some suggestions so that Liu could write about them in the *People's Daily*. Without hesitation, this young man said that in his view if China allowed the United States to manage it for fifty years, then things might be all right! Liu didn't say anything; he just burst out laughing. He probably understood why an ordinary Chinese had such a novel idea, but we didn't press him for his response to the driver.

Liu Binyan's speech was delivered to a standing-room-only audience of over a thousand people. Josephine and I had seats, but many people sat in the aisles. The students asked him many hard questions that demonstrated their dislike of the Chinese Communist Party, and Liu answered them as frankly as he could, pushing the envelope as far as possible at this time that turned out to be the peak of intellectual freedom in China before the next crackdown began in January 1987.

When we returned to Jinshan, as we stepped down from the taxi in front of the guest house, we heard some of the other Chinese conference participants loudly proclaiming that "Binyan has been out stirring up trouble again." Yes, indeed, he was very good at it.

In December 1986, at the end of the first term, we took our first trip—to Hangzhou and West Lake—on our way to Hong Kong for a month off and to pick up another group of students. At the Beijing train station, Josephine discovered she had forgotten her passport; she had to go back for it and, thus, missed events we witnessed that were perhaps a precursor of the tragic events of June 1989. We arrived at a college in Hangzhou in the late

afternoon, and our bus rolled through the campus gates just in time to witness a student march and demonstration for democracy. We had heard about these December demonstrations while in Beijing, and the US students were quite elated to see their Chinese counterparts marching by, carrying signs.
Of course, the *Liuban* people tried to steer us clear of the Chinese students. After dinner, however, many of our US charges slipped off to practice their Mandarin on the Hangzhou students. They came back with glowing reports of the students' demands for better living conditions and more political reforms.

I arrived at West Lake a day after the whole group. The air and the beautiful scenery made me feel like lingering around a little longer, but I had to catch up with Michael and the students. And yet, I thought I should try to buy some celebrated *Longjing* (Dragon Well) tea for our friends and for my mother before joining the group, and so I asked a clerk in a nearby tourist hotel what was the best way to do so. He found a taxi and told me that the driver would help me buy the best tea in town.

The taxi drove along a winding hilly road, and for a while I felt a bit worried, but we finally stopped at a small cleared area in the hills where a dozen or so men were scattered around. They were probably all *getihu* (independent entrepreneurs) tea growers and/or traders with sacks of tea leaves beside them and burners with kettles on for boiling water. No cups but empty food glass jars were prepared for tea. Some of them invited me to drink their prepared *Longjing* tea after they knew I wanted to buy some.

Right after I bought some tea from one of them, I saw a man nearby steeping a jar of tea. The color of his tea water was as green as that of fresh spring leaves. I approached him and wanted to buy some from him since I had never seen such a beautiful color of *Longjing* tea. But he refused to sell, telling me that his was "*gongpin, buneng mai*. It's a tribute article and cannot be sold." I laughed and said "*gong gei shei*, making tribute to whom?" "*Zhongnanhai gei Deng Xiaoping ah!*" Suddenly, I realized that the Chinese imperial practice of demanding that the best local products be sent up to the central leadership was continued in "socialist" China. And yet, if he was making tea here, why couldn't he sell some? I then tried to persuade him to sell me some by telling him that I was from Taiwan, that this was my first time to visit Hangzhou, and that my mother would be delighted if I could bring her some "*gongpin Longjing*," especially since she had not had the real *Longjing* since 1949. He smiled and told me: "*Ah, ni hen xiaoshun, keshi wo zhineng mai ni yidian.* You are very filial, but I can only sell you a little bit." I later divided the little amount into two smaller packages, and put them without thinking in a suitcase which had some moth balls. We never had the opportunity to ask our friends what the tea tasted like, but my mother said she threw hers away because it tasted like moth ball soup! So much for my "triumphant" story of buying *Longjing* tribute tea!

I re-joined Michael and the group in time before we took off to Shanghai for Christmas and then to Hong Kong. What we did not expect to experience was a bureaucratic wrestling match between our *Liuban* people and a Shanghai cadre officer. It had been pre-arranged for us to stay in the dormitory of a Shanghai college, but the local cadre officer wanted to charge additional fees for an extra Chinese language teaching staff member regardless of the fact that the Beijing office had a document asking them to accommodate the situation. We were kept sitting on the bus for at least two hours before being told that we could enter the dormitory. We did not know how our *Liuban* people struck a deal with the local cadre, but as much as we appreciated their hard work, we certainly did not envy their job. This experience, and many others like it, also convinced us of the utter lack of clout of any official document from the center. Local arrangements were always local arrangements, and someone always had to be found to take personal responsibility. Simply saying "I have a document from Beijing" would not cut it.

While we were in Hong Kong visiting Josephine's friends, we also learned that the result of the December student demonstrations was a new crackdown on those calling for faster reforms and more democracy in China. Secretary General Hu Yaobang was blamed for letting "bourgeois liberalization" get out of hand and was removed from office. Liu Binyan, Fang Lizhi and Wang Ruowang had their CCP memberships revoked and were deprived of any freedom of speech.

When we returned to Peking University in mid-January with a new group of students and a few who were there for the year, the whole atmosphere had changed. The intellectual excitement of 1986 was over, and the whole city was in the deep freeze. The *Liuban* people and the regular faculty people were not speaking again, since the *Liuban* was charged with watching the faculty for signs of "bourgeois liberalization." It was then that we learned that during the Cultural Revolution, the current staff of the *Liuban* was in on the repression of the current faculty of the Peking University Center for Teaching Chinese to Foreigners. These former persecutors and former victims all worked in the same *danwei* (organization) before and after the Cultural Revolution and would do so until retirement. It would be hard to imagine a worse working environment.

We could no longer safely visit Liu Binyan. That is, it was not safe for him to be seen having foreign visitors. The usual euphemism for being in political trouble was being in poor health, so every week until we met Liu again just before leaving Beijing we sent him a get well card with only the words *bao zhong*—take care of your health. Liu still believed in socialism at that time, but by November 1990 when he visited Vancouver and gave a lecture at UBC on "Reportage Fiction in My Life," sponsored by the Tiananmen University for Democracy in China Foundation, he had lived in the US long enough to begin to understand how human rights and the rule of law actually functioned.

Around this time, we visited with the editor of a major literary magazine, and he explained to us how the censorship system worked at the time. He received direct orders from the Propaganda Department detailing what stories or themes should not be published. For example, at that time he had been told not to print any more stories about high school romance. This editor had also been ordered not to publish any more stories dealing with national minorities. This was after Ma Jian's story "Stick Out Your Tongue" (*Liangchu Ni de Shetai*), about the dark side of Tibetan culture had been attacked by the Tibetan CCP leadership for "hurting the feelings" of the Tibetan people. The strategy for getting around censorship and publishing some truly interesting fiction and critical articles was very simple—put the good stuff in the middle of the journal. Start and end the journal with a hundred pages of low quality work and put the fifty or so pages of quality in the middle. It seems that even then the censors did not like to read all that much, and, as today, they did not really understand the more modernist works.

When we met Liu Binyan again in the early summer of 1987, he told Michael that he would be happy to take us to visit Shi Tiesheng, a fine writer who became paralyzed because of heavy duty work during the Cultural Revolution. Liu was very sympathetic with Shi's life and told us how difficult it must have been for Shi to sustain his writing, but Shi was just out for some air and we did not see him this time. All this time, Liu only asked Michael about his views on Shi's fiction, and did not talk about the recent revocation of his CCP party membership or all the problems he was subject to. That evening we said good-bye with the same "*Qing baozhong*, Please take care" to him. What else could one say when words were not enough to express one's feelings?

Before we left Beijing, a friend also took us to bid farewell to Wang

Zengqi, then an important writer of the *xungen* or "searching for roots" literature in the 1980s. He was Shen Congwen's student, and one can certainly spot the flavor of Shen's idyllic style in some of his works. It was July and Wang had just woken up from his afternoon nap. Michael and I both felt that we shouldn't stay long since the pressure of the Anti-Bourgeois Liberalization Campaign was still real. We talked about the *xungen* literature, and Wang smiled and told us he did not have to search for his roots because, unlike the young people who grew up during the Cultural Revolution, his roots were always there in the Chinese Confucian cultural tradition.

Wang gave us two of his Chinese literati-style paintings as parting gift. We waved good-bye hoping that we would soon see each other again in a happier atmosphere, but we never did and felt sorry to learn that he passed away in 1997.

I have often gazed at Wang's two painting gifts, trying to excavate the meaning of the phrases he wrote on them. On one painting, he wrote a phrase from a *shi* poem by Li Bai, the most renowned Tang Chinese poet. It reads: "*Chunfeng fukan luhua nong*, The flower is thick with dew when spring breezes brush by the balustrade." He signed and dated the poem 1978. It has both Michael's and my names on it.

Interestingly, on the other painting, with only my name on it, Wang wrote a phrase from a well known *ci* lyric by the famous Southern Song poet Xin Qiji: "*Tianliang hao ge qiu*, It's cold, what a chilly autumn!" Below the phrase he signed his name and then dated it July 1987.

Any educated Chinese would probably also read the poetic phrases on these two paintings as a metonym signifying Wang's inner feelings at the time, especially since the painting with spring flowers was oddly dated July 1978 and the cold autumn was dated July 1987. That is, the one with the spring flowers could well symbolize his high hopes for a new era of reform that Deng Xiaoping promised in 1978 while the other phrase pointed to the chilly cold of autumn brought on by the Anti-Bourgeois Liberalization Campaign of 1987. We never had the opportunity to confirm my speculation with him, but it would seem that the connection of spring flowers followed by a chilly autumn speaks for itself, especially when I recall the entire Xin Qiji couplet: "*Erjin shijin chou ziwei, yu shuo huan xiu, que dao tianliang hao ge qiu,* By now I have fully savored the taste of sorrow, I want to explain it, but swallow back the words, and simply say it's cold, what a chilly autumn!"

It's been twenty-five years since we lived at Beida in 1986-87. In this quarter of a century, our friends Liu Binyan, Shi Tiesheng and Wang Zengqi have passed away, while some other friends have shifted to a different life path. China has also dazzled the world with its economic achievements. Many Chinese today feel this is indeed their century, just as Li Bai felt about his age in that spring flower poem. And yet, for those Chinese who lost their freedom and whose voices are silenced, and for those who are still struggling to achieve a minimum level of subsistence or human dignity, we cannot help but wonder: Can that chilly autumn poem even remotely touch on the sorrow they have been subject to?

*Michael S. Duke* and *Josephine Chiu-Duke* are *Professor Emeritus of Chinese and Comparative Literature and Associate Professor of Chinese Intellectual History, respectively, at the University of British Columbia. His publications include The Iron House: A Memoir of the Chinese Democracy Movement and the Tiananmen Massacre. His literary translations include Raise the Red Lantern: Three Novellas by Su Tong, and The Fat Years by Koonchung Chan. Her publications include To Rebuild the Empire: Lu Chih's Confucian Pragmatist Approach to the Mid-T'ang Predicament, and a Festschrift she edited for Professor Lin Yü-sheng, Liberalism and the Humanistic Tradition, which received the United Daily News Award for Best Non-fiction Book of 2005.*